CW01084023

ENCYCLOPEDIA OF ISLAMIC DOCTRINE

VOLUME 3
THE PROPHET (ﷺ): COMMEMORATIONS, VISITATION AND HIS KNOWLEDGE OF THE UNSEEN
(*MAWLID, ZIYARA, ILM AL-GHAYB*)

SHAYKH MUHAMMAD HISHAM KABBANI

AS-SUNNA FOUNDATION OF AMERICA

Edited by Gabriel F. Haddad, Ph.D. (Columbia), Alexandra Bain, Ph.D. (Victoria), Karim K. Tourk, Jennifer McLennan

Library of Congress Cataloging in Publication Data

Kabbani, Shaykh Muhammad Hisham.
Encyclopedia of Islamic Doctrine Vol. 3. The Prophet: Commemorations, Visitation and His Knowledge of the Unseen (*mawlid, ziyara, ilm al-ghayb*)
[Arabic title: *al-Musuat al-islami aqida ahl al-sunnah wa al-jamaat*]
p.   cm.
    Indices.
Islam—doctrines. 2. Heretics, Muslim. 3. Wahhabiyah.
I. Kabbani, Shaykh Muhammad Hisham. II. Title.

ISBN: 1-871031-83-4

Published by
As-Sunna Foundation of America Publications
607A W. Dana St.
Mountain View, CA 94041
e-mail: asfa@sunnah.org
www: http://sunnah.org

Distributed by
KAZI Publications
3023 W. Belmont Avenue
Chicago, IL 60618
Tel: 773-267-7001; Fax: 773-267-7002
e-mail: kazibooks@kazi.org
www: http://www.kazi.org

CONTENTS

PREFACE   vii

INTRODUCTION   IX

    FATWA FROM THE AWQAF OF DUBAI: *MAWLID*: SHOULD WE
        CELEBRATE?   viii

    COMMENTARY AND EXPLANATION OF THE DUBAI *FATWA*   xxii

1. *MAWLID*: COMMEMORATING THE PROPHET'S BIRTHDAY   1

    1.1. TEN PROOFS FROM THE QURAN AND *SUNNA* THAT
    COMMEMORATING THE PROPHET'S BIRTHDAY IS
    ACCEPTED ISLAMIC PRACTICE   2

        1.1.1. THE OBLIGATION TO INCREASE THE LOVE AND
        HONOR OF THE PROPHET (ﷺ)   2

        1.1.2. THE PROPHET (ﷺ) EMPHASIZED MONDAY AS THE
        DAY HE WAS BORN   2

        1.1.3. ALLAH SAID: "REJOICE IN THE PROPHET"   4

        1.1.4. THE PROPHET (ﷺ) COMMEMORATED GREAT
        HISTORICAL EVENTS   4

        1.1.5. ALLAH SAID: "INVOKE BLESSINGS ON THE PROPHET"   4

        1.1.6. THE EFFECT ON DISBELIEVERS OF OBSERVING
        THE PROPHET'S BIRTHDAY   5

        1.1.7. THE OBLIGATION TO KNOW THE LIFE OF THE
        PROPHET (ﷺ) (*SIRA*) AND IMITATE HIS CHARACTER   6

        1.1.8. THE PROPHET (ﷺ) ACCEPTED POETRY IN HIS
        HONOR   6

            1.1.8.1. REMARKS: SINGING AND THE RECITATION OF
            POETRY   7

            1.1.8.2. REMARKS: RECITATION OF THE QURAN
            AND SINGING   8

            1.1.8.3. REMARKS: THE PROPHET (ﷺ) ALLOWED
            DRUM-PLAYING IF THERE WAS A GOOD
            INTENTION   9

        1.1.9. THE PROPHET (ﷺ) EMPHASIZED THE BIRTHDAY
        OF PROPHETS   9

            1.1.9.1. REMARKS: WHY BUKHARI EMPHASIZED
            DYING ON MONDAY   10

            1.1.9.2. REMARKS: THE PROPHET (ﷺ) EMPHASIZED
            THE BIRTHPLACES OF PROPHETS   10

1.1.10. THE UNANIMOUS ACCEPTANCE OF RELIGIOUS
SCHOLARS OF COMMEMORATING THE PROPHET'S
BIRTHDAY   10
1.2. HISTORY OF THE COMMEMORATION OF THE PROPHET'S
BIRTHDAY (*MAWLID*)   11
1.2.1. COMMEMORATION OF THE PROPHET'S BIRTHDAY IN
MAKKA ACCORDING TO MUSLIM HISTORIANS, AND
COMMEMORATION OF THE PROPHET'S BIRTHPLACE   11
1.2.2. EARLIEST MENTION OF PUBLIC *MAWLID*   11
1.2.3. IBN BATTUTA'S ACCOUNT OF THE *MAWLID*   12
1.2.4. THREE TENTH-CENTURY ACCOUNTS OF THE
MAWLID   12
1.2.5. THE *MAWLID* IN MUSLIM COUNTRIES TODAY   13
1.3. THE COMMEMORATION OF THE PROPHET'S BIRTHDAY AS
UNDERSTOOD BY "SALAFI" SCHOLARS AND MAINSTREAM
ISLAMIC SCHOLARS   14
1.3.1. IBN TAYMIYYA'S OPINION OF THE *MAWLID*
AND THE DEVIATION OF THE "SALAFIS" FROM HIS
OPINION   14
1.3.2. IBN TAYMIYYA'S VIEWS ON THE MEETINGS OF
REMEMBRANCE OF ALLAH (*DHIKR*)   15
1.3.3. IBN KATHIR PRAISES THE NIGHT OF *MAWLID*   15
1.3.4. ASQALANI'S AND SUYUTI'S EDICTS (*FATAWA*) ON THE
PERMISSIBILITY OF COMMEMORATING THE PROPHET'S
BIRTHDAY (*MAWLID*)   16
1.3.5. THE OPINION OF OTHER SCHOLARS ON THE *MAWLID*   17
1.3.6. IT IS RECOMMENDED TO COMMEMORATE THE PROPHET'S
BIRTHDAY (*MAWLID*)   18
1.3.7. CONCERNING THE CLAIM OF CONTEMPORARY "SALAFI"
WRITERS LIKE ALBANI, BIN BAZ, ABU BAKR JAZIRI,
MASHHUR SALMAN, UTHAYMIN AND OTHERS WHO FORBADE
THE *MAWLID*   19
1.3.8. QUESTIONS PERTAINING TO THE COMMEMORATION OF
THE PROPHET'S BIRTHDAY (*MAWLID*)   21
1.4. CONCERNING STANDING OF PEOPLE AT THE CONCLUSION
OF THE *MAWLID* WHILE SENDING BLESSINGS AND PEACE (*SALAM*) ON THE
PROPHET (ﷺ)   30
1.4.1. NAWAWI'S COMMENTARY ON STANDING   33
1.4.2. IBN AL-HAJJ'S OBJECTIONS TO STANDING   35
1.4.3. ASQALANI'S REFUTATION OF IBN AL-HAJJ   36
1.4.4. DOES STANDING WHILE INVOKING BLESSINGS
(*SALAWAT*) UPON THE PROPHET (ﷺ) SIGNIFY THAT HE IS
PRESENT IN PERSON?   45
1.4.5. USING THE PHRASE: "*AL-SALAMU ALAYKA
YA RASUL ALLAH* (PEACE BE UPON YOU O MESSENGER
OF ALLAH")   48

1.4.6. The Wahhabis' Tampering with the Gate to the
Prophet's Noble Grave (*Muwajaha al-
Sharifa*)   50
1.5. Conclusion: One May Not Object to Commemoration
of the Prophet's Birthday (*Mawlid*)   53

2. Visitation of the Prophet (ﷺ) in Madina (*Ziyara*)   55
2.1. Some Falsehoods of the "Salafis" Concerning
the Prophet's Grave and His Mosque   55
2.2. Shaykh Alawi al-Maliki's Excellent Words on
Traveling to Visit the Prophet (ﷺ)   59
2.3. The Praiseworthiness of Visiting the Prophet's
Blessed Grave   60
2.3.1. The Hadith Supporting the General Order
to Visit Graves   61
2.3.2. Traveling to Visit the Prophet's Grave   62
2.4. Hadith on Visiting Graves   65
2.5. Translating the Hadith "Do not make my grave
an *Id*"   66
2.6. al-Hafiz al-Qadi Iyad al-Maliki on Visitation (*Ziyara*)   68
2.7. Ibn Qunfudh al-Qusantini al-Maliki on *Ziyara*   70
2.8. Imam Malik's Preference of Madina Over Makka   72
2.9. Imam Malik's Additional Narrations on the Merits
of Madina in His *al-Muwatta*   74
2.9.1. The Prophet's Supplication (*Dua*) for Madina
and Its People   74
2.9.2. On Residing in Madina and Leaving It   75
2.9.3. The Making of Madina Sacrosanct (*Haram*)   76
2.9.4. The Epidemic of Madina   76
2.9.5. The Expulsion of the Jews from Madina   77
2.10. The Prophet's Grave Is the Holiest Site on Earth   77
2.11. Al-Shaykh Abd al-Qadir al-Jilani al-Hanbali
on *Ziyara*   78
2.11.1. Entering Madina the Illuminated   78
2.11.2. Explanation of Jilani's Supplication,
"I have come to Your House"   80
2.12. Al-Hafiz Abu al-Faraj Ibn al-Jawzi al-Hanbali
on *Ziyara*   82
2.12.1. Chapter on Visiting the Grave of the
Prophet (ﷺ)   82
2.12.2. Chapter on His Community's Greeting
Reaching Him   83
2.12.3. Chapter on Some Sayings That Were Retained
From the Visitors to His Grave and States They had
Experienced   84

2.13. SHAYKH AL-ISLAM AL-HAFIZ AL-IMAM MUHYI AL-DIN
    AL-NAWAWI AL-SHAFII ON VISITATION (ZIYARA)   85
2.14. "SALAFI" CORRUPTION OF THE TEXT OF NAWAWI'S
    ADHKAR   96
2.15. THE OPINION PROHIBITING TRAVEL TO VISIT THE PROPHET
    (ﷺ) IS NULL AND VOID   98
2.16. EDICT (FATWA) OF FORTY-FIVE SCHOLARS OF MAKKA,
    MADINA, EGYPT, SYRIA, AND INDIA ON THE
    PRAISEWORTHINESS OF TRAVELING TO VISIT
    THE PROPHET (ﷺ)   100
    2.16.1. SCHOLARS FROM INDIA   101
    2.16.2. SCHOLARS FROM MAKKA   101
    2.16.3. SCHOLARS FROM MADINA   101
    2.16.4. SCHOLARS FROM AL-AZHAR, EGYPT   102
    2.16.5. SCHOLARS FROM SYRIA   102
2.17. TEXT OF THE FATWA   102

3. THE PROPHET'S AND SAINTS' KNOWLEDGE OF THE UNSEEN (ILM
AL-GHAYB)   107
3.1. THE PROPHET'S KNOWLEDGE OF THE UNSEEN   107
    3.1.1. QADI IYAD AND ALI AL-QARI ON THE PROPHET'S
        KNOWLEDGE OF THE UNSEEN AND FUTURE EVENTS   116
    3.1.2. THE SIGHT OF THE PROPHET (ﷺ)   127
    3.1.3. CONCLUSION: THE PROPHET (ﷺ) "KNOWS" AND
        "CAN," BUT HE IS HUMBLE AND DOES NOT BOAST   128
3.2. THE SAINTS' UNVEILING OF THE UNSEEN   131
    3.2.1. IBN TAYMIYYA ON THE MIRACLES OF
        THE SAINTS (AWLIYA)   144
    3.2.2. AL-HARAWI AL-ANSARI ON THE LEVELS OF KASHF   145
    3.2.3. KNOWLEDGE OF THE UNSEEN
        (IBN HAJAR HAYTAMI)   147

APPENDIX 1: IBN QAYYIM ON VISITING AND GREETING THE
DECEASED AND THEIR INTERACTION WITH THE LIVING   151
GLOSSARY   159
BIBLIOGRAPHY   161
INDICES
    INDEX TO QURANIC VERSES   167
    INDEX TO HADITH   168
    GENERAL INDEX   174

PREFACE

Praise be to Allah, Lord of all the worlds, and peace and blessings upon His Prophet and Messenger Muhammad, his family and all his companions. In Islam there are two festivals (*id*): *id al-adha* and *id al-fitr*. Other commemorations like that of the Prophet's birthday (*mawlid*), are neither obligatory nor forbidden. However, we have come to a time in which there is much complaining about the remembrance of the Prophet's birthday. These objections stem from the "Salafi" movement whose followers search for anything that their scholars might consider doubtful and use it as an excuse to mock and denigrate the faith of other Muslims. Mainstream Muslims are labeled *mushrik* (polytheist), *kafir* (unbeliever), and *mubtadi* (innovator) simply because they accept the commemoration of the birth of the Prophet in accordance with the practices of Muslim scholars for over 1400 years.

To commemorate the Prophet's birthday is to celebrate Islam because the Prophet is the symbol of Islam. Imam Mutawalli Sharawi said:

> If living beings were happy for his coming (to this world) and every inanimate creation was happy at his birth and all plants were happy at his birth and all animals were happy at his birth and all angels were happy at his birth and all believing *jinn* were happy at his birth, why are you preventing us from being happy at his birth?[1]

The actual position of Islam on the celebration of the Prophet's birthday is permissibility based on *khilaf,* or diver-

---

1 Imam Mutawalli Sharawi, *Maidat al-fikr al-islamiyya* (p. 295).

gence of opinions among the scholars, which no one can change to prohibition. The following text will present the facts and proofs relating to the commemoration of the Prophet's birthday (*mawlid*) according to the Quran, the *sunna,* and the scholars of Islam. There are three statements that should be made:

1. Commemorating the mawlid of the Prophet is acceptable, to gather to hear his *sira* (life) and to listen to *madih* (praise) that has been written for him is acceptable, and giving food to people and bringing happiness to the Community on that occasion is acceptable.

2. The celebration of the Prophet's *mawlid* must not only be on the 12th of Rabi al-Awwal, but can and should be on every day of every month in every mosque, in order for people to feel the light of Islam and the light of Sharia in their hearts.

3. *Mawlid* gatherings are an effective and efficient means for calling people to Islam and educating children. These meetings offer a golden opportunity that must not be lost, for every scholar and *dai* to teach and remind the Community of the Prophet of his good character, his way of worshipping, and his way of treating people. This is a way to make children love and remember their Prophet through this celebration and by giving them food, juice and gifts to make them happy.

INTRODUCTION

FATWA[1] FROM THE *AWQAF* OF DUBAI: SHOULD WE CELEBRATE *MAWLID*?

Nowadays, we find publications filled with lies and deception which mislead many Muslims into thinking negatively about the honorable *mawlid* of the Prophet. These publications claim that to celebrate the *mawlid* is an act of innovation that goes against Islam. This is far from the truth, and it is therefore necessary for those who can speak clearly to help clarify and reverse the doubts surrounding this most blessed day. It is with this humble intention that I present the following proofs in support of celebrating our beloved Prophet's birthday.

The Prophet said, "He who innovates something in this matter of ours that is not of it will have it rejected." He also said, "Beware of innovations, for every innovation (*kull bida*) is misguidance." Those opposed to *mawlid* cite this saying and hold that the word "every" (*kull*) is a term of generalization, including all types of innovations, with no exception, and that therefore, celebrating *mawlid* is misguidance. By daring to say that, they accuse the scholars of Islam of innovation. At the top of the list of those they have accused, then, is our master Umar. Those in opposition to the *mawlid* quickly reply to this, "But we did not mean the Companions of the Prophet Muhammad (ﷺ)."

It follows, then, that the meaning of "every" (*kull*) cannot be taken in its general sense. Therefore,

1 *Fatwa* from the Office of Religious Endowments and Islamic Affairs, Dubai Administration of Ifta and Research, Dr. Isa al-Mani al-Humayri, Chairman of *awqaf*, Dubai. Reprinted with permission from The Muslim Magazine, Vol. 3, 1998.

although the Prophet (ﷺ) may not have said to celebrate his blessed birthday, it is nonetheless not an
innovation to do so. For, as the following examples
show, there were many actions and practices instituted by his close followers after his time that are not
deemed innovation.

Compiling the Quran

In a hadith, Zayd Ibn Thabit related that the
Prophet (ﷺ) passed away and the Quran had not been
compiled anywhere. Then Umar suggested to Abu
Bakr to compile the Quran in one book when a large
number of Companions were killed in the battle of
Yamama. Abu Bakr wondered, "How can we do something that the Prophet (ﷺ) did not do?" Umar said,
"By Allah, it is good." Umar persisted in asking Abu
Bakr until Allah expanded his chest for it (Allah made
him agree and accept these suggestions) and he sent
for Zayd Ibn Thabit and assigned him to compile the
Quran. Zayd said, "By Allah if they had asked me to
move a mountain, it would not have been more diffi-
cult than to compile the Quran." He also asked, "How
could you do something that the Prophet did not do?"
Abu Bakr said, "It is good, and Umar kept coming
back to me until Allah expanded my chest in regard to
this matter." This hadith is narrated in *Sahih
Bukhari*.

The Position of the *Maqam Ibrahim* (ﷺ)
in Relation to the Kabah

Al-Bayhaqi narrated with a strong chain of narrators from Aisha, "During the time of the Prophet
(ﷺ) and Abu Bakr, the *maqam* was attached to the
House, then Umar moved it back." *Al-Hafiz* Ibn Hajar
said in *al-Fath*, "The Companions did not oppose
Umar, neither did those who came after them, thus it
became unanimous agreement." He was also the first
to build the enclosure (*maqsura*) on it, which still
exists today.

ADDING THE FIRST CALL TO
PRAYER ON FRIDAY

In *Sahih Bukhari,* Al-Saib bin Yazid related, "During the time of the Prophet (☫), Abu Bakr and Umar, the call to Friday prayer used to occur when the Imam sat on the pulpit. When it was Uthman's time, he added the third call (considered third in relation to the first *adhan* and the *iqama*. But it is named first because it precedes the call to the Friday prayer)."

SALUTATIONS ON THE PROPHET (☫)
COMPOSED AND TAUGHT BY OUR MASTER ALI

The salutations have been mentioned by Said ibn Mansur and Ibn Jarir in *Tahzib al-athar*, and by Ibn Abi Assim and Yaqub ibn Shaiba in *Akhbar Ali* and by al-Tabarani and others from Salama al-Kindi.

THE ADDITION TO THE *TASHAHHUD* BY IBN MASUD

After *"wa rahmatullahi wa barakatu,"* and the Mercy of Allah and Blessings, Ibn Masud used to say, *"al-salamu alayna min rabbina* (peace upon us from our Lord). Narrated by al-Tabarani in *al-Kabir*, and the narrators are those of the sound transmitters, as it has been mentioned in *Majma al-zawaid*.

THE ADDITION TO THE *TASHAHHUD* BY
ABDULLAH IBN UMAR

Abdullah Ibn Umar added the *basmala* at the beginning of the *tashahhud*. He also added to the *talbia*, *"labbayka wa sadayka wa al-khayru bi yadayka wa al-raghbau ilayka wa al-amalu."* This is mentioned in Bukhari, Muslim, et al.

These are some of the developments instituted by the Prophet's Companions, the scholars, and the honorable members of his nation, which did not exist during the time of the Prophet (☫), and which they deemed good. Are they, then, misguided and guilty of bad innovation?

SAYINGS OF SCHOLARS CONCERNING
TYPES OF INNOVATION IN ISLAM

As for the claim that there is no such thing in religion as good innovation, here are some sayings of the brilliant scholars of Islam belying this claim. Imam Nawawi said in his commentary on *Sahih Muslim* (6-21).

"The Prophet's (☙) saying, 'Every innovation' is a general-particular and it is a reference to most innovations. The linguists say, 'Innovation is any act done without a previous pattern, and it is of five different kinds.'"

Imam Nawawi also said in *Tahzib al-asma wa al-sifat*, "Innovation in religious law is to originate anything which did not exist during the time of the Prophet (☙), and it is divided into good and bad." He also said, "*Al-muhdathat* (pl. of *muhdatha*) is to originate something that has no roots in religious law. In the tradition of religious law it is called innovation, and if it has an origin within the religious law, then it is not innovation. Innovation in religious law is disagreeable, unlike in the language where everything that has been originated without a previous pattern is called innovation regardless of whether it is good or bad."

Shaykh al-Islam Ibn Hajar al-Asqalani, the commentator on Bukhari, said, "Anything that did not exist during the Prophet's time is called innovation, but some are good while others are not."

Abu Naim, narrating from Ibrahim al-Junayd, said, "I heard al-Shafii saying, "Innovation is of two types: praiseworthy innovation and blameworthy innovation, and anything that disagrees with the *sunna* is blameworthy." Imam al-Bayhaqi narrated in *Manaqib al-Shafii* that he said, "Innovations are of two types: that which contradicts the Quran, the *sunna*, or unanimous agreement of the Muslims is an innovation of deception, while a good innovation does not contradict any of these things."

Sultan al-ulama, al-Izz ibn Abd al-Salam said at the end of his book, *al-Qawaid*, "Innovation is divided into obligatory, forbidden, recommended, disagreeable and permissible, and the way to know which is which is to match it against the religious law."

Clearly we see from the opinions of these righteous scholars that to define innovations in worship as wholly negative without exception is ignorant. For these pious knowers, among them Imam Nawawi and al-Shafii, declared that innovations could be divided into good and bad, based on their compliance with or deviance from religious law.

Moreover, the following prophetic saying as stated in *Sahih Muslim* is known even to common Muslims, let alone scholars: "He who inaugurates a good practice (*sanna fi al-Islam sunnatun hasana*) in Islam earns the reward of it, and of all who perform it after him, without diminishing their own rewards in the least." Therefore, it is permissible for a Muslim to originate a good practice, even if the Prophet (ﷺ) didn't do it, for the sake of doing good and cultivating the reward. The meaning of inaugurate a good practice is to establish a practice through personal reasoning (*ijtihad*) and derivation (*istinbat*) from the rules of religious law or its general texts. The actions of the Prophet's Companions and the generation following them which we have stated above is the strongest evidence. Those prejudiced against celebrating the Prophet's birthday have paved the way for their falsehood by deceiving the less-learned among the Muslims. The prejudiced ones claim that Ibn Kathir writes in his *al-Bidaya wa al-nihaya* (11-172) that the Fatimid-Ubaidite state, which descends from a Jewish man, Ubaydullah ibn Maymun al-Kaddah, ruler of Egypt from 357-567 A.H., innovated the celebration of a number of days, among them, the celebration of the Prophet's birthday. This treacherous lie is a grave insult to the scholarship of Ibn Kathir and the scholarship of all Islam. For in truth, Ibn Kathir writes about the Prophet's birthday in *al-Bidaya wa al-nihaya* [13-136], "The victorious king Abu Said Kawkaburi was one of the generous, distinguished masters, and the glorious kings; he left good impressions and used to observe the honorable *mawlid* by having a great celebration. Moreover, he was chivalrous, brave, wise, a scholar, and just." Ibn Kathir continues, "And he used to spend three hundred thousand dinars on the *mawlid*." In support, Imam Dhahabi writes of Abu Said Kawkaburi, in *Siyar alam al-nubala* [22-336], "He was humble, righteous, and loved religious learned men and scholars of prophetic saying."

SAYINGS OF THE RIGHTLY-GUIDED IMAMS REGARDING THE *MAWLID*
IMAM AL-SUYUTI IN *AL-HAWI LI AL-FATAWI*

Suyuti wrote a special chapter entitled, "The Good Intention in Commemorating the *Mawlid*," at the beginning of which he said, "There is a question being asked about commemorating the *mawlid* of the Prophet (ﷺ) in the month of Rabi al-Awwal: What is the religious legal ruling in this regard? Is it good or bad? Does the one who celebrates it receive spiritual reward or not?"

My answer is as follows: To commemorate the *mawlid*, which is basically gathering people together, reciting parts of the Quran, narrating stories about the Prophet's birth and the signs that accompanied it, then serving food, and afterwards departing is one of the good innovations; and the one who practices it is rewarded, because it involves venerating the status of the Prophet (ﷺ) and expressing joy for his honorable birth."

IBN TAYMIYYA IN *IQTIDA AL-SIRAT*
AL-MUSTAQIM [AL-HADITH PRINT, P. 266]

Ibn Taymiyya states, "As to what some people have innovated either to compete with Christians on the birth of Jesus or for the love of the Prophet and veneration for him, Allah might reward them for their love and *ijtihad*."

As far as we are concerned, we commemorate the *mawlid* for no other reason but what Ibn Taymiyya said, "Out of love and veneration of the Prophet." May Allah reward us according to this love and effort, and may Allah bless the one who said, "Let alone what the Christians claim about their prophet, and you may praise Muhammad in any way you want and attribute to his essence all honors and to his status all greatness, for his merit has no limits that any expression by any speaker might reach" [Imam al-Busiri].

HAFIZ IBN HAJAR AL-HAYTHAMI

In the same source previously mentioned, Suyuti said:

Someone asked Ibn Hajar about commemorating the *mawlid*. Ibn Hajar answered, 'Basically, commemorating the *mawlid* is an innovation that has not been transmitted by the righteous Muslims of the first three centuries. However, it involves good things and their opposites, therefore, whoever looks for the good and avoids the opposites then it is a good innovation.' It occurred to me (Suyuti) to trace it to its established origin, which has been confirmed in the two authentic books: *al Sahihayn* (*Sahih Bukhari* and *Sahih Muslim*). When the Prophet (ﷺ) arrived in Madina, he found that the Jews fast the day of Ashura. When he inquired about it they said, "This is the day when Allah drowned Pharaoh and saved Moses (ﷺ), therefore we fast it to show our gratitude to Allah." From this we can conclude that thanks are being given to Allah on a specific day for sending bounty or preventing indignity or harm. What bounty is greater than the bounty of the coming of this Prophet (ﷺ), the Prophet of Mercy, on that day?

This is regarding the basis of *mawlid*. As for the activities, these should consist only of things that express thankfulness to Allah, such as what has been previously mentioned: reciting Quran, eating food, giving charity, reciting poetry, praising the Prophet (ﷺ) or on piety which moves hearts and drives them to do good and work for the Hereafter." These are the derivations that those opposed to *mawlid* call false conclusions and invalid analogies.

IMAM MUHAMMAD BIN ABU BAKR ABDULLAH AL-QAYSI AL-DIMASHQI

He wrote *Jami al-athar fi mawlid, al-nabi al-mukhtar, al-lafz al-raiq fi mawlid khayr al-khalaiq,* and *Mawlid al-saadi fi mawlid al-hadi.*

IMAM AL-IRAQI

He wrote *al-Mawlid al-hani fi al-mawlid al-sani.*

MULLA ALI AL QARI

He wrote *al-Mawlid al-rawi fi al-mawlid al-nabawi*.

IMAM IBN DAHIYA

He wrote *al-Tanwir fi mawlid al-bashir al-nadhir*.

IMAM SHAM AL-DIN BIN NASIR AL-DIMASHQI

He wrote *Mawlid al-saadi fi mawlid al-hadi*. He is the one who said about the Prophet's estranged uncle, Abu Lahab, "This unbeliever who has been disparaged, 'perish his hands', will stay in hell forever. Yet, every Monday his torment is being reduced because of his joy at the birth of the Prophet. How much mercy can a servant expect who spends all his life joyous about the Prophet (ﷺ) and dies believing in the Oneness of Allah?"

IMAM SHAMS AL-DIN IBN AL-JAZRI

He wrote *Al-nashr fi al-qiraat al-ashr, urf al-tarif bi al-mawlid al-sharif*.

IMAM IBN AL-JAWZI

Imam Ibn al-Jawzi said about the honorable *mawlid*, "It is security throughout the year, and glad tidings that all wishes and desires will be fulfilled."

IMAM ABU SHAMA

Imam Abu Shama (Imam Nawawi's shaykh) in his book *al-Baith ala inkar al-bida wa al-hawadith* (pg.23) said, "One of the best innovations in our time is what is being done every year on the Prophet's birthday, such as giving charity, doing good deeds, displaying ornaments, and expressing joy, for that expresses the feelings of love and veneration for him in the hearts of those who are celebrating, and also, shows thankfulness to Allah for His bounty by sending His Messenger, the one who has been sent as a Mercy to the worlds."

IMAM AL-SHIHAB AL-QASTALANI

Al-Qastalani (Bukhari's commentator) in his book

al-Mawahib al-ladunniya (1-148) said, "May Allah have mercy on the one who turns the nights of the month of the Prophet's birth into festivities in order to decrease the suffering of those whose hearts are filled with disease and sickness."

There are others who wrote and spoke about *mawlid*, such as Imam al-Sakhawi, Imam Wajih al-Din bin Ali bin al-Dayba al-Shaybani al-Zubaydi, and many more, which we will not mention due to the limited space available.

From all of this evidence, it should have become clear that celebrating the *mawlid* is highly commendable and allowed. Surely we cannot simply shrug off as heretics the scholars and dignitaries of this nation who approved the commemoration of the *mawlid* and wrote countless books on the subject. Are all these scholars, to whom the whole world is indebted for the beneficial books they have written on prophetic sayings, jurisprudence, commentaries, and other sorts of knowledge, among the indecent who commit sins and evil? Are they, as those opposed to *mawlid* claim, imitating the Christians in celebrating the birth of Jesus? Are they claiming that the Prophet did not convey to the nation what they should do?

We leave answers to these questions up to you. We must continue to examine the errors which those opposed to *mawlid* utter. They say, "If celebrating the *mawlid* is from the religion, then the Prophet would have made it clear to the nation, or would have done it in his lifetime, or it would have been done by the Companions." No one can say that the Prophet (ﷺ) did not do it out of his humbleness, for this is speaking evil of him, so they cannot use this argument. Furthermore, that the Prophet and his Companions did not do a certain thing does not mean they made that thing prohibited. The proof is in the Prophet's saying, "Whoever establishes in Islam, a good practice. . . ." cited earlier. This is the strongest evidence that gives encouragement to innovate whatever practices have foundations in religious law, even if the Prophet and his Companions did not do them. Al-Shafii said, "Anything that has a foundation in religious law is not an innovation even if the Companions did not do it, because their refraining from doing it might have been for a certain excuse they had at the time, or they left it for something better, or perhaps not all of them knew about it." Therefore, whoever prohibits anything based on the concept that the Prophet (ﷺ) did not do it, his claim has no proof and must be rejected. Thus, we say to the rejecters of *mawlid*: based on the rule you have attempted to found, that is, that whoever does anything that the Prophet or his Companions did not do is committing innovation, it would follow that the Prophet (ﷺ) did not complete the religion for his nation, and that the Prophet (ﷺ) did not convey to the nation what they should do. No one says this or believes this except a heretic defecting from the religion of Allah. To the doubters of *mawlid* we declare, "Based on what you say, we convict you," for you have innovated in the basics of worship a large number of things that the Prophet (ﷺ) did not do nor did his Companions, the generation after the Companions, or the generation after them. For instance:

•Congregating people behind one Imam to pray *salat al-tahajjud* after *salat al-tarawih*, in the two Holy Mosques and other mosques.

•Reciting the prayer of completion of the Quran in *salat al-tarawih* and also in *salat al-tahajjud*.

•Designating the 27th night of Ramadan to complete reading the entire Quran in the two Holy Mosques.

•A caller saying, after *salat al-tarawih*, in the *qiyam* prayer, "May Allah reward you."

•The saying: "Oneness of Allah is divided into three parts: Oneness of Godhood; Oneness of Lordship; and Oneness of the Names and Attributes."

Is this found in a hadith, the statements of the Companions or the statements of the four Imams?

•Founding organizations which did not exist in the time of the Prophet, such as Islamic universities, societies for committing the Quran to memory, offices for missionary work, and committees for enjoining good and forbidding evil.

We are not objecting to these things, since they are forms of good innovation. We merely list these

innovations to point out that those who oppose
mawlid clearly contradict their own rule stating that
anything that neither the Prophet (ﷺ) nor his
Companions did is innovation. Since they claim that
all innovation is bad, they themselves are guilty.

Yet another claim they make is to say that those
who commemorate the *mawlid* are mostly indecent
and immoral. This is a vulgar statement and it only
reflects the character of the one saying it. Are all the
distinguished scholars that we have mentioned, from
the point of view of those opposed to *mawlid*, indecent
and immoral? We won't be surprised if this is what
they believe. This is a most serious slander.

We say, as the poet said, "When Allah wants to
spread a virtue that has been hidden, He would let
the tongue of an envious person know about it." Those
opposed to *mawlid*, may Allah guide them, have con-
fused some expressions, and claim that some religious
scholars associate partners with Allah. Take for
example the plea of Imam al-Busiri to Prophet
Muhammad(ﷺ), "Oh, most generous of creation, I
have no one to resort to, save you, when the prevailing event takes place."

They must examine carefully the saying of Imam
al-Busiri: "*Inda hulul al-hadith al-amami* (when the
prevailing event takes place)." What is *al-amam*? It
means that which prevails over the whole universe,
and all of creation, in referring to the Day of
Judgment. Imam al-Busiri is asking intercession
from the Prophet (ﷺ) on the Day of Judgment
because on that day we will have no one to resort to
or appeal to. Imam al-Busiri seeks his intercession to
Allah through the Prophet (ﷺ), for when all other
messengers and prophets will be saying, "Myself,
myself," the Prophet will be saying, "I am the one for
it, I am for it [the Intercession]."

It becomes even more clear now that the doubts of
those opposed to *mawlid* are unfounded, just as their
charges of associating partners with Allah are
unfounded. This is due to their blindness, both physical and spiritual. Another similar example can be
found in the well-known saying transmitted by the
distinguished Imam al-Kamal bin al-Hammam al-

Hanafi, author of *Fath al-qadir fi manasik al-farisi*, and *Sharh al-mukhtar min al-saada al-ahnaf*. When Imam Abu Hanifa visited Madina, he stood in front of the honorable grave of the Prophet (ﷺ) and said, "O, most honorable of the Two Weighty Ones (humankind and *jinn*)! O, treasure of mankind, shower your generosity upon me and please me with your pleasure. I am aspiring for your generosity, and there is no one for Abu Hanifa in the world but you." Again, we must not misinterpret this entreaty, but realize its true meaning.

Yet another misconception those opposed to *mawlid* hold can be seen in their statements such as these: "What occurs during *mawlid* is mixing between men and women, singing and playing musical instruments, and drinking alcohol." I myself know this to be a lie, for I have attended many *mawlid*s and have not seen any mixing and never heard any musical instruments.

As for drunkenness, yes, I have seen it, but not that of worldly people. We found people intoxicated with the love of the Prophet (ﷺ), a state surpassing even the agony of death, which we know overcame our master Bilal at the time of his death. In the midst of this sweet stupor he was saying, "Tomorrow I shall meet the loved ones, Muhammad (ﷺ) and his Companions."

To continue, those opposed to *mawlid* say, "The day of the Prophet's birth is the same day of the week as his death. Therefore, joy on this day is no more appropriate than sorrow, and if religion is according to one's opinion, then this day should be a day of mourning and sorrow." This kind of lame eloquence is answered by the Imam Jalal al-Din al-Suyuti in *al-Hawi li al-fatawi* (pg.193), "The Prophet's birth is the greatest bounty, and his death is the greatest calamity. Religious law urges us to express thankfulness for bounties, and be patient and remain calm during calamities. Religious law has commanded us to sacrifice an animal on the birth of a child [and distribute the meat to the needy], which is an expression of gratitude and happiness with the newborn, while it did not command us to sacrifice at the time of death. Also, it prohibited wailing and showing grief. Therefore, the rules of the divine Law indicate that it is recommended to show joy during the month of the Prophet's birth and not to show sorrow for his death."

Furthermore, Ibn Rajab, in his book *al-Lataif*, dispraising the rejecters of *mawlid* based on the above argument said, "Some designated the day of Ashura as a funeral ceremony for the murder of al-Husayn. But neither Allah nor His Prophet (ﷺ) commanded that the days of the prophets' great trials or deaths should be declared days of mourning, let alone those with lesser rank."

We conclude this article with a saying of the Prophet which has been narrated by Abu Yaala, from Hudhayfa and about which Ibn Kathir said, "Its chain of transmission is good." Abu Yaala said that the Prophet has said, "One of the things that concerns me about my nation is a man who studied the Quran, and when its grace started to show on him and he had the appearance of a Muslim, he detached himself from it, and threw it behind his back, and went after his neighbor with a sword and accused him of associating partners with Allah. I then asked, "Oh, Prophet of Allah, which one is more guilty of associating partners with Allah, the accused or the accuser?" The Prophet said, "It is the accuser.""

Completed, with all praises to Allah and salutations and peace be upon our master Muhammad and the Family of Muhammad and his Companions.

Isa al-Mani al-Humayri
Chairman of *Awqaf*, Dubai

COMMENTARY AND EXPLANATION OF THE DUBAI *FATWA*[2]

Every year Muslims throughout the world with profound love and abounding joy commemorate the birthday of our Beloved Prophet Muhammad (ﷺ). In keeping with Allah's Way, His *sunna* of recollecting the birthdays of the prophets as special events in the history of mankind, Muslims have found unique Islamic forms of worship to express their joy, their gratitude and their connection to the birth of the mercy to humanity.

His greatness reflects the greatness of His Creator. His purity outshines that of angels, mankind and spiritual beings. His advent on this earthly sphere was accompanied by extraordinary signs and miraculous occurrences, harbingers of the inestimable effect our perfect leader, the Prophet of Islam, the Guide of the believers, was to have on history.

MAWLID: INDEPENDENCE DAY OF THE MUSLIM COMMUNITY

Prophet Muhammad (ﷺ) is our hero, nay—our superhero! The people of each Muslim country rejoice in having achieved freedom from the colonialists who once held them in chains, considering their independence day the birth of their nation—a national holiday. In any Muslim country the emphasis on this is so strong that every child has memorized the date of independence and the events associated with it. The anniversary of that day represents their liberation from imperialism and having assumed their new identity as a young nation. On that holiday, flags fly on every street, the portrait of the founder of the nation is prominently displayed everywhere, names of other founding heroes and their stories are broadcast throughout the month, week and day. Everywhere the birth of a nation is commemorated by means of dazzling displays, parades, lights, decorations, fireworks, and military processions, as in America on the 4th of July. Glory be to Allah, objections are not made to the commemoration of Muslim national holidays. Therefore, does it not behoove the Muslims to commemorate the one who brought us independence from other than Allah, who took us from disbelief to faith, from idolatry to monotheism, founded our

2 Reprinted with permission from The Muslim Magazine, Vol. 3, 1998.

Community and gave us our identity as Muslims? Why not rejoice in that event, remember his greatness, his courage, his leadership and thank Allah for that day He favored and honored us to be of the Community-Nation (*umma*) of Muhammad (ﷺ)? As the best nation on earth, will we not enter paradise first for the greatness of our prophet?

ANNUAL GLOBAL *MAWLID* CONFERENCE

To further this discussion, it becomes essential to understand the difference between *halal* and *haram*, and the real meaning of innovation. As Islam progressed in America, many Islamic organizations sprang up, dedicated to reviving and supporting the spirit of Islam. All these organizations hold annual Islamic conventions and conferences. No one would deny these gatherings are rewarded by Allah, because they bring Muslims together to worship Allah in congregation in many ways: praying, studying Quran and hadith, studying *fiqh, sira, tafsir*, Islamic science, Islamic applications of secular science, Islamic politics and so on, invoking Allah in a gathering, introducing families to one other, increasing brotherly ties, and soliciting donations for building mosques, schools and Islamic institutions.

Most Islamic organizations hold their annual conference on the same day every year. Usually this day is a national holiday, such as Independence Day, Labor Day, Thanksgivin even Christmas. The dates these conferences are held on are so well-established that every American Muslim knows which national holiday is the day of the annual conference of each particular Islamic organization.

Not only is it ironic that the day is emphasized, but that the day emphasized is not an Islamic holiday! Most dangerous is that our youth attend such conferences in a hotel on Christmas where they are exposed to large, glamorous parties which promote drinking, dancing and other *haram* behavior. Yet attendees are often those who insist that to honor *mawlid* on the 12th of Rabi al-Awwal leads to harm? If Islamic gatherings can be held on the same secular or Christian holiday every year and Muslims will be rewarded for attending them, why not emphasize a particular day for communal supererogatory worship to commemorate the *mawlid* of the Prophet (ﷺ)? Is it Islamic justice to reject the 12th Rabi al-Awwal as commemoration of the birth of our Prophet (ﷺ) but to assign Christmas Day and other Christian and secular holidays such as Labor Day for a "35th Annual Convention" or Independence Day for the "15th Annual Ijtima?" Do we want our youth to consider these un-Islamic holidays as standard events for Muslims? The sponsoring organizations are proud of the numbers of conference attendees on that holiday, although that day was nowhere emphasized in Quran or *sunna*, nor in the practice of the *salaf*.

If we give credence to the claim, "In Islam there is no compromise," then why compromise on these dates? The same excuse of allowing annual Islamic events on secular U.S. or Christian holidays must be given for the *mawlid*. Therefore, Muslims can proudly say that this year, 1.2 billion Muslims will be attending the 1472nd Annual Global Conference for Commemorating the Birth of the Prophet (ﷺ) (i.e. 1419 years since the Hijra, plus 13 years in Makka added to the 40 years before the Prophet (ﷺ) received revelation). We are in support of the practices of commemorating *mawlid* and sponsoring Islamic conferences. We only present these facts here to provide a clear analogy (*qiyas*) of the fact that what is done every year by all Islamic organizations is no different than what is done to commemorate the Prophet's birth; thus, we must put an end to criticism of topics of whose scholarly roots the average reader may be unfamiliar.

EARLY COMMEMORATION OF
MAWLID IN MAKKA

Let us review some of the early sources mentioning public commemoration of the *mawlid* in Makka al-Mukarrama. One is Ibn Jubayr's (540-614) *Rihal* ("Travels"), wherein he describes his observation of *mawlid*: "This blessed place [the house of the Prophet (ﷺ)] is opened, and all enter to derive blessing from it (*mutabarrikin bihi*), on every Monday of the month of Rabi al-Awwal; for on that day and in that month was born the Prophet (ﷺ)."

The 7th-century historians Abu al-Abbas al-Azafi and his son Abu al-Qasim al-Azafi wrote in their *Kitab ad-durr al-munazzam*: "Pious pilgrims and prominent travelers testified that, on the day of the *mawlid* in Makka, no activities are undertaken, and nothing is sold or bought except by the people who are busy visiting his noble birthplace and rush to it. On this day the Kabah is opened and visited."

The famous 8th-century historian Ibn Battuta relates in his *Rihla*: "On every Friday, after the *juma* prayers and on the birthday of the Prophet (ﷺ), the door of the Kabah is opened by the head of the Banu Shayba, the doorkeepers of the Kabah, and that on the *mawlid*, the Shafii *qadi* (head judge) of Makka, Najmuddin Muhammad Ibn al-Imam Muhyiddin al-Tabari, distributes food to the *shurafa* (descendants of the Prophet) and to all the other people of Makka."

THREE 10TH-CENTURY
ACCOUNTS OF *MAWLID*

The following description consolidates eyewitness accounts by three 10th-century authorities: the historian Ibn Huhayra from his *Al-Jami al-latif fi fasl makka wa ahliha*; al-Hafiz Ibn Hajar al-Haytami from his *Kitab al-mawlid al-sharif al-muazzam*, the historian al-Nahrawali from *al-Ilam bi alam bayt Allah al-haram*. A fourth account by al-Diyarbakri (d. 960) in his *Tarikh al-khamis* correlates exactly with the following: "Each year on the 12th of Rabi al-Awwal, after the evening prayer, the four *qadi*s of Makka (representing the four Sunni schools) and large groups of people including the scholars (*fuqaha*) and notables (*fudala*) of Makka, shaykhs, *zawiya* teachers and their students, magistrates (*ruasa*), and scholars (*mutaammamin*) leave the mosque and set out collectively for a visit to the birthplace of the Prophet (ﷺ), shouting out *dhikr* and *tahlil* (*la ilaha illa Allah*)." The houses on the route are illuminated with numerous lanterns and large candles, and a great many people are out and about. They all wear special clothes and they take their children with them. Having reached the birthplace, inside a special sermon for the occasion of the birthday of the Prophet (ﷺ) is delivered, mentioning the miracles (*karamat*) that took place on that occasion. Hereafter, the invocation for the Sultan (i.e. the Caliph), the Amir of Makka, and the Shafii *qadi* is performed and all pray humbly. Shortly before the night prayer, the whole party returns from the birthplace of the Prophet (ﷺ) to the Great Mosque, which is almost overcrowded, and all sit down in rows at the foot of the *maqam Ibrahim*. In the mosque, a preacher first mentions the *tahmid* (praise) and the *tahlil*, and once again the invocation for the Sultan, the Amir, and the Shafii *qadi* is performed. After this the call for the night prayer is made, and after the prayer the crowd disperses."

Similar events are recorded as having taken place in Makka and Madina up to the year 1917. Only then did these traditions and practices cease in these two holiest cities, though they are still held in the homes of many Hijazi families, attended by many Muslims who come from around the world. At that time, *muqriin* (reciters) of the Quran and *maddahin* (those who praise the Prophet (ﷺ)) from Egypt, Syria, Pakistan and many other countries visit Makka and Madina and participate in these private ceremonies. Until today in Muslim countries around the globe, government offices, universities and businesses are closed on that day.

MAWLID IS ALLAH'S SUNNA

A community is only as great as its greatest man or woman. What then of a community whose greatness is derived from the incomparable Perfect Man, whose creation preceded all others? His very nature was not simply heroic, not just great—no, it was magnificent—not as appreciated by limited minds of men, but by the Creator Himself, for Allah praised our Holy Prophet (ﷺ) in countless verses of the Quran, and He swore an oath by his perfect character when He said, "*And lo! Thou art of a tremendous nature!*" (68:4). And the Prophet (ﷺ) was most pleased when he was mentioned in the Holy Quran in *Surah al-Isra*, attributed as "*abd*", saying, "*Glorified be He Who carried His servant by night from the Inviolable Place of Worship to the Far Distant Place*" (17:1).

One might ask, "How is *mawlid* part of the sunna?" But recall the day of freedom and independence of the Bani Israil, the 10th of Muharram, the day on which Moses (ﷺ) saved his people from the bondage of Pharoah, who drowned. The Jews of Madina observed this as a special day on which they fasted, in gratitude for Moses' salvation.

When the Prophet (ﷺ) migrated to Madina, he found the Jews fasting that day. Upon inquiring as to the reason, the Prophet (ﷺ) ordered his community to fast that day, saying "We have more right to Moses (ﷺ) than they do." Thus, the day of independence for Bani Israil became a day of worship for the Muslims.

As the followers of Muhammad (ﷺ), is it not appropriate for us to say, "We have more right on commemorating Muhammad (ﷺ) than any other community in commemorating their prophet?" Yes, and let us praise Allah on that day and rejoice in His mercy as He ordered, *"Of the favor and the mercy of Allah let them rejoice"* (10: 58). This order came because joy makes the heart grateful for Allah's mercy. What greater mercy did Allah grant to mankind than the Holy Prophet (ﷺ) himself, about whom He says, *"We did not send you except as a mercy to human beings?"* (21:107). Let us recall then, with love and fervor, joy and deep emotion, the birth of our Beloved Prophet, as Allah Himself commemorates without cease, in His final revelation, the birth of Prophet John (ﷺ), *"So peace on him the day he was born, the day that he dies, and the day that he will be raised up to life (again)!"* (19: 15). And similarly, Jesus (ﷺ) *"So peace is on me the day I was born, the day that I die, and the day that I shall be raised up to life (again)"* (19:33). Similarly the conception of Ishmael (ﷺ), Isaac (ﷺ) and of the Virgin Mary, peace be upon her, were mentioned in the Quran. We also find another birth commemorated in the verse, *"In pain did his mother bear him, and in pain did she give him birth"* (46:15). Ibn Abbas in his Quranic commentary explains that this verse was revealed in reference to *al-Siddiq al-Akbar* (Abu Bakr). What then of the one who is higher in station, who is the Seal of the Prophets and Master of all Mankind?

The mention of the Prophet's birth in the Quran is more subtle and more exalted, closer to the angelic realm where Allah said, *"Indeed, there has come to you Light and a clear Book from Allah"* (5:15). Quranic commentators have concluded that the *"Light"* as mentioned here is the Holy Prophet (ﷺ), and his birth is the turning point of a new cycle in the history of humanity: bringing the divine message of Islam and the Holy Quran.

The Quran relates the supplication of Jesus (ﷺ) on behalf of his disciples when he said, *"O Allah, send for us a heavenly table that we will eat from; and it will be a feast (id) for the first of us and for the last of us"* (5:114). That feast was held in honor of a heavenly table sent down from paradise full of food: seven loaves of bread and seven fish, as mentioned in traditional commentary on that verse. For a table of food, an *id* was held. What then for the coming to mankind of one who would serve not their worldly needs, but one sent by Allah as the intercessor for all nations? Does not this day deserve at least an annual commemoration?

Allah also mentions in the Holy Quran how He brought together the souls of the prophets before creating their physical forms: *"Behold! Allah took the covenant of the prophets, saying: 'I give you a Book and Wisdom; then comes to you a messenger, confirming what is with you; do ye believe in him and render him help?' Allah said: "Do ye agree, and take this My Covenant as binding on you?" They said: "We agree." He said: "Then bear witness, and I am with you among the witnesses."'* (3:81). If Allah mentioned his birth before this worldly life, in the presence of the souls of all prophets on the Day of Promises, does that day not deserve commemoration, as it is commemorated in the Quran? What of Allah's mention of the Prophet's birth in hadith, when He told Adam (ﷺ), "If he comes in your time you must follow him." If Allah is reminding us of this great event, who are we to say "forget it?"

We know there are only two *id*s in Islam and no others: *id al-adha* and *id al-fitr*. Therefore, people must not confuse *id* with commemoration (*dhikra*). The Prophet Muhammad's birthday is not an *id*, but it is an exceedingly important event that took place for humanity in the Light sent with him—the message of Islam—which brought the two *id*s. What then can we recall of the birth of the Prophet (ﷺ)?

What is known of it? According to Ibn Kathir's, *al-Bidaya wa al-nihaya* and *Dhikra mawlid rasulillah*, "Paradise and the skies were decorated and angels moved about in continuous processions, the palace of Chosroes was shaken and the fire of 1000 years ceased to burn." All these events happened on the night and within the moment of the Prophet's birth. So, it is not an *id* on a particular day, but it is a universal blessing from Allah to humanity, for which reason its commemoration is needed. He was the most honored and perfect creation that Allah created as a servant, and raised him by putting his name with His Name, elevated him on the night of the Ascension and revealed to him the Holy Quran. If Allah's creation rejoiced at the advent of the Prophet (ﷺ) on the day of his birth, what about us, for whom his birth is the greatest favor, and the means by which we were granted the religion of Islam? Is it not illogical to say, "We must not rejoice on that day," when all heavens and all creations do so in the most auspicious manner?

Imam al-Fakhr al-Razi said, "The Prophet's importance is a favor for all human beings and Allah has honored the Arabs by him and improved their status for the sake of the Prophet(ﷺ). From bedouins raising sheep as shepherds, they became leaders raising nations. For the sake of the Prophet (ﷺ), He took them from utter ignorance to the station of knowledge, enlightenment and leadership. He put them over all other nations, better than Jews and Christians, who were always proud of Moses (عليه السلام) and Jesus (عليه السلام) and the Torah and the Gospel. Allah made them better than everyone, so He made the Arabs and Muslims proud of their Prophet (ﷺ) above anyone.

EVIDENCE FOR *MAWLID* FROM THE *SUNNA* OF THE PROPHET(ﷺ)

Muslim narrated that Abu Qatada said that the Prophet (ﷺ) was asked about fasting on Monday and he said "That was the day I was born." This hadith is clear evidence of the importance of the commemoration of the Prophet's birthday through worship. *Al-Hafiz* ibn Rajab al-Hanbali, in his book *Lataif al-maarif* (p. 98), in explaining this hadith of Muslim said, "It is good to fast on the days that Allah honored and favored His servants." It is incumbent not only on Muslims but on all human beings to rejoice in his advent, the day of his birth. As *al-Hafiz* ibn Rajab al-Hanbali said, "The best favor that Allah has granted this nation is the birth of Prophet Muhammad (ﷺ) when he was sent to humanity. So we review and recall Allah's favor of sending the Prophet (ﷺ) by fasting on that day."

Thus, commemoration of the Prophet's birthday by any form of worship, starting with fasting, was derived analogously by the great scholars of jurisprudence, who concluded that all forms of worship according to the Quran and *sunna* are meritorious to perform on that day. This includes recitation of the Quran, loudly or quietly, individually or in congregation, praising the Prophet (ﷺ) amongst the most meritorious forms of worship, feeding people, charity and remembering Allah. Allah's injunction stands unceasingly, *"Verily, Allah and His*

angels are praying on the Prophet. O believers, pray on him"
(33:56). This clear order to praise the Prophet (ﷺ) includes
remembering who the Prophet (ﷺ) was and what he did. Thus,
coming together and sitting in a session in which the *sira* is told
and the Prophet's excellent character is recalled, and his person is praised, even through excessive *salawat*, is a form of worship.

Similarly, fasting on the day of the Prophet's birth or on any
Monday is an act of worship related to his birthday, which
brings nearness to Allah, as the Prophet (ﷺ) explicitly stated.
Similarly, the Prophet (ﷺ) slaughtered an *aqiqa* on his own
behalf, forty years after his birth, though one had been slaughtered by his grandfather when he was born. This is a firm evidence from the *sunna* for increasing acts of worship and
remembrance of his birth, for the *aqiqa* is an act of worship
associated with a birth. By analogy (*qiyas*), any worship
increased on Monday or on the day of the Prophet's birth, is
acceptable and meritorious. Thus, sitting in commemoration of
the Prophet (ﷺ)—by remembering his *sira*, praising him, offering food to people, giving donations to the poor—are all forms
of worship in the commemoration of the Prophet's birth,
whether it be every Monday, every month or every year, or even
every day of the year.

RECITATION OF POETRY IN PRAISE
OF THE PROPHET (ﷺ) IS *SUNNA*

Recitation of poetry in the Prophet's honor is one of the meritorious acts recommended by the *sunna*. Thus, we find it is one
of the primary means of observing the *mawlid* in almost all
Muslim nations. Here we cite a few examples from the *sira* and
hadith in which the Prophet (ﷺ) listened to poetry in his
praise. The Prophet's uncle al-Abbas composed poetry praising
the birth of the Prophet (ﷺ), in which are found the following
lines: "When you were born, the earth was shining, and the firmament barely contained your light, and we can pierce
through, thanks to that radiance and light and path of guidance." [Suyuti's, *Husn al-maqsid*, Ibn Kathir's *Mawlid*, Ibn
Hajar's *Fath al-bari*].

Ibn Kathir mentions the fact that according to the
Companions, the Prophet (ﷺ) praised his own name and recit-

ed poetry about himself in the middle of the battle of Hunayn in order to encourage the Companions and scare the enemy. That day he said: "I am the Prophet! This is no lie. I am the son of Abd al-Muttalib!" [Ibn Kathir, *Dhikra mawlid al-nabi*] The Prophet (ﷺ) was therefore happy with those who praised him because it is Allah's order, and he rewarded them from what Allah was providing him by praying for them and giving them gifts. Ibn Qayyim al-Jawziyya relates that the Prophet (ﷺ) prayed that Allah support Hassan ibn Thabit with the *ruh al-qudus* (the divine spirit) as long as he would support the Prophet (ﷺ) with his poetry. Similarly, the Prophet (ﷺ) rewarded Kab ibn Zuhayr's poem of praise with a robe (*burda*).

Hasan ibn Thabit recited this poetry about the Prophet (ﷺ) on the day of his death saying: "I say, and none can find fault with me. But one lost to all sense: I shall never cease to praise him. It may be for so doing I shall be forever in paradise, with the Chosen One for whose support in that I hope, and to attain to that day I devote all my efforts" [Ibn Hisham, notes to his *Sira*, p. 797, Karachi: Oxford Press].

As mentioned in the Dubai *fatwa*, al-Hafiz Shams al-Din Muhammad ibn Nasr al-Din al-Dimashqi in reference to the Prophet's uncle, Abu Lahab, noted in his book, *Mawlid al-saadi*, that his punishment in hell is lessened every Monday because upon hearing the good news of his nephew, the Prophet's birth, he released his handmaiden Thuwayba out of joy. For his celebration of the Prophet's birth his punishment is reduced on the day of his birth. "What then," he asks, "of the believer who all his life was joyful for the existence of the Prophet and died believing in the Oneness of Allah?" With these hadith in mind, people constantly relate the Prophet's *sira*, speak to their children about the importance of the Prophet (ﷺ) in their lives, offer food, help people, recite poetry in his praise and recite *salawat* (*darud*) excessively. *Alhamdulillah*, according to the principles of the Quran and *sunna*, this is considered an acceptable and effective approach to revive the love of the Prophet (ﷺ) and his message, in our ears and in our lives.

Regarding praise of the Prophet (ﷺ) and other subjects, we would like to share here what Shaykh Muhammad bin Abd al-Wahhab declared in *Muallafat al-Shaykh Muhammad ibn Abd al-Wahhab, al-Rasail al-shakhsiyya*, published by the Islamic University of Muhammad ibn Saud, on the occasion of "Shaykh Muhammad ibn Abd al-Wahhab Week," 1980. "I was never against *tawassul* nor against praising the Prophet, nor against *Dalail al-khayrat* [a book of prayers on the Prophet (ﷺ)], but all these I accept. I never said I reject the four schools and that I claim *ijtihad* and that I am exempt from *taqlid* [obligation to follow one of the schools of *fiqh*], and I do not say 'differences among the *ulama* are a curse' and I do not call *kafir* those who seek *tawassul* through the pious, and I don't call al-Busiri, who wrote *al-Mudariyya* and *al-Burda*, *kafir* for saying, 'O Most honored of creation,' and I never forbade the visit of the Prophet's tomb, and I never said, 'burn *Dalail al-khayrat* and *Rawd al-rayyahin* [books of praise of the Prophet (ﷺ)],' and I never said that Ibn al-Farid and Muhyiddin ibn Arabi were *kafir*s.' So, as Muhammad Ibn Abd al-Wahhab, student of Ibn Taymiyya, did not reject all of these things, why do some contemporary scholars reject them today? This is an unambiguous article published by a Saudi Arabian university on the occasion of Muhammad ibn Abd al-Wahhab Week, 1980. In fact, we must ask: if Muhammad ibn Abd al-Wahhab has a special week to commemorate his life and work, why then is it "wrong" with having one day—the 12th of Rabi al-Awwal to commemorate the life and work of the Greatest Perfect Human Being, Prophet Muhammad (ﷺ)?

ISLAMIC FUNDRAISERS AND *MAWLID*

Nowadays, we often see Muslims gather on specific days to serve food, give speeches on the life of the Prophet (ﷺ) and on Islam, to pray, recite the Quran and Islamic poetry, chant *qasidas* or *naat*, tell some jokes, and also collect money for the purchase of a mosque or an Islamic school. However, if one looks in the *sira*, the Prophet (ﷺ) never held a fundraising dinner. When he needed finances for a battle, to build a mosque or for whatever purpose, he asked his Companions to donate and they would give. Some gave all, some gave half, others gave what they could afford. Without the "bait" of delicious food or some show in a fancy hotel, they gave of their wealth—they simply obeyed.

No one has ever condemned fundraising dinners as a reprehensible innovation, although it is a newly-developed form of worship and an encouragement for worship (donation, *sadaqa*), without precedent in the life of the Prophet (ﷺ), his Companions, or the pious predecessors. Those who judge fairly and without bias must acknowledge there is no genuine difference between a fundraiser and a traditional *mawlid* ceremony commemorating the Prophet's birthday. One is a dinner and remembrance of the Prophet's birthday by means of different kinds of worship. However, a fundraising dinner might even involve mixing of men and women, women uncovered, and hosting non-Muslims as guests of honor, in whose attendance all take pride and for whom attendees stand in admiration and respect. If one wishes to be very strict, then we must apply the rules evenly and not discriminate. After all, what is more deserving of a dinner, a function or a ceremony—building a new mosque, or building love of the one who taught us to worship in mosques, peace be upon him?

CONCLUSION

In 1998, 50 years of the occupation of al-Quds was marked across the U.S. by many Islamic organizations. If al-Quds can be commemorated, cannot the one who was blessed by Allah to visit al-Quds and ascend from there to the heavens be commemorated on a special day? Imam Mutawalli Sharawi said in his book, *Maidat al-fikr al-islamiyya* (p. 295), "If living beings were happy for his coming (to this world) and every inanimate creation was happy at his birth and all plants were happy at his birth and all animals were happy at his birth and all angels were happy at his birth and all believing *jinn* were happy at his birth, why are you preventing us from being happy at his birth?"

We quote again from Mutawalli Sharawi: "Many extraordinary events occurred on his birthday as evidenced in hadith and history, and the night of his birth is not like the night of any other human being's birth." These events and the hadith pertaining thereto, such as the shaking of Chosroes' court, the extinction of the 1,000-year old fire in Persia, etc. are related in Ibn Kathir's work *al-Bidaya*, Vol. 2, pages 265-268. We hold the hope that every house, every *masjid*, every street, every school, college and university, every store and factory, every office and government department will shine with lights of happiness and rejoice in the person of the Prophet (ﷺ), just as the Kabah was illuminated in the time of our ancestors, and as paradises and skies were illuminated with stars on the day of the Prophet's birth.

The evidence we have quoted proves beyond a shadow of a doubt that the celebration of the *mawlid* and all that pertains thereto of praise and respect for the Prophet (ﷺ) of Islam such as *salawat*, prayers on the Prophet (ﷺ), *sira* (life story), *qasida* (poetry), and *madih* (praise) is not only permissible but according to most opinions is praiseworthy and recommended! Thus Muslims are encouraged to celebrate and commemorate their Prophet (ﷺ) with pride and joy and not to go into dispute in matters that create discord and confusion.

We conclude with the hadith of Muslim, "The Prophet (ﷺ) said 'Whoever innovates something good in Islam will have its reward and the reward of all those who act according to it, and whoever innovates something evil will have its sin and the sin of those who act according to it.'"

This is a clear statement, along with the numerous proofs presented here and in the *fatwa* of the *Awqaf* of Dubai, supported by the opinions of the most highly regarded scholars of Islam, of the acceptability of *mawlid* and of its deserving reward. This article was not written to cause division and discord, but rather to end the arguments revolving around this topic. Let everyone follow their heart and let us unify ourselves and keep Allah's order in the Holy Quran to *"Hold fast to the rope of Allah and do not separate."* Let us pray for Heavenly Support for a better Islamic world in which everyone can find a place for himself or herself, based on the accepted schools of thought and the *ijtihad* of scholars.

1. *MAWLID*: COMMEMORATING THE PROPHET'S BIRTHDAY

This chapter addresses the following issues among others:

Is there evidence for the commemoration of the Prophet's birthday (*mawlid*) in the Quran and the *sunna*?

What do the imams and scholars of the recognized schools say about the permissibility of commemorating the Prophet's birthday (*mawlid*)? What about the handful of modern "Salafis" like Albani, Bin Baz, al-Jazairi, Mashhur Salman, Uthaymin and their followers who forbid it on the grounds that it is an innovation?

What about "Salafis" who tolerate the commemoration of the Prophet's birthday (*mawlid*), but forbid people from standing at the conclusion of the commemoration while sending blessings (*salawat*) and peace (*salam*) on the Prophet (ﷺ)?

What about the objection by those influenced by the "Salafis" to using the phrase, "*Al-salamu alayka ya rasul Allah* (peace be upon you, O Messenger of Allah)," and their claim that one cannot call the Prophet (ﷺ) with the term *ya* (O)?

1.1. TEN PROOFS FROM THE QURAN AND SUNNA THAT COMMEMORATING THE PROPHET'S BIRTHDAY IS ACCEPTED ISLAMIC PRACTICE

1.1.1. THE OBLIGATION TO INCREASE THE LOVE AND HONOR OF THE PROPHET (ﷺ)

First, Allah asks the Prophet (ﷺ) to remind his Community that it is essential for those who claim to love Allah to love His Prophet (ﷺ), *"Say to them, 'If you love Allah, follow (and love and honor) me, and Allah will love you'"* (3:31).

The commemoration of the Holy Prophet's birth is motivated by this obligation to love the Prophet (ﷺ), to obey him, to remember him, to follow his example, and to be proud of him as Allah is proud of him. Allah has boasted about him in His Holy Book saying, *"Truly you are of a magnificent character"* (68:4).

Love of the Prophet (ﷺ) is what differentiates the believers in the perfection of their *iman*. In an authentic hadith related in Bukhari and Muslim, the Prophet (ﷺ) said, "None of you believes until he loves me more than he loves his children, his parents, and all people." In another hadith in Bukhari he said, "None of you believes until he loves me more than he loves himself." Umar ibn al-Khattab said, "O Prophet (ﷺ), I love you more than myself."

Perfection of faith is dependent on love of the Prophet (ﷺ) because Allah and His angels are constantly raising his honor, as is clear in the verse, *"Allah and His angels are praying on the Prophet"* (33:56). The divine order, *"O believers, pray on him,"* that immediately follows makes it clear that the quality of being a believer is dependent on and manifested by sending blessings to the Prophet (ﷺ).

1.1.2. THE PROPHET (ﷺ) EMPHASIZED MONDAY AS THE DAY HE WAS BORN

Second, Abu Qatada al-Ansari narrates that the Prophet (ﷺ) was asked about the fast of Monday, and he answered,

"That is the day that I was born and that is the day I received the prophecy."[1]

Shaykh Mutawalli Sharawi writes, "Many extraordinary events occurred on his birthday as evidenced in hadith and history, and the night of his birth is not like the night of any other human being's birth."[2]

According to Ibn al-Hajj,

> It is an obligation that on every Monday of Rabi al-Awwal we increase our worship to thank Allah for what He gave us as a great favor–the favor of sending us His beloved Prophet (ﷺ) to direct us to Islam and to peace . . . The Prophet (ﷺ), when answering someone questioning him about fasting on Mondays, mentioned, "I was born on that day." Therefore that day gives honor to that month, because that is the day of the Prophet (ﷺ) . . . and he said, "I am the master of the children of Adam and I say that without pride" . . . and he said, "Adam and whoever is descended from him are under my flag on the Day of Judgment." These hadiths were transmitted by the *shaykhayn* [Bukhari and Muslim]. And Muslim quotes in his *Sahih* that the Prophet (ﷺ) said,"On that day, Monday, I was born and on that day the first message was sent to me."[3]

The Prophet (ﷺ) emphasized the day of his birth and thanked Allah for the favor of bringing him to life by fasting on that day, as mentioned in the hadith of Abu Qatada. The Prophet (ﷺ) expressed his happiness for that day by fasting, which is a kind of worship. Since the Prophet (ﷺ) emphasized that day by fasting, worship in any form to emphasize that day is also acceptable. Even if the form is different, the essence remains the same. Therefore, fasting, giving food to the poor, coming together to praise the Prophet (ﷺ), or coming together to remember his good manners and good behavior, are all considered ways of emphasizing that day.[4]

---

1 *Sahih Muslim, Kitab al-siyam.*

2 These events and the hadith pertaining thereto, such as the shaking of Chosroe's court, the extinction of the 1,000-year old fire in Persia, etc. are related in Ibn Kathir's work *al-Bidaya*, Vol. 2, pages 265-268.

3 Ibn al-Hajj, in the book *Kitab al-madkhal* (1:261).

4 See also the hadith "Dying on Monday" below.

1.1.3. ALLAH SAID: "REJOICE IN THE PROPHET"

Third, expressing happiness about the advent of the Prophet (ﷺ) is an obligation given by Allah through Quran, as He said, *"Of the favor and mercy of Allah let them rejoice"* (10:58).

This order came because joy makes the heart grateful for the mercy of Allah. What greater mercy did Allah give than the Prophet (ﷺ) himself, of whom Allah says, *"We did not send you except as a mercy to human beings"* (21:107).

Since the Prophet (ﷺ) was sent as a mercy to all mankind, it is incumbent not only upon Muslims, but upon all human beings to celebrate his person. Unfortunately, today it is a few Muslims who are foremost in rejecting Allah's order to rejoice in His Prophet (ﷺ).

1.1.4. THE PROPHET (ﷺ) COMMEMORATED GREAT HISTORICAL EVENTS

Fourth, the Prophet (ﷺ) always made the connection between religious and historical events, so that when the day of a significant event arrived, he reminded his Companions (*sahaba*) to celebrate that day and to emphasize it, even if it happened in the distant past. This principle can be found in the following hadith:

> When the Prophet (ﷺ) reached Madina, he saw the Jews fasting on the day of Ashura. He asked about that day and they told him that on that day, Allah saved their Prophet, Moses (ﷺ), and drowned their enemy. Therefore they were fasting on that day to thank Allah for that favor.[5]

At that time the Prophet (ﷺ) responded with the famous hadith, "We have more right to Moses (ﷺ) than you," and he used to fast that day and the day preceding it.

1.1.5. ALLAH SAID: "INVOKE BLESSINGS ON THE PROPHET"

Fifth, remembrance of the birth of the Prophet (ﷺ) encourages us to send blessings to the Prophet (ﷺ) and to praise him,

---

5 Bukhari and others.

which is an obligation according to the verse, *"Allah and His angels pray on (and praise) the Prophet; O believers! Send blessings to (and praise) him and send him utmost greetings"* (33:56). As coming together and remembering the Prophet (ﷺ) leads us to send blessings to him and to praise him, it accords with Allah's command. Who has the right to deny the obligation which Allah has ordered us to fulfill through the Holy Quran? The benefit brought by obeying an order of Allah, and the light that it brings to the heart cannot be measured. That obligation, furthermore, is mentioned in the plural, Allah and His angels are praying on and praising the Prophet (ﷺ)—in a gathering. It is entirely incorrect, therefore, to say that sending blessings to and praising the Prophet (ﷺ) cannot be done in a group and must be done alone.

1.1.6. THE EFFECT ON DISBELIEVERS OF OBSERVING THE PROPHET'S BIRTHDAY

Sixth, expressing happiness and commemorating the Prophet (ﷺ) on his birthday causes even unbelievers, by Allah's favor and mercy, to gain some benefit.[6] Bukhari said in his hadith that every Monday, Abu Lahab is released from punishment in his grave because he freed his handmaid Thuwayba, the Prophet's wet-nurse. Some scholars, such as Ibn Kathir and Ibn Nasir al-Din al-Dimashqi, said that this was because Abu Lahab rejoiced when she brought him the news of the birth of a nephew. However, it is more likely that the manumission occurred in the Prophet's adulthood, at the time of his migration to Madina.[7]

The *hafiz* Shams al-Din Muhammad ibn Nasir al-Din al-

---

6 This is mentioned in *Sahih Bukhari*.

7 This hadith is mentioned in Bukhari in the book of *Nikah* and elsewhere, and Ibn Kathir mentions it in his books *Sirat al-nabi* (1:124), *Mawlid al-nabi* (p. 21), and *al-Bidaya* (p. 272-273). There is doubt as to the connection of Thuwayba's manumission with the Prophet's birth. Bukhari's narration, as well as similar narrations in Muslim, Nasai and Ahmad, are ambiguous in that regard: Narrated Ursa: Thuwayba was the freed slave girl of Abu Lahab whom he had manumitted, and she suckled the Prophet. When Abu Lahab died, one of his relatives saw him in a dream in a very bad state and asked him, "What have you found?" Abu Lahab said, "I have not found any rest since I left you, except that I have been given water to drink in this (the space between his thumb and other fingers) and that is because of my manumitting Thuwayba." Evidence from Ibn Sad, *Tabaqat* does indicate that Abu Lahab manumitted Thuwayba in connection with the Prophet's migration. The source for this is the notice in Ibn Hajar, *al-Isaba*, book of the Women, under "Thuwayba" (8:36), citing the narration from Ibn Sad in his *Tabaqat*, chapter of "those who nursed the Prophet":

Dimashqi wrote the following verse, about this "If this, a *kafir* who was condemned to hell eternally with '*Perish his hands*' [*sura* 111], is said to enjoy a respite every Monday because he rejoiced in Ahmad, what then do you think of the servant who, all his life, was happy with Ahmad, and died saying, 'One'?"[8]

1.1.7. THE OBLIGATION TO KNOW THE LIFE OF THE PROPHET (ﷺ) (*SIRA*) AND IMITATE HIS CHARACTER

Seventh, we are asked to know about our Prophet (ﷺ), about his life, about his miracles, about his birth, about his manners, about his faith, about his signs (*ayat wa dalail*), about his seclusions, and about his worship. Is this knowledge not an obligation for every Muslim?

What is better than celebrating and remembering his birth, which represents the essence of his life, in order to understand his life? To remember his birth reminds us of everything else about him, and thus enables us to know the Prophet's *sira* better. We will be more prepared to take the Prophet (ﷺ) as our exemplar, to correct ourselves, and to imitate him. That is why the celebration of his birthday is a great favor sent to all Muslims.

1.1.8. THE PROPHET (ﷺ) ACCEPTED POETRY IN HIS HONOR

Eighth, it is well-known that, in the time of the Prophet (ﷺ), poets came to him with all kinds of works praising him, and wrote about his campaigns and battles and about the Companions. This is evident in the numerous poems quoted in the Life of the Prophet (ﷺ) (*sira*) of Ibn Hisham, al-Waqidi, and others. The Prophet (ﷺ) was happy with good poetry, as it is reported in Bukhari and elsewhere that he said: "There is wisdom in poetry."[9] The Prophet's uncle al-Abbas composed poetry praising the birth of the Prophet (ﷺ), including the following lines:

> When you were born, the earth was shining,

"Thuwayba was the Prophet's milk-nurse and he would treat her as his family while he was in Makka, and Khadija would treat her with great respect; at that time she was owned by Abu Lahab and Khadija asked him to sell her to her, but he refused. When the Prophet migrated, Abu Lahab manumitted her."

8 Hafiz Shamsuddin Muhammad ibn Nasir al-Din al-Dimashqi in his book *Mawrid al-sadi fi mawlid al-hadi*.

9 *al-Adab al-mufrad*.

and the firmament barely contained your light,
and we can pierce through,
thanks to that radiance and light and path of
guidance.[10]

Ibn Kathir mentions the fact that, according to the
Companions, the Prophet (ﷺ) praised his own name and recited poetry about himself in the middle of the battle of Hunayn
in order to encourage the Companions and scare the enemies.
That day he said, "I am the Prophet! This is no lie. I am the
son of Abd al-Muttalib!"

The Prophet (ﷺ) was happy with those who praised him
because it is Allah's order, and he gave them some of what
Allah was providing him. Allah is well pleased with those who
gather and attempt to know and love the Prophet (ﷺ) of Allah.

1.1.8.1. Remarks: Singing and the Recitation of Poetry

It is established that the Prophet (ﷺ) instructed Aisha to
let two ladies sing on the day of *id*. He said to Abu Bakr, "Let
them sing, because for every nation there is a holiday, and this
is our holiday." Ibn Qayyim comments that the Prophet (ﷺ)
also gave permission to sing at wedding celebrations, and
allowed poetry to be recited to him.[11] He heard Anas and the
Companions praising him and reciting poems while digging
before the famous battle of the Trench (*khandaq*); he heard
them say, "We are the ones who gave allegiance (*baya*) to
Muhammad for jihad as long as we are living."

Ibn Qayyim also mentions Abdullah ibn Rawaha's recitation of a long poem in praise of the Prophet (ﷺ) as he entered
Makka, after which the Prophet (ﷺ) prayed for him. The
Prophet (ﷺ) prayed that Allah support Hassan ibn Thabit with
the holy spirit as long as he would support the Prophet (ﷺ)
with his poetry. Similarly, the Prophet (ﷺ) rewarded Kab ibn
Zuhayr's poem of praise with a robe. The Prophet (ﷺ) asked al-
Sharid ibn Suwayd al-Thaqafi to recite a poem of praise one
hundred verses long that Umayya ibn Abi al-Salt had com-

---

10 This text is found in Suyuti, *Husn al-maqsid* p. 5 and in Ibn Kathir's *Mawlid*
p. 30 as well as Ibn Hajar, *Fath al-bari*.
11 Ibn Qayyim, in *Madarij al-salikin*.

posed.[12] Ibn Qayyim continues, "Aisha always recited poems praising him and he was happy with her."

Umayya ibn Abi al-Salt is a poet of Jahiliyya who died in Damascus before Islam. He was a pious man who had relinquished the use of wine and the worship of idols.[13] Part of the funeral eulogy that Hassan ibn Thabit recited for the Prophet (ﷺ) states:

I say, and none can find fault with me
But one lost to all sense:
I shall never cease to praise him.
It may be for so doing I shall be forever in paradise
With the Chosen One for whose support in that I hope.
And to attain to that day I devote all my efforts.[14]

1.1.8.2. REMARKS: RECITATION OF
THE QURAN AND SINGING
Ibn al-Qayyim says in his book, *Madarij al-salikin*:

> Allah gave permission to His Prophet (ﷺ) to recite the Quran in a melodious way. Abu Musa al-Ashari one time was reciting the Quran in a melodious voice and the Prophet (ﷺ) was listening to him. After he finished, the Prophet (ﷺ) congratulated him on reciting in a melodious way and said, "You have a good voice." And he said about Abu Musa al-Ashari that Allah gave him a '*mizmar*' (flute or horn) from Dawud's *mizmar*s. Then Abu Musa said, "O Messenger of Allah, if I had known that you were listening to me, I would have recited it in a much more melodious and beautiful voice such as you have never heard before."

Ibn Qayyim also relates that the Prophet (ﷺ) said, "Decorate the Quran with your voices," and "Who does not sing the Quran is not from us." Ibn Qayyim comments:

> To take pleasure in a good voice is acceptable, as is taking pleasure in a nice scenery, such as moun-

---

12 Narrated by Muslim.
13 Related by Dhahabi in *Siyar alam al-nubala* (2:23).
14 Ibn Hisham's notes to his *Sirat rasul Allah*, trans. A. Guillaume, 9th printing (Karachi: Oxford U. Press, 1990) p. 797.

tains or nature, or from a nice smell, or from good food, as long as it conforms to the Sharia. If listening to a good voice is forbidden (*haram*), then taking pleasure in all these other things is also forbidden (*haram*).

1.1.8.3. REMARKS: THE PROPHET (ﷺ) ALLOWED DRUM-PLAYING IF THERE WAS A GOOD INTENTION

Ibn Abbad the *Muhaddith* gave the following edict (*fatwa*) in his "Letters." He begins with the hadith,

> A lady went to the Prophet (ﷺ) when he was returning from one of his battles and she said,"*Ya rasul Allah*, I have swore an oath that if Allah sends you back safe, I would play this drum near you." The Prophet (ﷺ) said, "Fulfill your oath."[15]

Ibn Abbad continues:

> There is no doubt that the playing of a drum is a kind of entertainment, even though the Prophet (ﷺ) ordered her to fulfill her oath. He did that because her intention was to honor him for returning safely, and her intention was a good intention, not with the intention of a sin or of wasting time. Therefore, if any-one celebrates the time of the birth of the Prophet (ﷺ) in a good way, with a good intention, by reading *sira* and praising him, it is accepted.

1.1.9. THE PROPHET (ﷺ) EMPHASIZED THE BIRTHDAY OF THE PROPHETS

Ninth, the Prophet (ﷺ) emphasized in his hadith both the day and the place of birth of previous prophets. In regard to the greatness of the day of Friday (*juma*), the Prophet (ﷺ) said, "On that day [i.e. *juma*], Allah created Adam." Thus Friday is emphasized because Allah created Adam on that day. That day is emphasized because it saw the creation of a prophet and the father of all human beings. What about the day when the greatest of prophets and best of human beings was created? The Prophet (ﷺ) said, "Truly Allah made me the Seal of Prophets while Adam was between water and clay."[16]

---

15 The hadith is found in Abu Dawud, Tirmidhi, and Ahmad.
16 This hadith is related by Ahmad in the *Musnad*, Bayhaqi in *Dalail al-*

1.1.9.1. REMARKS: WHY BUKHARI EMPHASIZED DYING ON MONDAY

Imam Qastallani said in his commentary on Bukhari:

> In his book on *Janaiz* (Funerals), Bukhari named an entire chapter "Dying on Monday." In it there is the hadith of Aisha relating her father's (Abu Bakr al-Siddiq) question, "On which day did the Prophet (ﷺ) die?" She replied, "Monday." He asked, "What day are we today?" She said, "O my father, this is Monday." Then he raised his hands and said, "I beg you, O Allah, to let me die on Monday in order to coincide with the Prophet's day of passing."

Imam Qastallani continues:

> Why did Abu Bakr ask for his death to be on Monday? So that his death would coincide with the day of the Prophet's passing, in order to receive the blessing (*baraka*) of that day . . . Does anyone object to Abu Bakr's asking to pass away on that day for the sake of blessings? Now, why are people objecting to celebrating or emphasizing the day of the Prophet's birth in order to receive blessings?

1.1.9.2. REMARKS: THE PROPHET (ﷺ) EMPHASIZED THE BIRTHPLACE OF PROPHETS

A hadith authenticated by the *hafiz* al-Haythami states that, on the night of the Night Journey (*isra* and *miraj*), the Prophet (ﷺ) was ordered by Gabriel to pray two cycles (*rakat*) in Bethlehem (*Bayt Lahm*) Gabriel asked him, "Do you know where you prayed? When the Prophet (ﷺ) asked him where, he told him, "You prayed where Jesus was born."[17]

1.1.10. THE UNANIMOUS ACCEPTANCE OF RELIGIOUS SCHOLARS OF COMMEMORATING THE PROPHET'S BIRTHDAY

Tenth, remembering the Prophet's birthday is an act that all religious scholars (*ulama*) of the Muslim world accept and still accept. For this reason it is considered a holy day in all

---

Nubuwwa and others, and is sound and established as authentic.

17 Narrated from Shaddad ibn Aws by al-Bazzar, Abu Yala, and Tabarani. Haythami said in *Majma al-zawaid* (1:47): "Its narrators are the men of the sound collections." Ibn Hajar mentioned this hadith in his *Fath al-bari* (7:199) without saying

Muslim countries. Allah accepts it, according to the saying of Ibn Masud, "Whatever the majority of Muslims see as right, then this is good to Allah, and whatever is seen by the majority of Muslims as wrong, it is wrong to Allah."[18]

1.2. HISTORY OF THE COMMEMORATION OF THE PROPHET'S BIRTHDAY (*MAWLID*)

1.2.1. THE COMMEMORATION OF THE PROPHET'S BIRTHDAY IN MAKKA ACCORDING TO MUSLIM HISTORIANS, AND COMMEMORATION OF THE PROPHET'S BIRTHPLACE

Makka, the Mother of Cities, may Allah bless and honor her, is the leader of other Islamic cities in the celebration of *mawlid*, as in other things. The third-century historian of Makka, al-Azraqi, mentions the house where the Prophet (ﷺ) was born (*mawlid al-nabi*) among the many places in Makka where the performance of prayer (*salat*) is desirable (*mustahabb*).[19] According to him, the house had previously been turned into a mosque by the mother of the caliphs, Musa al-Hadi and Harun ar-Rashid.

The Quranic scholar al-Naqqash (266-351) mentions the birthplace of the Prophet (ﷺ) as a place where supplication (*dua*) by noon on Mondays is answered.[20]

1.2.2. EARLIEST MENTION OF PUBLIC *MAWLID*

The oldest source that mentions a public commemoration of the *mawlid* is in Ibn Jubayr's (540-614) *Rihal* ("Travels"):

> This blessed place [the house of the Prophet (ﷺ)]
> is opened, and all men enter it to derive blessing from
> it (*mutabarrikin bihi*), on every Monday of the month
> of Rabi al-Awwal; for on that day and in that month
> was born the Prophet (ﷺ).[21]

The seventh-century historians Abu al Abbas al-Azafi and his son Abu al Qasim al-Azafi wrote:

> Pious pilgrims and prominent travelers testified

anything against it.
18 Related in Imam Ahmad's *Musnad* with a sound chain.
19 Al-Azraqi, in his book *Akhbar Makka*, Vol. 2, p. 160.
20 Al-Naqqash is quoted in al-Fasis *Shifa al-gharam* Vol. 1, p. 199, and others.
21 Ibn Jubayr, *Ribal*, p. 114-115.

that, on the day of the *mawlid* in Makka, no activities are undertaken, and nothing is sold or bought, except by the people who are busy visiting his noble birth-place, and rush to it. On this day the Kabah is opened and visited.[22]

1.2.3. Ibn Battuta's Account
of the *Mawlid*

The famous eighth-century historian, Ibn Battuta, relates that on every Friday after the *salat*, and on the birthday of the Prophet (ﷺ), the door of Kabah was opened by the head of the *Banu Shayba*, the doorkeepers of the Kabah. On the *mawlid*, he relates that the head judge (*Shafii qadi*) of Makka, Najmuddin Muhammad Ibn al-Imam Muhyiddin al-Tabari, distributed food to the descendants of the Prophet (ﷺ) (*shurafa*) and to all the other people of Makka.[23]

1.2.4. Three Tenth-century
Accounts of the *Mawlid*

The following description consolidates the eyewitness accounts of three tenth-century authorities: the historian Ibn Zahira al-Hanafi, Imam Ibn Hajar al-Haytami, and the historian al-Nahrawali.

> Each year on the 12th of Rabi al-Awwal, after the evening prescribed prayer (*salat al-maghrib*), the four *qadi*s of Makka (each representing one of the schools of law) and large groups of people including the scholars (*fuqaha*) and notables (*fudala*) of Makka, shaykhs, *zawiya* teachers and their students, magistrates (*ruasa*), and scholars (*mutaammamin,* literally, 'turbaned ones') leave the mosque and set out collectively for a visit to the birthplace of the Prophet (ﷺ), shouting out invocations (*dhikr*) and *tahlil* (*la ilaha illallah*). The houses on the route are illuminated with many lanterns and large candles. A great many people are out and about. They all wear special clothes and take their children with them. Having reached the birthplace, inside a special sermon for the

---

22 Abul Abbas al-Azafi and his son Abul Qasim al-Azafi in their unpublished *Kitab ad-durr al-munazzam*.

23 Ibn Battuta, in his *Rihla* (1:309 and 1:347).

occasion of the birthday of the Prophet (ﷺ) is delivered, mentioning the miracles (*karamat*) that took
place on that occasion. Hereafter the supplication
(*dua*) for the Sultan (i.e. the Caliph), the Amir of
Makka, and the Shafii *qadi* is performed and all pray
humbly. Shortly before the night prescribed prayer
(*salat al-isha*), the whole party returns from the
birthplace of the Prophet (ﷺ) to the Great Mosque,
which is almost overcrowded, and all sit down in rows
at the foot of the Station of Abraham (*maqam
ibrahim*). In the mosque, a preacher first mentions
the *tahmid* (*al-hamdulillah*) and the *tahlil*, and once
again the supplication for the Sultan, the Amir and
the Shafii *qadi* is performed. After this the call for the
night prescribed prayer (*salat al-isha*) is made. After
the prayer, the crowd disperses.[24]

1.2.5. THE *MAWLID* IN
MUSLIM COUNTRIES TODAY

In every Muslim country today, there are people celebrating
the Prophet's birthday. This is true of Egypt, Syria, Lebanon,
Jordan, Palestine, Iraq, Kuwait, the Emirates, Saudi Arabia,[25]
Sudan, Yemen, Libya, Tunisia, Algeria, Morocco, Mauritania,
Djibouti, Somalia, Turkey, Pakistan, India, Sri Lanka, Iran,
Afghanistan, Azerbaijan, Uzbekistan, Turkestan, Bosnia,
Indonesia, Malaysia, Brunei, Singapore, and most other
Islamic countries. In most Arab countries it is a national holi-
day. As all these countries celebrate this event, it is odd that
today a vocal minority can rule that it is forbidden (*haram*).
Who are these scholars who speak against *mawlid*, as opposed
to the hadith masters (*huffaz*) and scholars of the Community
like Abu Shama, Asqalani, Suyuti, Sakhawi, Haytami,
Shawkani, and al-Qari, who declare the commemoration of the
mawlid praiseworthy? How can any of the "Salafis" condemn
something that even the strictest of their scholars, Ibn
Taymiyya, allowed under certain conditions, and that Ibn al-
Jawzi and Ibn Kathir encouraged, each of them by writing a
booklet entitled *Mawlid* consisting of poems and passages from
the life of the Prophet (ﷺ) (*sira*)?

---

24 Ibn Zahira al-Hanafi, *al-Jami al-latif fi fasl Makka wa ahliha*, p. 326, Imam
Ibn Hajar al-Haytami, *Kitab al-mawlid al-sharif al-muazzam,* Al-Nahrawali, *al-Ilam
bi-alam bayt Allah al-haram*, p. 205. A similar description is given by al-Diyarbakri
(d. 960) in his *Tarikh al-Khamis.*
25 Not officially, but in the majority of homes.

1.3. THE COMMEMORATION OF THE PROPHET'S BIRTHDAY AS UNDERSTOOD BY "SALAFI" SCHOLARS AND MAINSTREAM ISLAMIC SCHOLARS

1.3.1. IBN TAYMIYYA'S OPINION OF THE *MAWLID* AND THE DEVIATION OF "SALAFIS" FROM HIS OPINION

The following is Ibn Taymiyya's opinion about the *mawlid*, as illustrated in his *Fatawa*:[26]

> And similarly what some people innovate by analogy with the Christians who celebrate the birth of Jesus, or out of love for the Prophet and to exalt him, and Allah may reward them for this love and effort, not on the fact that it is an innovation . . . To celebrate and to honor the birth of the Prophet and to take it as an honored season, as some of the people are doing, is good and in it there is a great reward, because of their good intentions in honoring the Prophet.

For all their cleaving to Ibn Taymiyya, the "Salafis" cannot seem to forgive him for saying this. One "Salafi" editor of the *Iqtida,* Muhammad Hamid al-Fiqqi, writes a two-page footnote to this text in which he exclaims, *Kayfa yakunu lahum thawabun ala hadha??* . . . *Ayyu ijtihadun fi hadha??* "How can they possibly obtain a reward for this?? . . . What kind of effort is in this??" Contemporary "Salafi" scholars are cut from the same cloth of intemperance and deviation regarding the commemoration (*mawlid*), substituting their own ruling in place of Ibn Taymiyya's although his should be sufficient for them. Another "Salafi" author, Mashhur Salman, explodes in the same way in his edition of Abu Shama's *al-Baith ala inkar al-bida* (Assault on all innovations), because instead of censoring the commemoration, Abu Shama declares, "Truly it is a praiseworthy innovation and a blessed one."

Further on in the above mentioned text, Ibn Taymiyya mentions an edict (*fatwa*) given by Imam Ahmad ibn Hanbal, the

---

26 From the Collected *Fatwas, Majma Fatawa Ibn Taymiyya*, Vol. 23, p. 133 and his *Iqtida al-sirat al-mustaqim*, p. 294-295, Section entitled: "The innovated festivities of time and place" *(ma uhditha min al-ayad al-zamaniyya wa al-makaniyya).*

Imam of Ibn Taymiyya's school of law when the people told Imam Ahmad about a prince who spent 1000 dinars on the decoration of Quran he said, "That is the best place for him to use gold."

Was Ibn Taymiyya promoting innovation (*bida*) when he permitted the commemoration of the *mawlid* "as some of the people are doing?" No. Not only did he allow it, but he mentioned that their commemoration of the *mawlid* "is good and in it there is reward." Was Imam Ahmad making innovation (*bida*) when he allowed the decoration of the Quran? The answer to both questions is no.

The permission of commemorating the birthday of the Prophet (ﷺ) by Ibn Taymiyya, whom his supporters misrepresent as a critic of the *mawlid*, has been pointed out by Sunni scholars, among them Said Hawwa, Muhammad ibn Alawi al-Maliki, Abd al-Karim Jawad, al-Sayyid Hashim al-Rifai, and the two shaykhs of al-Qarawiyyin Abd al-Hayy al-Amruni and Abd al-Karim Murad.[27]

1.3.2. Ibn Taymiyya's Views on the Meetings of the Remembrance of Allah (*dhikr*)

The following is Ibn Taymiyya's opinion on meetings for the purpose of remembrance of Allah (*dhikr*):

> Ibn Taymiyya was asked about people that gather in a mosque (*masjid*) remembering Allah (*dhikr*) and reading the Quran, praying to Allah and taking their turbans off their heads (leaving their heads bare) and crying, while their intention is not pride nor showing off but seeking to draw closer to Allah: is it acceptable or not? He answered: "Praise to Allah, it is good and recommended according to the Sharia (*mustahabb*) to come together to read the Quran, remember Allah (*dhikr*), and supplicate."[28]

1.3.3. Ibn Kathir Praises the Night of *Mawlid*

Imam Ibn Hajar al-Asqalani mentions that Ibn Kathir, a *muhaddith* from among the followers of Ibn Taymiyya, "in the

---

27 Said Hawwa, *al-Sira bi lughati al-shir wa al-hubb;* ibn Alawi al-Maliki, *Mafahim yajib an tusahhah;* al-Sayyid Hashim al-Rifai, *Adilla ahl al-sunna wa al-jamaa*, and Abd al-Hayy al-Amruni and Abd al-Karim Murad in their book *Hawla kitab al-hiwar ma al-maliki.*

28 Ibn Taymiyya, *Majmuat fatawa Ibn Taymiyya* 22:523. King Khalid ibn Abd al-Aziz edition.

last days of his life wrote a book entitled *Mawlid rasul Allah*
which was spread far and wide.[29] That book mentioned the permissibility and recommendation of commemorating the
mawlid."[30]

In Ibn Kathir's book, he says, "The Night of the Prophet's
birth is a magnificent, noble, blessed and holy night, a night of
bliss for the believers, pure, radiant with lights, and of immeasurable price."[31]

1.3.4. ASQALANI'S AND SUYUTI'S EDICTS (*FATAWA*) ON THE PERMISSIBILITY OF COMMEMORATING THE PROPHET'S BIRTHDAY (*MAWLID*)

Jalal al-Din al-Suyuti said,

> The Shaykh of Islam and hadith master of his
> age, Ahmad ibn Hajar (Asqalani) was asked about the
> practice of commemorating the birth of the Prophet
> (ﷺ), and gave the following written reply:
> As for the origin of the practice of commemorating
> the Prophet's birth, it is an innovation that has not
> been conveyed to us from any of the pious early
> Muslims of the first three centuries, despite which it
> has included both features that are praiseworthy and
> features that are not. If one takes care to include in
> such a commemoration only things that are praise-
> worthy and avoids those that are otherwise, it is a
> praiseworthy innovation, while if one does not, it is
> not.
> An authentic primary textual basis from which its
> legal validity is inferable has occurred to me, namely
> the rigorously authenticated (*sahih*) hadith in the col-
> lections of Bukhari and Muslim that the Prophet (ﷺ)
> went to Madina and found the Jews fasting on the
> tenth of Muharram (Ashura), so he asked them about
> it and they replied, "It is the day on which Allah
> drowned Pharaoh and rescued Moses (ﷺ), so we fast
> in it to give thanks to Allah Most High," which indi-
> cates the validity of giving thanks to Allah for the
> blessings He has bestowed on a particular day in pro-
> viding a benefit, or averting an affliction. We repeat
> our thanks on the anniversary of that day every year,

29 Ibn Hajar al-Asqalani, *al-Durar al-kamina fi ayn al-Miat al-thamina.*
30 Ibn Kathir, *Mawlid Rasul Allah*, ed. Salah al-Din Munajjad (Beirut: dar al-
kitab al-jadid, 1961).
31 *Ibid*. p. 19.

giving thanks to Allah with various forms of worship such as prostration, fasting, giving charity or reciting the Quran . . . Then what blessing is greater than the birth of the Prophet (ﷺ), the Prophet (ﷺ) of mercy, on this day? In light of which, one should take care to commemorate it on the day itself in order to conform to the above story of Prophet Moses (ﷺ) and the tenth of Muharram, [but] those who do not view the matter thus do not mind commemorating it on any day of the month, while some have expanded its time to any of day the year, whatever exception may be taken at such a view."[32]

1.3.5. The Opinion of Other Scholars on the *Mawlid*

According to the *mufti* of Makka, Ahmad ibn Zayni Dahlan, "To commemorate the birthday of the Prophet (ﷺ) (*mawlid*) and to remember the Prophet (ﷺ) is accepted by all the religious scholars (*ulama*) of the Muslims."[33]

Imam Subki said, "When we celebrate the Prophet's birthday, a great familiarity (*uns*) comes to our hearts, and we feel something special."

Imam Shawkani said, "It is permissible to celebrate the Prophet's birthday."[34] He mentioned that Mullah Ali Qari held the same opinion in a book entitled *al-Mawrid ar-rawi fi al-mawlid al-nabawi*, written specifically to support the celebration of the Prophet's birthday.

Imam Abu Shama, the shaykh of Imam Nawawi, said:

> The best innovation in our day is the remembrance of the Prophet's birthday. On that day, people give many donations, worship a great deal, show much love for the Prophet (ﷺ), and give much thanks to Allah Almighty for sending them His Messenger to keep them on the *sunna* and Sharia of Islam.[35]

Imam Sakhawi said, "The commemoration of the Prophet's birthday (*mawlid*) was begun three centuries after the Prophet (ﷺ). All Muslim nations celebrated it and all *ulama* accepted it,

---

32 Suyuti, *al-Hawi li al-fatawi* as cited in al-Misri, *The Reliance of the Traveller*, trans. Nuh Ha Mim Keller, section w58.0.

33 Ahmad ibn Zayni Dahlan, *al-Sira al-nabawiyya wa al-athar al-muhammadiyya*, page 51. Most of the following quotations are taken from that work.

34 Imam Shawkani, in his book *al-Badr al-tali*.

35 Imam Abu Shama, in his book on innovations entitled: *al-Baith ala inkar al-bida wa al-hawadith*.

by worshipping Allah alone, by giving donations and by reading the Prophet's *sira*."

Hafiz Ibn Hajar al-Haytami said, "As Jews celebrated the day of Ashura by fasting to thank Allah, we also have to celebrate the day of *mawlid*." He quoted the aforementioned hadith, "When the Prophet (ﷺ) came to Madina . . ." Ibn Hajar continues:

> One gives thanks to Allah for the favor that He gave on a particular day either through a great good, or through the averting of a disaster. That day is celebrated every year thereafter. Thanksgiving entails various forms of worship like prostration, fasting, charity, and the recitation of Quran, and what greater good is there than the advent of that Prophet (ﷺ), the Prophet (ﷺ) of Mercy, on the day of *mawlid*?

Ibn al-Jawzi (d. 597) wrote a booklet of poems and *sira* to be read at *mawlid* celebrations. It is entitled *Mawlid al-arus*[36] and begins with the words, *al-hamdu lillah al-ladhi abraza min ghurrati arusi al-hadrati subhan mustanira* "Praise be to Allah Who has manifested from the radiance of the bridegroom of His Presence a light-giving daybreak . . ."

1.3.6. It is Recommended to Commemorate the Prophet's Birthday (*MAWLID*)

Imam Suyuti says:

> The reason for gathering for *tarawih* prayers is *sunna* and a way to seek nearness to Allah (*qurba*) . . . and similarly we say that the reason for gathering to commemorate *mawlid* is recommended (*mandub*) and an act of drawing near (*qurba*). . . and the intention to celebrate *mawlid* is excellent (*mustahsana*) without a doubt.[37]

Imam Suyuti continues:

> I have derived the permissibility of *mawlid* from another source of the *sunna* [besides Ibn Hajar's deduction from the hadith of Ashura], namely, the

---

36 Ibn al-Jawzi, *Mawlid al-arus*, Damascus: Maktabat al-hadara 1955.
37 Imam Suyuti, *Husn al-maqsid fi amal al-mawlid*, p. 54 and 62.

hadith found in Bayhaqi, narrated by Anas, "The Prophet (ﷺ) slaughtered a sacrifice for newborns (*aqiqa*) for himself after he received the prophecy," although it has been mentioned that his grandfather Abd al-Muttalib did that on the seventh day after he was born, and the *aqiqa* cannot be repeated.[38] Thus the reason for the Prophet's action is to give thanks to Allah for sending him as a mercy to the worlds, and to give honor to his Community, in the same way that he used to pray on himself. It is recommended for us, therefore, that we also show thanks for his birth by meeting with our brothers, by feeding people, and other such good works and rejoicing.[39]

This hadith confirms the aforementioned hadith of the Prophet's emphasis of Monday as the day of his birth and of his prophethood.

1.3.7. CONCERNING THE CLAIM OF THE CONTEMPORARY "SALAFI" WRITERS LIKE ALBANI, BIN BAZ, ABU BAKR JAZIRI, MASHHUR SALMAN, UTHAYMIN AND OTHERS WHO FORBADE THE *MAWLID*

The claim that commemoration of the *mawlid* is an innovation is not only an innovative departure from what the majority of the past scholars have said on the question. It is, first and foremost, defective in its logic and reasoning, since the scholars have defined innovations as being sometimes good, sometimes bad, and sometimes indifferent. Therefore it is not allowed to prohibit something solely on the ground that it is an innovation without first defining what kind of innovation it is.

There is an excellent innovation (*bida hasana*), according to the majority of the scholars who have written about innovation (*bida*), though some, like Ibn al-Jawzi and Ibn Taymiyya, consider all innovation (*bida*) to be innovation of misguidance (*bida dalala*). Their position in this is anomalous (*shadhdh*) and deviating from the norm, as the following evidence shows:

1 Harmala ibn Yahya said, I heard al-Shafii saying:

al-bidatu bidatan: bida mahmuda wa bida madhmuma, fa ma wafaqa al-sunna fa huwa mahmud, wa ma khalafa al-

---

38 The *hadith* is in Bayhaqi, *Sunan*, Vol. 9 p. 300, and in Haythami, *Majma al-zawaid*, Vol. 4, p. 59, who says that al-Bazzar and Tabarani relate it, the latter with a sound chain of transmission.

39 Suyuti, p. 64-65.

sunna fa huwa madhmum (Innovation is of two kinds: the praiseworthy innovation and the blameworthy innovation. Whatever conforms to the *sunna* is praiseworthy, and whatever contravenes the *sunna* is blameworthy).[40]

2. *Al-Hafiz al-Izz* Ibn Abd al-Salam said:
There are five types of innovation (*bida*):
Haram (forbidden)
Makhruh (disliked)
Mubah (permitted)
Mandub (praiseworthy)
Wajib (obligatory).[41]

3. Others who admitted the possibility of praiseworthy innovation (*bida*) are:

Abu Shama. He divided it into *bida mustahsana / hasana* on the one hand, and *bida mustaqbaha*, itself subdivided into *muharram* and *makruh,* on the other.[42]

Al-Turkumani al-Hanafi. He divided it into either *bida mustahsana* (approved), such as *mubaha yuthab alayha* (per-

---

40 Sources: *Al-hafiz* Abu Nuaym al-Asbahani cites it in *Hilyat al-awliya* (9:113); *al-hafiz* Ibn Hajar al-Asqalani also in *Fath al-bari* (13:253); *al-hafiz* Ibn Rajab al Hanbali also in *Jami al-ulum wa al-hikam* (p. 291); *al-hafiz* Abu Shama in *al-Baith ala inkar al-bida wa al-hawadith,* ed. Mashhur Hasan Salman (Riyadh: Dar al-Raya, 1990/1410) p. 93; Cairo edition, p. 12; *al-hafiz* al-Turtushi al-Maliki, *Kitab al-hawadith wa al-bida* (p. 158-159); He himself divided the *bida* into *muharrama* (forbidden), *makruha* (disliked), and *wajiba* (obligatory): p. 15; *al-hafiz* al-Suyuti alludes to it in the introduction to his *fatwa* on *mawlid* entitled *Husn al-maqsid fi amal al-mawlid* in *al-Hawi li al-fatawi; al-hafiz* Ibn Taymiyya, *Dar taarud al-aql wa al-naql,* ed. Muhammad al-Sayyid Julaynid (Cairo: Muassasat al-ahram, 1409/1988) p. 171: "Bayhaqi narrated it in *al-Madkhal* with a sound chain"; *al-hafiz* al-Bayhaqi, *Manaqib al-Shafii* (1:469) in these words: *"Al-muhdathatu min al-umuri darbani ahaduhuma ma uhditha yukhalifu kitaban aw sunnatan aw atharan aw ijmaan fa hadhihi al-bidatu al-dalalat wa al-thaniyatu ma uhditha min al-khayri la khilafa fihi li wahidin min hadhihi wa hadhihi muhdathatun ghayru madhmuma.* (Innovated matters are one of two kinds: one is an innovation which contravenes something in the Quran or the *sunna* or a report from a Companion or the consensus of the scholars: this is the innovation of misguidance *(bida dalala);* the other kind is whatever good has been innovated which contravenes none of the above, and this is an innovation that is not blameworthy *(muhdathatun ghayru madhmuma))."*

41 Sources: *Al-hafiz* al-Shatibi, *Kitab al-itisam* (Beirut ed.) 1:188; *al-hafiz* al-Imam al-Nawawi, *Kitab al-Adhkar* (Beirut: al-Thaqafiyya) p. 237; and *Tahdhib al-asma wa al-lughat* ([Cairo]: Idarat al-Tibaah al-Muniriyah, [1927]?) 3: 22; *al-hafiz* Ibn Abidin, *Radd al-muhtar* (Kuitah, Pakistan ed.?) 1:376; *al-hafiz* al-Suyuti mentions it in the introduction to his *fatwa* on *mawlid* entitled *Husn al-maqsid fi amal al-mawlid* in *al-Hawi li al-fatawi.*

42 Abu Shama, *al-Baith ala inkar al-bida wa al-hawadith* Cairo ed. (p. 13).

mitted innovation which merits reward), or *bida mustaqbaha* (disapproved), such as *makruha* or *muharrama*.[43]

Ibn al-Hajj al-Abdari al-Maliki, who followed Ibn Abd al-Salam's classification.[44]

Al-Tahanawi al-Hanafi, who also followed *al-Izz* Ibn Abd al-Salam.[45]

Al-Hafiz Ibn Hajar al-Asqalani, in his commentary of Umar's saying about *salat al-tarawih,* "What a fine innovation this is" *(nimat al-bida hadhih):*[46]

> The root meaning of innovation is what is produced without precedent. It is applied in the law in opposition to the *sunna* and is therefore blameworthy. Strictly speaking, if it is part of what is classified as commendable by the law then it is a good innovation (*hasana*), while if it is part of what is classified as blameworthy by the law then it is blameworthy (*mustaqbaha*), otherwise it falls in the category of what is permitted indifferently (*mubah*). It can be divided into the known five categories.[47]

1.3.8. QUESTIONS PERTAINING TO THE COMMEMORATION OF THE PROPHET'S BIRTHDAY (*MAWLID*)

1.3.8.1.

Q. Certain people still object saying, "What about the hadith *kullu bidatin dalala* 'Every innovation is a misguidance'? Doesn't the term 'every' include all innovations?"

A. Such an objection stems from the misinterpretation of the term *kullu* ("every") to mean "all-encompassing without exception," whereas in Arabic it may mean "nearly all" or "the vast majority." This is how al-Shafii understood it; otherwise he would have never allowed any innovation whatsoever to be considered good. Moreover, he is considered a *hujja* or "proof;" that is, a resource without equal for questions regarding the Arabic

43 Al-Turkumani al-Hanafi, *Kitab al-luma fi al-hawadith wa al-bida* (Stuttgart, 1986) 1:37.

44 Ibn al-Hajj al-Abdari al-Maliki, *Madkhal al-shar al-sharif* (Cairo, 1336 H) 2:115.

45 Al-Tahanawi al-Hanafi, *Kashshaf istilahat al-funun* (Beirut, 1966) 1:133-135.

46 Related by Bukhari.

47 Ibn Hajar, *Fath al-bari* (Cairo: al-Halabi, 1378 /1959) 5:156-157; (Beirut: Dar al-kutub al-ilmiyya, 1410/1989) 4:318.

language. Imam Bayhaqi narrated:[48]

> Al-Hasan ibn Habib related from Mahmud al-Misri–and he was one of those gifted with eloquence–that Mahmud said, "I saw al-Shafii when I was little, and I heard Ibn Hisham–and I never set eyes on one from whom I took wisdom such as Ibn Hisham–say, 'I was al-Shafii's sitting-companion for a long time, and I never heard him use a word except that if that word were carefully considered, one would not find (in its context) a better word than it in the entire Arabic language.'" Mahmud also said,"I also heard Ibn Hisham say, 'Al-Shafii's discourse, in relation to language, is a proof in itself.'"
>
> It is also related from al-Hasan ibn Muhammad al-Zafarani: A group of the people of pure Arabic (qawmun min ahl al-arabiyya) used to frequent al-Shafii's gathering with us and sit in a corner. One day I asked their leader, "You are not interested in scholarship; why do you keep coming here with us?" They said, "We come to hear al-Shafii's language."

The stylistic figure of indicating the part by the whole, or synecdoche in English, is in Arabic abbara an al-kathrati bi al-kulliyya. This is illustrated by the use of kull in verse 46:25 of the Quran, in a selective or partial sense, not a universal sense:

> Destroying all things by commandment of its Lord. And morning found them so that naught could be seen save their dwellings.

Thus the dwellings were not destroyed although "all" things had been destroyed. "All" here specifically refers to the lives of the unbelievers of Ad and their properties, but not their houses. The same applies in Surah al-Naml (27:23) with the hoopoe-bird's saying that Bilqis has been given in abundance from "everything," while she was not given any power over Solomon (ﷺ) nor any share of his kingdom. Similarly, when Allah says, "Every soul (kullu nafsin) shall taste death" (3:185), it is understood though not mentioned that Allah Himself is excluded from the meaning.

---

48 Imam Bayhaqi, in his Manaqib al-shafii (2:42-46).

In conclusion, the position of the majority of the scholars is clear. "To invent" *(ahdatha)* a "new practice" *(bida)* may refer either to the matter that is new, linguistically speaking *(lafzan)*, e.g. stone *masjid*s, all the Islamic sciences, writing books about religion, etc., or to the matter that is new legally speaking *(sharan)*, e.g. a sixth daily prayer. Since *bida* usually applies to innovations in religion in the legal sense, the first kind of "new matter" does not qualify as a *bida* and therefore is not prohibited.

Ibn Hisham and others narrate that Asim said:

> They took out Khubayb as far as al-Tamim to crucify him. He asked them to give him time to make a couple of prayer-cycles, and they agreed. He performed two excellent bowings and then turned to the people saying, "Were it not that you would think that I only delayed out of fear of death I would have prolonged my prayer." Khubayb ibn Adi was the first to establish the custom of performing two bowings at death. Then they raised him on the wood and when they had bound him he said, "O Allah, we have delivered the message of Thy Messenger, so tell him tomorrow what has been done to us." Then he said, "O Allah, reckon them by number and kill them one by one, let none of them escape." Then they killed him, Allah have mercy on him."[49]

The above is the ruling of all the major scholars on the definition of *bida*. Whoever denies this consensus is either ignorant or creating a new definition that is not from the majority of scholars but from his own whim.

1.3.8.2.

Q. Since the purpose of *mawlid* is to promote love of and obedience to the Prophet (ﷺ), why did the first generations of Muslims not celebrate it? Undoubtedly, love and obedience of the Prophet (ﷺ) were not lacking at that time.

A. The answer is in the question itself. If the people of today could practice love and obedience of the Prophet (ﷺ) the way

---

49 From *The Life of Muhammad: A Translation of Ibn Ishaq's Sirat Rasul Allah,* trans. A. Guillaume, p. 428.

the Salaf did, then they would not need the celebration of *mawlid* to remind them.

The same applies to knowledge and belief. In the first generations, knowledge and belief were pure and safe from the dangers of forgetfulness and innovation. When these evils appeared, the jurists stepped forth and did their great work to protect the Community from error. The Companions themselves had no need of formal schools of Law.

The same applies to morals. Doing without (*zuhd*) was a characteristic of all the Companions and the natural state of the Prophet (ﷺ). When it became a rare thing, the imams of self-purification (*tazkiyat al-nafs/tasawwuf*) codified *zuhd*, and encouraged people to return to the excellent manners and simplicity of earlier times. All of these, *ulum al-fiqh*, *ulum al-tasawwuf*, and *mawlid*, did not exist formally in the first centuries because there was no need for them. The love and imitation of the Prophet (ﷺ) were certainly far greater then.

Beware of those who say that *mawlid* is wrong because it did not exist in the first three centuries. To claim that something goes against the *sunna* because it was not present in the first three centuries indicates an incorrect understanding of "following the *sunna*." For instance, it is impermissible to claim that the Prophet (ﷺ) did not celebrate his birthday, since it is established in sound hadith that he commemorated his birthday by fasting on Mondays.

1.3.8.3.

Q. There was no such thing as *mawlid* before the Fatimi regime in Egypt started it. Aren't they denounced by Sunnis as deviants?

A. The Fatimis ruled in Egypt from about 360 to 560 AH. However, there is a precedent for the practice of celebrating the *mawlid* from before their rule. For instance, the historian of Makka al-Azraqi (third century) mentioned the *mawlid* in reference to the house where the Prophet (ﷺ) was born. He said that *salat* in that house was declared desirable *(mustahabb)* by the scholars for seeking special blessing *(tabarruk)*.[50] Also, the *mufassir* al-Naqqash (266-351) said that the birthplace of the

---

50 See Al-Azraqi, *Akhbar makka* (2:160).

Prophet (ﷺ) *(mawlid al-nabi)* is a place where *dua* on Mondays is answered.[51] Ibn Jubayr (540-640) mentions the *mawlid* as a public commemoration taking place in Makka in the House of the Prophet (ﷺ) "every Monday of the month of Rabi al-Awwal."[52] The 7th century father-and-son historians Abul Abbas and Abul Qasim al-Azafi said that "On the day of the *mawlid* in Makka, no activities are undertaken, the Kabah is opened and visited, etc."[53]

Furthermore, the fact that the Fatimis committed a particular action does not mean that the action is not good. Regarding *mawlid* in particular, refer to the Maliki jurist of Alexandria under the Fatimis, Abu Bakr Muhammad ibn al-Walid al-Turtushi (d. 520). He wrote a comprehensive book on the innovations of his time under the Fatimi regime, entitled *Kitab al-hawadith wa al-bida*.[54] Al-Turtushi's book constitutes one of the early comprehensive treatises on innovations in religion. It had immeasurable influence on the style and structure of later books on the same subject, both in and outside his school, such as those authored by Ibn Rushd, Abu Shama, Ibn Taymiyya, Ibn al-Hajj, al-Shatibi, Ahmad Zarruq, and al-Suyuti.

Turtushi is strict and extremely thorough in his listing of innovations in religion under the Fatimis, whether great or small. He lists, among other innovations:

—Reciting the Quran with melody *(tatrib* or *qiraa bi al-alhan*)
—Numbering the *surah*s and punctuating the Quran
—Building *mihrab*s in and embellishing mosques
—Placing a collection-box in the mosques
—Eating and drinking in the mosques
—Selling goods in the mosques,
—The *alfiyya* prayer of mid-Shaban and the Raghaib of Rajab,
—Stopping work on Friday *(juma)*

51 Al-Naqqash, *Shifa al-gharam* (1:199).
52 Ibn Jubayr, *Kitab al-rihal* (p. 114-115).
53 Abul Abbas and Abul Qasim al-Azafi, *Kitab al-durr al-munazzam*.
54 This book has received two editions, one in Tunis (M. Talbim 1959), and one in Beirut (A.M. Turki, 1990).

—Pronouncing *tathwib*, '*al-salatu khayrun min al-nawm* ' in the *adhan* of *fajr*[55]
—Raising the hands and voice during *dua*
—Wearing the turban without passing the longest extremity under the chin
—Dragging one's clothes behind oneself on the ground
—Mixing of the sexes in the mosques on the nights of *tarawih*
—Renting the services of a person to perform the pilgrimage by proxy, etc.

He defends *tarawih* as not being an innovation because the *Shiis* had attacked it as such.

Al-Turtushi never mentions nor condemns the *mawlid*, although he must have witnessed it since it was a regular public celebration during his life in Egypt, and although it involved more people than many of the innovations he does mention! This is a glaring omission in view of the fact that he was especially intent on censoring the innovations that he deemed were connected to the Fatimi regime. Al-Turtushi's omission is an indication that, although he opposed the Fatimis, he considered *mawlid* under the Fatimis to be neither an innovation, nor blameworthy. This constitutes tacit approval of *mawlid* on his part.

1.3.8.4.

Q. What are the opinions on *mawlid* of those whom the "Salafis" consider their authorities?

A. The subject has already been touched on above. Following are additional remarks with reference to *Hafiz* al-Dhahabi and Imam Ibn Kathir.

Dhahabi's and Ibn Kathir's favorable views on *mawlid* can be ascertained in their comments about Muzaffar the King of Irbil, who was famous for his sumptuous celebration of the Prophet's birthday. Dhahabi writes:

He [Muzaffar] loved charity (*sadaqa*) . . . and built

---

55 Al-Wansharisi, a later Maliki who died in 914, finally accepts it as a *bida mustahsana*: see his *al-Mustahsan min al-bida* (The innovations that are considered good).

four hospices for the poor and sick . . . and one house for women, one for orphans, one for the homeless, and he himself used to visit the sick . . . He built a *madrasa* for the Shafiis and the Hanafis . . . He would forbid any reprehensible matter to enter into his country . . . As for his celebration of the noble *mawlid al-nabawi*, words are too poor to describe it. The people used to come all the way from Iraq and Algeria to attend it. Two wooden daises would be erected and decorated for him and his wife . . . the celebration would last several days, and a huge quantity of cows and camels would be brought out to be sacrificed and cooked in different ways . . . Preachers would roam the field exhorting the people. Great sums were spent (as charity). Ibn Dihya compiled a "Book of *mawlid*" for him for which he received 1,000 dinars. He [Muzaffar] was modest, a lover of good, and a true Sunni who loved scholars of jurisprudence and scholars of hadith, and was generous even to poets. He was killed in battle according to what is reported.[56]

Ibn Kathir said in *al-Bidaya wa al-nihaya*:

He [Muzaffar] used to celebrate the noble *mawlid* in Rabi al-Awwal and organize huge festivities for it. He was a wise king, brave, a fierce fighter, intelligent, learned, and just. May Allah have mercy on him and ennoble his grave. Shaykh Abu al-Khattab ibn Dihya compiled for him a book on the *mawlid* of the Prophet (ﷺ) and named it *al-Tanwir fi mawlid al-bashir al-nadhir* (The illumination concerning the birthday of the Bringer of glad tidings and warner) and the king rewarded him with 1,000 dinars for it. His rule lasted until he died in the year 630 [Hijri] as he was besieging the French in the city of Acca [Acre, Palestine] after a glorious and blameless life.[57]

More importantly, Ibn Kathir himself composed a text on *mawlid* that consisted of hadiths, invocations of blessings on the Prophet (ﷺ), and poetry in praise of him.[58]

56 Al-Dhahabi, *Siyar alam al-nubala*, ed. Shuayb Arnaut (Beirut: Muassasat al-Risalah, 1981) 22:335-336.
57 Ibn Kathir, *al-Bidaya wa al-nihaya* (Beirut and Riyad: Maktabat al-maarif and Maktabat al-nasr, 1966) 13:136-137.
58 Ibn Kathir, *Mawlid rasulillah sallallahu alayhi wa sallam*. It was edited and published by Salah al-Din al-Munajjad (Beirut: Dar al-kitab al-jadid, 1961).

1.3.8.5.

Q. Who are the scholars of the major schools that accept the celebration of *mawlid al-nabi* as permissible or recommended?

A. They are the overwhelming majority of Sunnis. Among them are the following, listed with the title of the works where their position is stated:

1.3.8.5.1. Hanafis

Imam Qutb al-Din al-Hanafi, *al-Ilam bi alam bayt Allah al-haram*

Imam Muhammad ibn Jar Allah ibn Zahira, *al-Jami al-latif*

Abd al-Haqq *Muhaddith* Dihlawi, *Ma thabata min al-sunna*

Shah Abd al-Rahim Dihlawi, *al-Durr al-thamin*

Shah Wali Allah Dihlawi, *Fuyud al-haramayn*

Mufti Inayat Allah Kakurawi, *Tarikh habib Allah*

Mufti Muhammad Mazhar Allah Dihlawi, *Fatawa mazhari*

Mulla Ali al-Qari, *al-Mawrid al-rawi fi mawlid al-nabi.*

Haji Imdad Allah Muhajir Makki, *Shamaim imdadiyya*

Muhaddith Abd al-Hayy al-Lucknawi, *Fatawa Abd al-Hayy*

1.3.8.5.2. Malikis

Hafiz Ibn Dihya al-Kalbi, *al-Tanwir fi mawlid al-bashir al-nadhir*

Imam al-Turtushi, *Kitab al-hawadith wa al-bida* (indirectly)

Imam al-Faqih Abu al-Tayyib Muhammad ibn Ibrahim al-Sabti (d. 695), as quoted by al-Adfawi in Suyuti's *Husn al-maqsid*

Abu Abd Allah Sayyidi Muhammad ibn Abbad al-Nafzi, *al-Rasail al-kubra*

Shaykh Jalal al-Din al-Kattani, *Rawdat al-jannat fi mawlid khatim al-risalat,* also quoted in Sakhawi's *Subul al-huda*

Shaykh Nasir al-Din ibn al-Tabbakh, quoted in Sakhawi's *Subul al-huda*

Shaykh Muhammad ibn Alawi al-Makki, *al-Ihtifal bi dhikra al-mawlid*

Note: Among other similar works of *mawlid* by the authorities is that by Ibn Hajar al-Haytami entitled *Mawlid al-nabi* (Damascus, 1900), and that by the Hanbali *hafiz* Abu al-Faraj Ibn al-Jawzi entitled *Mawlid al-arus* (Cairo, 1850). The latter received a commentary entitled *Fath al-samad al-alim ala mawlid al-shaykh Ibn al-Qasim* also known as *al-Bulugh al-fawzi li-bayan alfaz mawlid Ibn al-Jawzi* by Muhammad Nawawi ibn Umar ibn Arabi (Cairo: Tubia bi nafaqat Fada Muhammad al-Kashmiri al-Kutubi, 1328/1910).

1.3.8.5.3. Shafiis

Hafiz Abu Shama, *al-Baith ala inkar al-bida wa al-hawadith*

Hafiz Shams al-Din al-Jazari, *Urf al-tarif bi al-mawlid al-sharif.*

Hafiz Shams al-Din ibn Nasir al-Din al-Dimashqi, *al-Mawrid al-sadi fi mawlid al-hadi*; *Jami al-athar fi mawlid al-nabi al-mukhtar*; *al-lafz al-raiq fi mawlid khayr al-khalaiq*

Hafiz Zayn al-Din al-Iraqi, *al-Mawrid al-hani fi al-mawlid al-sani*

Hafiz al-Dhahabi, *Siyar alam al-nubala* (indirectly)

Hafiz Ibn Kathir, *Kitab mawlid an-nabi*, and *al-Bidaya* p. 272-273.

Hafiz Ibn Hajar al-Asqalani, as quoted by Suyuti in *al-Hawi*. Qastallani, *al-Mawahib al-laduniyya*

Hafiz al-Sakhawi, *Subul al-huda*, also quoted in Qari, *al-Mawrid al-rawi*

Imam Ibn Hajar al-Haytami, *Fatawa hadithiyya*; *al-nimat al-kubra ala al-alam fi mawlid sayyid waladi Adam*; *Tahrir al-kalam fi al-qiyam inda dhikr mawlid sayyid al-anam*; *Tuhfat al-akhyar fi mawlid al-mukhtar*

Hafiz Wajih al-Din Abd al-Rahman al-Zabidi al-Dayba (d. 944), *Kitab al-mawlid.*

Zahir al-Din Jafar al-Misri, quoted in Sakhawi's *Subul al-huda*

Muhammad ibn Yusuf al-Salihi al-Shami, quoted in Sakhawi's *Subul al-huda*

Kamal al-Din al-Adfawi, *al-Tali al-said*

Hafiz al-Suyuti, *Husn al-maqsid fi amal al-mawlid* in his *al-Hawi li al-fatawi*

Al-Zarqani, *Sharh al-mawahib*

Abu Zura al-Iraqi, as quoted in Muhammad ibn Siddiq al-Ghumari's *Tashnif al-adhan*

1.3.8.5.4. Hanbalis

Hafiz Ibn Taymiyya, *Iqtida al-sirat al-mustaqim* (in some cases)

1.3.8.6.

Q. Reading about the life of the Prophet (ﷺ) and the recitation of poems in the Prophet's honor take place during the *mawlid* commemoration. Is there a precedent in the *sunna* for this practice?

A. It has been shown conclusively that the recitation of poetry in honor of the Prophet (ﷺ) is a *sunna* that he and the Companions practiced.[59] As for reading about his life, it falls within the obligation upon every Muslim to know their Prophet (ﷺ) and to love him.

It is narrated by Ibn Umar that:

> The Prophet (ﷺ) used to deliver his sermons while standing beside the trunk of a datepalm. When he had the pulpit made, he used it instead. The trunk started crying and the Prophet (ﷺ) went to it, rubbing his hand over it (to stop its crying).[60]

If a dead tree could cry when distanced from the Prophet (ﷺ), what about a human being? How distant from the Prophet (ﷺ) are we in comparison to those who lived in his time? If some would accuse mainstream Muslims of innovation when they want to remember the Prophet (ﷺ) on his birthday and on any other day by reciting his *sira*, sending salutations (*salawat*) in groups, singing *qasida*s of praise, and longing for him, then let them accuse the tree trunk of *bida* and stop it from its sorrow. The mainstream Muslims rejoice his advent into this world and lament his passing for we miss him and seek the day of meeting with him. May Allah perfume his blessed grave and endow it with ever more lights and peace.

It is from the *sunna* to long for the Prophet (ﷺ) after his passing from this life. This is documented in an authentic hadith in which Abu Hurayra narrated that the Prophet (ﷺ) said, "A time will come when any of you will long to see me more than to have his family and property doubled."[61]

1.4. CONCERNING THE STANDING OF PEOPLE AT THE CONCLUSION OF THE *MAWLID* WHILE SENDING BLESSINGS AND PEACE (*SALAM*) ON THE PROPHET (ﷺ)

Some also criticize people's standing at the conclusion of *mawlid*, and their addressing salutations and blessings to the

---

59 See further below, in the section on *Nat*, the list of over a hundred Companions who composed and recited such poetry.
60 *Sahih Bukhari*, Vol. 4, Book 56, Number 783.
61 *Sahih Bukhari*, Vol. 4, Book 56, Number 787.

Prophet (ﷺ). It should be apparent that no one can object to an act of obedience and worship that has specifically been enjoined by Allah when He said, *"O believers, send blessings and utmost salutations on him!"* (33:56). He also spoke in praise of *"those who remember Allah standing, and sitting, and on their sides"* (3:191). Since remembering Allah and sending blessings on His Prophet (ﷺ) are acts of worship, the objection to standing for the sake of fulfilling one of Allah's orders and greeting the Prophet (ﷺ) according to Allah's order is dismissed.

It is known that anyone who visits the Prophet (ﷺ) in Madina is obliged to stand in front of him with utmost respect when he gives him greetings and salutations. There is no difference in the greeting of *salam* being given to the Prophet (ﷺ) in front of him in Madina and the one given to him from thousands of miles away. This is affirmed in many sound hadith, among them the following:[62]

> Whoever invokes blessings on me at my grave, I hear him, and whoever invokes blessings on me from afar, I am informed about it.[63]
> No one greets me except Allah has returned my soul to me so that I can return his salam.[64]

Suyuti said that *radda* means *ala al-dawam*, or permanently, and not temporarily.[65] In other words, Allah does not return the Prophet's soul and take it back, then return it again and then take it back again, but He has returned it to him permanently. Thus the Prophet (ﷺ) is alive permanently and not intermittently as some people have suggested. To those who would differ with Imam Suyuti it is said, his proof is irrefutable, since there are people at prayer in the world twen-

---

62 Several of these are mentioned above in the section on *Ziyara* or Visitation of the Prophet.

63 Abu al-Shaykh cites it in *Kitab al-salat ala al-nabi (Jala al-afham* p. 22), and Ibn Hajar says in *Fath al-bari* (6:379): "Abu al-Shaykh cites it with a good chain *(sanad jayyid)*." Bayhaqi mentions it in *Hayat al-anbiya* and *Shuab al-iman* (2:218 #1583) with *ublightuhu* instead of *bullightuhu* in the end.

64 Abu Hurayra in Abu Dawud (*Manasik* #2039) with a sound chain; Ibn Asakir, *Mukhtasar tarikh dimashq* 2:407; Ahmad, *Musnad* 2:527; Abu Nuaym, *Akhbar asbahan* 2:353; Ibn al-Najjar, *Akhbar al-madina* p. 145; Bayhaqi, *Shuab al-iman* #4161; Haythami, *Majma al-zawaid* 10:162; Ibn Kathir, *Tafsir* 6:464; al-Mundhiri, *al-Targhib wa al-tarhib* 2:499; *Talkhis al-habir* 2:267.

65 Suyuti, *Anba al-adhkiya bi hayat al-anbiya.*

ty-four hours a day, and sending salutations (*salawat*) to the Prophet (ﷺ) is part of prescribed prayer (*salat*). It follows that people are invoking blessings and greetings on the Prophet (ﷺ) without stop, and that he is constantly returning them. This shows that the hadith of the Prophet (ﷺ) on the return of his soul considers the continuity of prayer concomitant with the revolution of the prayer times around the world, and that he is indeed alive in permanence, since Allah has entitled him to return every single *salam* that is made to him.

Finally, it is appropriate to stand and offer salutations not only at the commemoration of his birth (*mawlid*), but at any time, such as after *salat*, after Friday (*juma*) prayer, individually or in congregation. It is a voluntary act of worship that no one can forbid others from performing for the sake of obeying Allah.

Ibn Qunfudh al-Qusantini al-Maliki (d. 810) wrote:

> The Community is unanimous concerning the obligation to magnify and exalt the Prophet (ﷺ), his Family, and his Companions. It was the practice of the Pious Predecessors and the imams of the past that whenever the Prophet (ﷺ) was mentioned in their presence they were overwhelmed by reverence, humbleness, stillness, and dignity. Jafar ibn Muhammad ibn Ali ibn al-Husayn ibn Ali ibn Abi Talib (Jafar al-Sadiq) would turn pale whenever he heard the Prophet (ﷺ) mentioned. Imam Malik would not mention a hadith except in a state of ritual purity. Abd al-Rahman ibn al-Qasim ibn Muhammad ibn Abu Bakr al-Siddiq would turn red and stammer whenever he heard the Prophet (ﷺ) mentioned. As for Amir ibn Abd Allah ibn al-Zubayr ibn al-Awamm al-Asadi (one of the early Sufis), he would weep until his eyes had no tears left in them. When any hadiths were mentioned in their presence they would lower their voices. Malik said, "His sacredness (*hurmat*) is in death is as his sacredness was in life."[66]

Another reason why it is desirable and recommended to be

---

[66] Abu al-Abbas Ahmad ibn al-Khatib, known as Ibn Qunfudh al-Qusantini al-Maliki, *Wasilat al-islam bi al-nabi alayhi al-salat wa al-salam* (The means to Islam with the Prophet, blessings and peace upon him) (Beirut: Dar al-gharb al-islami, 1404/1984) p. 145-146.

seen standing at the time of greeting the Prophet (ﷺ) is that he himself ordered the Companions to stand up when Sad ibn Muadh came to him. He said, as related by Bukhari in his *Sahih, Qumu ila sayyidikum* or "Stand up for your master."[67] What better master to stand for than the Prophet (ﷺ)? Imam Nawawi demonstrated at length that standing out of respect for scholars was not only permissible but desirable in his book *al-Tarkhis fi al-ikram bi al-qiyam.* The full title reads, "The Permissibility of Honoring, By Standing Up, Those Who Possess Excellence and Distinction Among the People of Islam: In the Spirit of Piousness, Reverence, and Respect, Not in the Spirit of Display and Aggrandizement." The following discussion on the subject of standing out of respect is taken from Nawawi's *Tarkhis,* as well as his *Sharh sahih Muslim,* Ibn Hajar's sections of *Fath al-bari* following up on Nawawi's *Tarkhis,* and Sakhawi's own biography of Ibn Hajar entitled *al-Jawahir wa al-durar:*

1.4.1. Nawawi's Commentary on Standing

• From Amr ibn Shuayb from his father from his grandfather: The Prophet (ﷺ) said: "He is not of us who did not show mercy to our young ones and ignored the honor of our elders."[68]

• From Maymun ibn Abi Shabib: A beggar passed by Aisha and she gave him a chunk of bread. Another time a handsomely dressed man passed by her and she invited him to sit and eat. She was asked about it and she said, "The Prophet (ﷺ) said, *anzilu al-nasa manazilahum* 'Treat people according to their station.'"[69]

• Abu Said al-Khudri said: The people of Qurayza submitted to Sad ibn Muadh's arbitration, so the Prophet (ﷺ) sent for Sad who came riding on his donkey. When he approached the mosque, Allah's Messenger said to the Ansar, "Stand up for your chieftain—or for the best among you—." Then he said,

---

67 The hadith is also narrated as *Qumu li sayyidikum* which means the same thing. See Tahawi, *Mushkil al-athar* (2:38), Ibn Kathir, *al-Bidaya wa al-nihaya* (4:122), and al-Zabidi, *Ithaf al-sada al-muttaqin* (7:142).

68 Tirmidhi (*Birr wa silat* 4:322 #28) said: *hasan sahih* (fair and sound). Ahmad (2:185) narrates it but the second part is: "and ignored the right of our elders." Nawawi said: we related (by a chain) from Bukhari that he said: "I saw Ahmad ibn Hanbal and Ali ibn al-Madani and Ishaq ibn Rahawayh cite the hadith of Amr ibn Shuayb from his father from his grandfather as a proof—and who are those who came after them!" Another version from Ibn Abbas has: ". . .and does not treat our elders with reverence. . ." Tirmidhi (4:322 #28), but with a weaker chain.

69 Abu Dawud related it with an interrupted *(munqati)* chain; Muslim mentions

"These people have submitted to your decision . . ."[70]
Nawawi's Commentary:

> There is in this hadith the proof for honoring per-
> sons of merit by standing up for them upon receiving
> them while they are coming towards us. Thus have
> the overwhelming majority of the scholars used this
> as a proof for the desirability of standing up. Qadi
> Iyad said: "This is not the kind of standing that is for-
> bidden. The latter is only when one sits and the oth-
> ers remain standing all through his sitting." I say:
> Standing up for the person of merit who is approach-
> ing is desirable; many hadith have been related sup-
> porting it, while there is not one sound explicit prohibi-
> tion against it.

• Anas said that none was dearer to them than Allah's
Messenger, and they would not stand up when they saw him
due to their knowledge that he disliked it.[71]
Nawawi's Commentary:

> This is the hadith most readily cited as a proof
> against standing up. There are two answers:
> 1 The Prophet (ﷺ) feared confusion for them and
> for their successors in their exaggeration in magnify-
> ing him, as he said in another hadith, 'Do not praise
> me in the fashion that the Christians praised Jesus
> son of Mary.'[72] He disliked their standing for him for
> that reason. However, he did not dislike their stand-
> ing for each other, and he even stood for some of them,
> and also they stood for others in his presence without
> his prohibiting it. Rather he approved it, and he
> ordered it in the hadith of standing up for Sad ibn

it without chain in the introduction to his *Sahih*. Sakhawi says in his introduction (p.
5) to *al-Jawahir wa al-durar* (The diamonds and the pearls), his biography of his
teacher Ibn Hajar al-Asqalani: "This is a fair *(hasan) hadith*... Nawawi reports Ibn al-
Salah's opinion that it is not definitely established as sound [although it satisfies
Muslim's criterion], however, al-Hakim definitely establishes it as sound in the part
that deals with the 16th kind of sound narration of his book *Marifat ulum al-hadith*
(Knowledge of the Sciences of Hadith) where he also says: "Ibn Khuzayma declared it
sound; al-Bazzar extracted it in his *Musnad*; so did Abu Dawud in his *Sunan.*; al-
Askari in his *Kitab al-amthal*; Abu Yala in his *Musnad*; Bayhaqi in *al-Adab*; Abu
Nuaym in the *Hilya*."

70 Muslim narrated it in his *Sahih* (Bk. 32 *Jihad*, Ch. 22 #1728).
71 Tirmidhi (*Adab* - 5:90 # 44) said it is *hasan sahih* (fair and sound).
72 Bukhari 6:478 Bk. 60 *Anbiya* #48 and Ahmad 1:23, 24.

Muadh . . . This is a clear answer in which none will see doubt except an ignorant or stubborn person.

2 There was between the Prophet (ﷺ) and his Companions a perfect state of love and purity which does not suffer addition through honoring by standing up, since there was no purpose being achieved by standing up, as opposed to standing up for someone else. One's companion who is near this state has no need of standing up.

1.4.2. IBN AL-HAJJ'S OBJECTIONS TO STANDING

1 This answer is not complete except if it is first conceded that the Companions rose up for no one. If they got up for him then, it would be exaggeration. However, Nawawi affirms that they did this for other than him; how then does he deem it permissible for them to do with other than the Prophet (ﷺ) what leaves no protection against exaggeration, while they do not do it with him? For if they do this to honor someone, then the Prophet (ﷺ) is worthier of such honor, as we know from the source-texts which order us to honor him above everyone else. It seems that their rising for other than him was therefore only for a necessity caused by their arrival, or to congratulate them, and so forth, not for the reason that is being questioned [i.e. not due to respect].

2 Nawawi's explanation can be reversed and it can be said that the Companion whose devotion to the Prophet (ﷺ) has not been ascertained and who has not yet realized the stature of the Prophet (ﷺ) is excused for not standing up, as opposed to him whose devotion is ascertained and whose station is greater in relation to the Prophet (ﷺ) and his worth is known: he would apply himself (to respect him), because he would be certain that he deserves more piety and honor and reverence than any other. But Nawawi's saying makes it necessary that whoever is likelier to show respect to the Prophet (ﷺ) and is closer in station to him, should show him less reverence than he who is far from him, due to intimacy and

complete affection. The reality is other than that according to the authentic reports, as occurred in the story of the Prophet's oversight, whereas while Abu Bakr and Umar were present among the people, they were too afraid to speak to him, Dhu al-Yadayn ("He of the Long Hands"– perhaps al-Khirbaq al-Sulami) spoke to him despite his remoteness from the Prophet (ﷺ) in station in comparison to Abu Bakr and Umar.[73]

1.4.3. ASQALANI'S REFUTATION OF IBN AL-HAJJ

1 This objection of Ibn al-Hajj does not stand, because Imam Nawawi never said that the Companions' rising for the Prophet (ﷺ) is considered exaggeration in order for Ibn al-Hajj to say, "This answer is not complete except if it is first conceded that the Companions rose up for no one. If they got up for him then, it would be exaggeration." What Imam Nawawi said is that the Prophet (ﷺ) feared lest their rising should lead to exaggeration. That is why he forbade it to them, fearing exaggeration, lest they should fall into excess and confusion. Yes, he is worthier of being honored than any other, except that he feared that their showing him this particular mark of honor might lead to exaggeration and that is why he forbade it to them.

2 With the second objection Ibn al-Hajj has contravened the universal custom of people in their companionship and their love. It is definitely known that the stronger the companionship and love between two people, the more superfluous certain formalities become between them. This is clear and needs no exposition. On the contrary, if companionship is weak and mutual acquaintance limited, a human being in that case needs to win his companion's love and affection with all kinds of honorific acts. This is because obtaining a person's love and affection is upheld by the transmitted reports dealing with giving honor. Now when love reaches the level where it is no longer

---

73 A reference to the hadith in Bukhari (English 1:278-279) and Muslim whereby the Prophet prayed Asr and gave *salam* after two cycles (*rakat*); this Companion said to him: "O Messenger of Allah, has the prayer been shortened or did you forget?" The Prophet replied that neither applied, then he prayed the remaining two cycles.

increased by honorific acts, the latter are no longer necessary.

3 As for Ibn al-Hajj's objection that "Nawawi's saying makes it necessary that whoever is likelier to show respect to the Prophet (ﷺ) and is closer in station to him, should show him less reverence than he who is far from him, due to intimacy and complete affection": it is an invalid necessity. That some formalities become superfluous between friends and loved ones does not mean that mutual reverence and respect become superfluous. This is clear and needs no exposition. Rather, the contrary is true: because the lover is of all people the most aware of the attributes of his beloved, and when the latter is graced with praiseworthy, high attributes, and people flock to give him proper respect and reverence, the lover is the most intense of all in respect and reverence due to his added knowledge of the attributes of the beloved.

4 As for Ibn al-Hajj's inference from the hadith of the Prophet's oversight, it does not impose itself due to the possibility that Abu Bakr and Umar's silence may be for a reason other than fear, such as their knowledge that he disliked questioning, or their knowledge that he does not settle on a mistake except Allah certainly informs him of it, or for another reason. Moreover, Ibn al-Hajj's inference contradicts what has been related concerning his attributes, namely that those who were far from him feared him, and that those who grew near him, frequented him, and saw his humbleness and the nobility of his manners, immediately were at ease with him and loved him. Here are some proofs:

Ibn Majah narrated (2:1101 Bk. 29, *atima,* Ch. 30) from Ibn Masud that a man came to speak to the Prophet (ﷺ) and he began to shake with fear. The Prophet (ﷺ) said to him: "Put yourself at ease, for I am not a king, I am the son of a woman who ate sun-dried meat." Tirmidhi narrated (5:599 - Bk. 50 *manaqib* ch. 8) from Ali at the end of his description: "Whoever saw him from afar was awed by him, and whoever mixed with him and grew to know him, loved him." The reason for this is the presence in the Prophet (ﷺ) of the attributes of majesty and sanctity despite great humbleness before all who saw him.

5 Abu Mijlaz said: Muawiya went out to meet Ibn al-Zubayr and Ibn Amir. The latter stood up while the former remained seated. Muawiya said to Ibn Amir, "Sit, for I heard the Prophet (ﷺ) say, "Whoever likes for men to stand up for him let him take his place in the fire."[74]

Nawawi's Commentary:

Most people in disfavor of standing are fond of quoting this hadith. It is answered in many ways, (1) the soundest and best—nay, the one answer which makes all others superfluous is that there is no proof against standing up in this hadith. Its plain, outward meaning is the explicit condemnation and harsh threat against any man who likes people to get up for him. There is neither prohibition nor other than pro-hibition concerning standing itself, and there is agree-ment about this . . . The gravity of the condemnation is in what takes place inside the mind of the person who likes people to stand for him. If there is no such thing in his mind there is no blame on him—all this whether they get up or not . . . The prohibition revolves around the love of adulation not the act of standing. Therefore there is no proof in this hadith against the permissibility of standing.

2 Another answer is that the hadith is disordered (*mudtarib*—many incompatible narrations) according to the two imams of hadith Abu Bakr ibn Abi Asim and Abu Musa al-Asbahani, and this is a necessary cause for the weakness of the hadith. However, this answer is open to question since both Tirmidhi and Abu Dawud have graded the hadith fair (*hasan*) and have spoken concerning it. Moreover, the disparity does not result in a disorder of the kind that makes it necessarily weak, and Allah knows best.

3 The sayings of the imams and luminaries con-cerning whose eminence there is unanimity among the people of intellect and discernment: Abu Nasr Bishr ibn al-Harith al-Hafi al-Zahid, Abu Sulayman Hamd ibn Muhammad ibn Sulayman al-Khattabi,

---

74 Tirmidhi's version mentions Ibn al-Zubayr and Safwan, and both get up. Abu Dawud narrated it (*Adab*, 4:385), also Tirmidhi (*Adab*, 5:90 #44) who said: *hasan* (fair) and Ahmad (4:94, 100).

Abu Muhammad al-Husayn ibn Masud al-Baghawi, and Abu Musa Muhammad ibn Umar al-Asbahani the *hafiz*, may Allah be well pleased with all of them: [after quoting the *isnad*] Ahmad ibn al-Mughlis said, Abu Nasr ibn al-Harith said, after I mentioned this hadith in front of him, "He only disliked the standing from the perspective of arrogance, but from the perspective of sincere love, he did not, since he himself stood up for Ikrima ibn Abu Jahl . . . and he said, "Stand for your chief," and he said, "He who likes people to stand for him . . ." indicating that whoever likes people to stand for him, you must not stand for him." As for Baghawi and Khattabi as we mentioned with our *isnad* they spoke to the effect that the hadith concerns only those who order others from the perspective of pride and arrogance. Abu Musa said: "The meaning of the hadith is those who make men stand around them like courtiers stand around kings."

4 From Abu Amama: The Prophet (ﷺ) came out leaning on a stick and we rose up for him. He said, "Do not get up in the manner of the foreigners who aggrandize each other."[75]

Nawawi's Commentary:

The answer is in two beautiful ways:

1 The two imams Abu Bakr ibn Abi Asim and Abu Musa al-Asbahani said that this is a weak hadith which cannot be used as a proof. Abu Bakr said, "This hadith cannot be established and its sub-narrators are unknown." I say, to this is added the fact that it is "*mudtarib*" (disordered–see above), and it would suffice that only one of these two factors were present to grade it as weak, let alone two.

2 The hadith in itself is crystal-clear as to its intent as opposed to that of the rest; namely, it purports to condemn those who stand for the purpose of aggrandizement. That is why he said, "Do not get up in the manner of the foreigners who aggrandize each other." There is no doubt as to what is being condemned. And Allah knows best.

---

75 Abu Dawud narrated it (*Adab*, 4:358). Ibn Majah's version (*Dua* #34, 2:1261): "Do not do as the Persians do with their great ones."

From (Nafi) Abu Bakra, the Prophet (ﷺ) said, "Let no man stand from his seat for another."[76]

Nawawi's Commentary:

> The answer to this is the same two answers as the preceding section . . . There is possibly a third way to answer it reasonably. The meaning would be, "Do not get up from the place of prayer, of listening to a sermon and to remembrance and knowledge et cetera, for it is disliked that one should give up one's seat in such cases, or leave it and take another farther away from the imam.
>
> The same is true of all gestures that are similar to these, and we consider this to muster the general agreement of scholars, as opposed to giving up one's food and drink and other things related to one's personal lot: to give those up is a most desirable thing, one of the marks of the righteous and among the manners of saints and knowers, concerning which this verse was revealed, *"They prefer others above themselves though poverty become their lot"* (59:9).
>
> The difference between the two types of sacrifice is that the right, in the person's nearness, belongs to Allah the Exalted, and to transfer it is not permissible, as opposed to food and the like where the right belongs to the person, although in some cases it belongs to Allah even then . . .

Nawawi also said:

> Al-Shaykh Abu Muhammad told us: Abu Taher al-Khashawi told us: Abu Muhammad al-Akfani told us: *Al-hafiz* Abu Bakr al-Khatib al-Baghdadi told us by permission not hearing: Al-Husayn ibn Ali al-Jawhari told us: Amr ibn al-Abbas al-Khazzaz related to us: Abu Bakr al-Sawli told us: Ishaq ibn Ibrahim al-Qazzaz told us: Ishaq al-Shahidi related to us: I would see Yahya al-Qattan – may Allah the Exalted have mercy on him–pray the midafternoon prayer, then sit with his back against the base of the minaret of his mosque. Then Ali ibn al-Madini, al-Shadhakuni, Amr

---

76 Abu Musa al-Asbahani narrated it with his chain. *Al-hafiz* Abu al-Qasim Ibn Asakir said in his book *al-Atraf* that Abu Dawud narrated in the book of *Adab* (4:258). The chain has Abu Abd Allah Mawla Al Abi Burda, who is unknown. See *al-Taqrib* #8215.

ibn Ali, Ahmad ibn Hanbal, Yahya ibn Main, and others would stand before him and ask him questions about hadith standing on their feet until it was time for the sunset prayer. He would not say to a single one of them "Sit" nor would they sit, out of awe and reverence.

It is related that when Abu Hanifa visited Sufyan after the death of the latter's brother Sufyan stood up, went to greet him, embraced him, and bade him sit in his place, said to those who questioned this act, "This man holds a high rank in knowledge, and if I did not stand up for his science I would stand up for his age, and if not for his age then for his Godwariness *(wara)*, and if not for his Godwariness then for his jurisprudence *(fiqh)*."[77]

Al-Hakim narrates that when al-Dhuhli went to see Imam Ahmad the latter stood up for him and the people were astounded. Then he told his son and his companions, "Go to Abu Abd Allah [al-Dhuhli] and write his narrations."[78]

Nawawi also said the *hafiz* Abu Musa al-Asbahani (d. 581) recited:

> *Qiyami wa al-azizi ilayka haqqun* (I swear by the All-Powerful that my standing for you (O Prophet (ﷺ)) is right and true) *wa tarku al-haqqi ma la yastaqimu* (and to leave truth and right is to embrace error) *fa hal ahadun lahu aqlun wa lubbun wa marifa yaraka fa la yaqumu?* (I ask: can anyone possessed of a mind and a heart and knowledge, upon seeing you, not stand up?).[79]

The author holds, as Ibn Hajar al-Asqalani, Nawawi and Abu Musa al-Asbahani, that no one of heart and mind can

77 It is narrated by Suyuti in *Tabyid al-sahifa* (p. 32) and al-Tahanawi in his book *Inja al-watan* (1:19-22).

78 Al-Hakim, *Marifat ulum al-hadith* (p. 104).

79 See the following sources: Nawawi's *al-Tarkhis fi al-ikram bi al-qiyam li dhawi al-fadl wa al-maziyya min ahl al-islam ala jihat al-birr wa al-tawqir wa al-ihtiram la ala jihat al-riya wa al-izam* (The permissibility of honoring, by standing up, those who possess excellence and distinction among the people of islam: in the spirit of piousness, reverence, and respect, not in the spirit of display and aggrandizement) ed. Kilani Muhammad Khalifa (Beirut: Dar al-Bashair al-islamiyya, 1409/1988); Nawawi's *Sharh sahih Muslim*; Ibn Hajar al-Asqalani's *Fath al-bari sharh sahih Bukhari* (The victory of the Creator: commentary on Bukhari's collection of sound *hadiths*); Shams al-Din al-Sakhawi's *al-Jawahir wa al-durar fi tarjamat shaykh al-islam Ibn Hajar* (The diamonds and the pearls: biography of Shaykh al-Islam Ibn Hajar).

object to standing for the sake of the Prophet (ﷺ). This was desirable and recommended not only in the time of the Prophet (ﷺ) but is recommended until the end of time. Observe that the *hafiz* Abu Musa died in 581, more than five centuries after the time of the Prophet (ﷺ), and yet stands for him in the present tense and mentions "seeing him." This seeing the Prophet (ﷺ) by pious believers both in a sleeping and a wakeful state is attested to in the Sharia, as has been mentioned by the scholars. Al-Haytami is among them:

> He was asked, "Is it possible to meet the Prophet (ﷺ) while awake in our time?" He replied, "Yes, it is possible. It has been asserted as part of the miracles of saints (*karamat al-awliya*) by Ghazali, al-Barizi, al-Taj al-Subki, and al-Yafii among the Shafiis, and by al-Qurtubi and Ibn Abi Jamra among the Malikis. It has been narrated that one of the saints (*awliya*) was sitting in the assembly of a jurist (*faqih*) while the latter related a hadith, whereupon the saint (*wali*) said, "This hadith is false." The jurist asked, "How do you know that?" The *wali* replied, "There is the Prophet (ﷺ) standing right next to you, and he is saying, "I never said this." When he said this the sight of the *faqih* was unveiled and he could see the Prophet (ﷺ)."[80]

This kind of testimony constitutes evidence that the Prophet (ﷺ) hears and sees us, as stated in *hadith*s that describe his seeing our actions, his hearing our greetings and blessings, and his interceding on our behalf.[81] In summary, as it is meritorious to stand as a sign of respect for others in religion, the Prophet (ﷺ) is alive and hears us, and he himself ordered the Companions to stand for their *sayyid*, it is certainly allowed and indeed praiseworthy to stand for the Prophet (ﷺ).

The following is further sound evidence that the Prophet (ﷺ) is alive in his grave.

---

80 Ibn Hajar al-Haytami, *Fatawa hadithiyya* (Cairo: Halabi, 1390/1970) p. 297.
81 The Prophet's intercession is discussed below, in the section on *ziyara*.

> Allah has defended the earth from consuming the bodies of prophets.[82]

Another version in Ibn Majah adds, "And the Prophet (ﷺ) of Allah is alive and provided for *(fa nabiyyullahi hayyun yurzaq)*."[83]

> The prophets are alive in their graves, praying to their Lord.[84]

Suyuti adds, "The life of the Prophet (ﷺ) in his grave, and [also] that of the rest of the prophets is known to us as definitive knowledge *(ilman qatiyyan)*."

> (The night I was enraptured to my Lord) I saw Moses standing in prayer in his grave.[85]

Nawawi said in his explanation of this *hadith*, "The work of the next world is all remembrance of Allah (*dhikr*) and supplication (*dua*)."[86]

> No one greets me except Allah has returned my soul to me so that I can return his *salam*.[87]

This hadith has been adduced by the scholars as the legal proof for the validity and modality of visiting and greeting the Prophet (ﷺ), although the hadith does not mention the necessity of physically visiting the Prophet (ﷺ) in Madina.

In reference to the translation of "has returned," Suyuti

82 A sound (*sahih*) tradition related on the authority of Aws ibn Aws al-Thaqafi by: Ahmad in his *Musnad*, Ibn Abi Shayba in the *Musannaf*, Abu Dawud in the *Sunan*, Nisai in his *Sunan*, Ibn Majah in his *Sunan*, Darimi in his *Musnad*, Ibn Khuzayma in his *Sahih*, ibn Hibban in his *Sahih*, Hakim in the *Mustadrak*, Tabarani in his *Kabir*, Bayhaqi in *Hayat al-anbiya*, Suyuti in *Anba al-adkhiya*, Dhahabi who confirmed Hakim's grading, and Nawawi in the *Adhkar*.

83 Bayhaqi mentions it also in the *Sunan al-kubra*.

84 A sound (*sahih*) tradition related on the authority of Anas ibn Malik by: al-Bazzar in his *Musnad*, Abu Yala in his *Musnad*, Ibn Adi in *al-Kamil fi al-duafa*, Tammam al-Razi in *al-Fawaid*, al-Bayhaqi in *Hayat al-anbiya fi quburihim*, Abu Nuaym in *Akhbar Asbahan*, Ibn Asakir in *Tarikh Dimashq*, al-Haythami in *Majma al-zawaid* (8:211), Suyuti in *Anba al-adhkiya bi-hayat al-anbiya* (#5), and al-Albani, in *Silsilat al-ahadith al-sahiha* (#621).

85 A sound (*sahih*) tradition related on the authority of Anas and others by Muslim, Nasai, Bayhaqi in the *Dalail al-nubuwwa* and the *Hayat al-anbiya*, and others. Some mention the beginning (in parentheses), while others omit it.

86 *Sharh sahih Muslim* 1/73/267.

87 Abu Hurayra in Abu Dawud (*Manasik* #2039) with a sound chain; Ibn Asakir, *Mukhtasar tarikh Dimashq* 2:407; Ahmad, *Musnad* 2:527; Abu Nuaym, *Akhbar*

and Haytami said that *radda* means *ala al-dawam*, or permanently, and not temporarily.[88] In other words, Allah does not
return the soul and take it back, then return it again and then
take it back again, but He returned it to the Prophet (ﷺ) permanently, so that the Prophet (ﷺ) is alive permanently.

Sakhawi, Ibn Hajar al-Asqalani's student, said, "As for us
[Muslims of the major schools] we believe and we confirm that
he is alive and provided for in his grave."[89] Ibn al-Qayyim said:

> It is obligatory knowledge to know that his body is
> in the earth tender and humid (i.e. as in life), and
> when the Companions asked him, "How is our greet-
> ing presented to you after you have turned to dust" he
> replied, "Allah has defended the earth from consum-
> ing the flesh of prophets," and if his body was not in
> his grave he would not have given this answer."[90]

Ibn Hajar al-Haythami wrote:

> The proofs and the transmitted texts have been
> established as authentic in the highest degree that
> the Prophet (ﷺ) is alive and tender . . . that he fasts
> and performs the pilgrimage every year, and that he
> purifies himself with water which rains on him.[91]

Whoever invokes blessings on me at my grave, I hear him,
and whoever invokes blessings on me from afar, I am informed
about it.[92]

> Whoever visits my grave, my intercession
> becomes guaranteed for him.[93]

Asbahan 2:353; Ibn al-Najjar, *Akhbar al-Madina* p. 145; Bayhaqi, *Shuab al-iman*
#4161; Haythami, *Majma al-zawaid* 10:162; Ibn Kathir, *Tafsir* 6:464; al-Mundhiri, *al-
Targhib wa al-tarhib* 2:499; *Talkhis al-habir* 2:267.

88 Suyuti in *Anba al-adhkiya bi hayat al-anbiya,* and Haytami in *al-Jawhar al-
munazzam.*

89 Sakhawi, *al-Qawl al-badi* p. 161.

90 Ibn al-Qayyim, *Kitab al-ruh* p. 58.

91 Ibn Hajar al-Haythami, *al-Jawhar al-munazzam.* End of quote.

92 Abu al-Shaykh cites it in *Kitab al-salat ala al-nabi* ("*Jala al-afham*" p. 22), and
Ibn Hajar says in *Fath al-bari* (6:379): "Abu al-Shaykh cites it with a good chain *(sanad
jayyid)*." Bayhaqi mentions it in *Hayat al-anbiya* and *Shuab al-iman* (2:218 #1583)
with *ublightuhu* in the end.

93 *Hadith hasan.* Narrated by al-Daraqutni, al-Dulabi, al-Bayhaqi, Khatib al-
Baghdadi, al-Uqayli, Ibn Adi, Tabarani, and Ibn Khuzayma in his *Sahih,* all through
various chains going back to Musa ibn Hilal al-Abdi from Ubayd Allah Ibn Umar, both

This is one of the proof-texts adduced by the religious scholars (*ulama*) of Islam to support the obligation or recommendation of visiting the Prophet's grave and seeking him as an intermediary or means of nearness to Allah (*wasila*).[94] Sakhawi said:

> The emphasis and encouragement on visiting his noble grave is mentioned in numerous hadiths, and it would suffice to show this if there was only the hadith whereby the truthful and anointed Prophet (ﷺ) of Allah promises that his intercession among other things becomes guaranteed for whoever visits him, and the Imams are in complete agreement from the time directly after his passing until our own time that this is among the best acts of drawing near to Allah.[95]

1.4.4. DOES STANDING WHILE INVOKING BLESSINGS (*SALAWAT*) UPON THE PROPHET (ﷺ) SIGNIFY THAT HE IS PRESENT IN PERSON?

Some of those who forbid standing for the Prophet (ﷺ) do so because they imagine that people who stand think the Prophet (ﷺ) is actually present at that time. However, this is not the reason why people stand and no one claims it as such. Rather, those who stand are expressing happiness, love, respect, and dedication at the mention of the Prophet (ﷺ) in the august assembly of those who remember him. They stand to attention

---

from Nafi, From Ibn Umar. Dhahabi declared this chain *hasan* (fair) as narrated, in *Mizan al-itidal*, vol. 4, p. 226 and he said: *"Huwa salih al-hadith"* which means: "He – Musa ibn Hilal – is good in his narrations." This is also Imam Ahmad's opinion as related by Shawkani in *Nayl al-awtar* 5:95. Imam Sakhawi confirmed Dhahabi's grading in the *Maqasid al-hasana*, and al-Lucknawi also declared it *hasan* in his commentary on Jurjani entitled *Zafr al-amani* p. 422 (3rd ed.) while al-Subki declared it *sahih* as stated by Samhudi in *Saadat al-darayn* 1:77, and Shawkani said: "Ibn al-Sakan, Abd al-Haqq (ibn al-Kharrat al-Ishbili), and Taqi al-Din al-Subki have declared this hadith sound *(sahih)*." Ibn Adi said in *al-Kamil fi al-Duafa* (6:2350): "He [Musa ibn Hilal] is most likely acceptable; other people have called him "unknown" [i.e. Abu Hatim al-Razi and al-Uqayli] and this is not true . . . He is one of the shaykhs of Imam Ahmad and most of them are trustworthy." Even the "Salafi" Albani declared him *thabit al-riwaya* (of established reliability) in his *Irwa* (4:338). About Ubayd Allah ibn Umar al-Umari: Dhahabi calls him *saduq hasan al-hadith* [truthful, of fair narrations] in *al-Mughni* 1:348; Sakhawi says of him *salih al-hadith* [of sound narrations] in *al-Tuhfa al-latifa* 3:366; Ibn Main said to Darimi about him: *salih thiqa* [sound and reliable] in *al-Kamil* 4:1459.

94 As cited in the present book from the chapters on visiting the Prophet's grave in Nawawi's book *al-Adhkar* and *al-Idah* and in Qadi Iyad's book *al-Shifa*.

95 Sakhawi, *al-Qawl al-badi* (p. 160).

in awe of the light that dawns upon creation for the one whose fame Allah has highly exalted. They stand as a sign of gratitude for the immense mercy bestowed on creation through the person of the Prophet Muhammad (ﷺ).

Furthermore, it is not permissible to deny the freedom of the soul in the isthmus (*barzakh*) to travel wherever it pleases by Allah's permission. According to the sayings reported by Ibn al-Qayyim, Salman al-Farisi said, "The souls of the believers are in an isthmus of land from where they go wherever they wish," and Imam Malik said, "I have heard *(balaghani)* that the soul is set free and goes wherever it wishes."[96]

Standing or dancing out of joy for the Prophet (ﷺ), or for what is connected to him or proceeds from him, is supported by clear proofs in the *sunna*, including:

• The Ethiopians put on a dancing display with spears out of joy *(farahan)* when he came to Madina. This is narrated by Abu Dawud with a good chain.[97]

• They played again in the Prophet's mosque on the day of *id al-fitr*, whereupon they danced while the Prophet (ﷺ) and his wife looked on, and the Prophet (ﷺ) encouraged them with the words *dunakum ya bani arfada*, "Jump to it, O sons of Arfada!" thus indicating that what they were doing was harmless and permissible. This is narrated by Muslim in the book of *Salat al-idayn* in his *Sahih* from Aisha.

• Similarly, they would bang the drum, sing, and play in front of him on the day of *id*. This is narrated by Ahmad and Ibn Majah from Qays ibn Sad ibn Ubada.

All this was not for any other reason than joy at being around the Prophet (ﷺ), as confirmed by the act of the women of the Banu Najjar when the Prophet (ﷺ) came to Madina:

> Anas narrates that when the Prophet (ﷺ) first came to Madina the Ansar came out, men and women, and they were all saying: "With us, O Messenger of Allah!" [i.e. come stay with us.] The Prophet (ﷺ) said, "Let the camel choose, for she has her orders." The camel alighted at the door of Abu Ayyub. Anas continued, (After he went in) the women of Banu al-Najjar

---

96 Imam Malik, *Kitab al-ruh* (p. 144).
97 Abu Dawud, in the book of *Adab* in his *Sunan* from Anas.

came out banging their drums and singing:
Nahnu jawar min bani al-najjar
ya habbadha muhammadin min jar
We are the girls of the Sons of Najjar
O delight of Muhammad for a neighbor!
The Prophet (ﷺ) came out and said, "Do you love
me?" *(atuhibbuni)*?
They replied:
Ey wallah ya rasul Allah
Yea, by Allah, O Messenger of Allah!
At this he said:
Wa ana uhibbukum
Wa ana uhibbukum
Wa ana uhibbukum
And I love you.

In another version he said: *Allahu yalamu anna qalbi yuhibbukunna* or Allahu *yalamu anni la uhibbukunna* i.e. Allah knows that my heart loves you that in truth I love you.[98]

• Several female Companions came up to the Prophet (ﷺ) after he came back from his campaigns and said that they had vowed to bang the drum before him if he came back safe and sound, and the Prophet (ﷺ) allowed them.[99]

• Ali said: I visited the Prophet (ﷺ) with Jafar (ibn Abi Talib) and Zayd (ibn Haritha). The Prophet (ﷺ) said to Zayd, "You are my freedman" *(anta mawlay)*, whereupon Zayd began to hop on one leg around the Prophet (ﷺ) *(hajala)*. The Prophet (ﷺ) then said to Jafar, "You resemble me in my creation and my manners" *(anta ashbahta khalqi wa khuluqi)*, whereupon Jafar began to hop behind Zayd. The Prophet (ﷺ) then said to me, "You are part of me and I am part of you" *(anta minni wa ana minka)* whereupon I began to hop behind Jafar.[100]

There is no doubt that such singing, dancing, reciting of poetry, and banging the drum was for joy at being with the

---

98 It is narrated by Bayhaqi with two chains in *Dalail al-nubuwwa* (2:508), Ibn Kathir in *al-Bidaya wa al-Nihaya* (3:199-200), and Suyuti in *al-Khasais al-kubra* (1:190). Shaykh Muhammad ibn Alawi al-Maliki in *al-Bayan wa al-tarif fi dhikra al-mawlid al-sharif* (p. 24-25) said that al-Hakim documents it, Abu Sad al-Nisaburi mentions it in his *Sharaf al-mustafa*, and Ibn Majah narrates it in his *Sunan*, book of *Nikah* (#1889).

99 This is narrated by Tirmidhi from Burayda and he said: *hasan sahih gharib*, also Abu Dawud, and Bukhari.

100 Imam Ahmad related it in his *Musnad* (1:108) and Ahmad Muhammad Shakir declared it sound *(sahih)* in his Riyadh, 1949 edition; it is related also by Uqayli, Abu Nuaym from Jabir, and Ibn Sad in his *Tabaqat* with a sound chain to Muhammad al-Baqir.

Prophet (ﷺ); nor did he condemn or frown upon such displays in any way. These are common displays of happiness and lawful forms of merriment. Similar to standing up at the mention of the Prophet's birth, they are ordinary acts that show love and gladness and symbolize the joy of creation. None of these constitutes worship or law. That is why the savant al-Barzanji said in his famous poem of *mawlid*:

> *wa qad sanna ahl al-ilmi wa al-fadli wa al-tuqa*
> *qiyaman ala al-aqdami maa husni imani*
> *bi tashkhisi dhati al-mustafa wa huwa hadirun*
> *bi ay maqamin fihi yudhkaru bal dani*
> It is the usage of the excellent people of
>   knowledge and piety
> To stand on their feet in the best demeanor
> Acting as if the Prophet (ﷺ) were actually present
> Every time they mention him, and visualizing
>   him coming to them.

Al-Barzanji's reference to acting as if the Prophet (ﷺ) were present, and visualizing him, suggests calling his gracious form and qualities to mind so as to increase and perfect the motion of the hearts and body in respecting and loving him.

1.4.5. USING THE PHRASE, "*AL-SALAMU ALAYKA YA RASUL ALLAH* (PEACE BE UPON YOU, O MESSENGER OF ALLAH)"

The answer is that it is permissible, excellent, praiseworthy, and highly meritorious to invoke blessings upon the Prophet (ﷺ) with the phrases:

Ya rasul Allah (O Messenger of Allah),
Ya habib Allah (O Beloved Lover of Allah),
Ya nabi Allah (O Prophet of Allah),
Ya safi Allah (O Elect Friend of Allah),
Ya khalil Allah (O Intimate Friend of Allah),
Ya naji Allah (O Confidant of Allah).

These and any such phrases may be used at all times and in all places, but most especially in gatherings of *dhikr* where such phrases increase the love of the Prophet (ﷺ) in the heart by untold amounts. Muslims are obliged to love him more than our children, parents, and life itself. The scholars of *Manasik,* or rites of Pilgrimage, recommend these phrases, moreover, when visiting the Prophet (ﷺ) in Madina. It is established that Abdullah ibn Umar would say, *as-salamu alayka ya rasul allah* upon each of his visits to the Prophet (ﷺ), and a similar phrase upon visiting Abu Bakr and his father. Those who object to using "*YA*" with the Prophet (ﷺ) are injuring themselves and others by subscribing to inconsistency and innovation. This is true for the following reasons:

Apparently they have overlooked the fact that Muslims are required to say *tashahhud* in their *salat* as the prayer is invalid without it. At least nine times a day, Muslims say in *tashahhud*: *as-salamu alayka ayyuha al-nabi wa rahmatullah wa barakatuh* The phrase *ayyuha al-nabi* is the same as *ya nabi*.

Allah orders Muslims not to call upon the Prophet (ﷺ) in the same way as they call upon each other: *la tajalu duaa al-rasuli baynakum ka duai badikum badan* (*Make not the calling of the Messenger among you as your calling one of another*) (24:63).

This is proof that Allah did not prohibit people from calling upon the Prophet (ﷺ), for were it an absolute prohibition, it would not need to be qualified further. Allah Himself shows us the etiquette of addressing the Prophet (ﷺ) by calling him "*Ya ayyuha al-nabi*," or O Prophet (ﷺ), and by referring to him as "The Messenger" in the Quran, while He calls other prophets by name *ya Ibrahim, ya Yahya, ya Musa, ya Isa*, ("O Abraham, O John, O Moses, O Jesus)," etc. The religious scholars (*ulama*) have explained that in doing this Allah established an honorific difference between the Seal of Prophets and those who preceded him, blessings and peace of Allah upon him and upon all of them.[101] They have also said that it is the reason why it should be preferred to say, *ya rasul allah* instead of *ya Muhammad*.

As mentioned in the volume on *tawassul*, the Prophet (ﷺ) taught a blind man to supplicate in which he has to say, "*Ya Muhammad*." This is a well-known, well-authenticated hadith that cannot be refuted. The invocation is as follows:

---

101 See Qadi Iyad, *al-Shifa*; Bayhaqi, *Shuab al-iman*; Ibn al-Jawzi, *al-Wafa*; Qastallani, *al-Mawahib al-laduniyya*; Suyuti, *al-Khasais al-kubra*; and others, chapters concerning Allah's bestowal of precedence and preference to His Prophet.

> O Allah, I am asking you and turning to you by
> means of your Prophet Muhammad, the Prophet of
> mercy; O Muhammad, I am turning with you to my
> Lord regarding my present need so that He will fulfill
> it; O Allah, allow him to intercede (with You) for
> me![102]

The words "O Muhammad" are missing from the version in
Tirmidhi.[103] It is a grammatically faulty omission because
without the vocative "O Muhammad," the sense of the direct
address continues to be "O Allah." This makes no sense since in
the latter part he says, "I am turning *with you* to my Lord,"
which clearly does not mean "O Allah, I am turning with You to
my Lord."

1.4.6. THE WAHHABIS' TAMPERING WITH THE GATE TO THE PROPHET'S NOBLE GRAVE (*MUWAJAHA AL-SHARIFA*)

Muslims should take note of the following heinous act related to the issue of *"ya Muhammad,"* because it is established
without doubt as one of the greatest slights upon the Prophet
(ﷺ) in our time. In looking at an old picture of the golden gate
at the entrance of the Prophet's grave, one will see, at the top
of each door, intertwined, the invocations in Arabic calligraphy:

YA ALLAH
YA MUHAMMAD

If one looks at the top of each door today, one will notice that
the Arabic letter *Y* (Ar. *ya*) in the initial position of the word *YA*
in *"Ya Muhammad"* has been cut away, but the *A* (Ar. *alif*) and
the bottom two dots of the *Y* have been left in place. Now one
will read:

YA ALLAH
A MUHAMMAD

A picture of the old gate, before the Wahhabis defaced it, is
published on the front cover of *Islamic Beliefs and Doctrine
According to Ahl al-Sunna: A Repudiation of "Salafi"*

---

102 Related by Ahmad (4:138 #17246), Tirmidhi (Daawat Ch. 119), Ibn Majah
(*Iqamat al-salat wa al-sunnat*, Ch. on *Salat al-hajat*), Nasai (*Amal al-yawm wa al-laylat* p. 417-418), al-Hakim (1:313), and rigorously authenticated as sound (*sahih*) by
nearly fifteen hadith masters including Ibn Hajar, Dhahabi, Shawkani, and Ibn
Taymiyya.

103 Cf. Tirmidhi's *Aridat al-ahwadhi* (13:81) with *al-hafiz* Abu Bakr ibn al-Arabi's
commentary.

Innovations. It is a high-quality, clear color picture that, it is hoped, can be seen and understood by all Muslims.

The above mentioned invocation using the vocative *YA* in front of the Prophet's name was also used after the Prophet's death, as is proven by the following sound (*sahih*) *hadith*:[104]

> A man would come to Uthman ibn Affan for a certain need, but the latter would not pay him any attention nor look into his need, upon which he complained of his condition to Uthman ibn Hunayf who told him: "Go and make ablution, then go to the mosque and pray two cycles (*rakat*), then say (this *dua*)," and he mentioned the invocation of the blind man, "then go (to Uthman again)."

The man went, did as he was told, then came to Uthman's door, upon which the door-attendant came, took him by the hand, and brought him to Uthman who sat him with him on top of the carpet, and said, "Tell me what your need is." After this the man went out, met Uthman ibn Hunayf again, and said to him, "May Allah reward you! Previously he would not look into my need nor pay any attention to me, until you spoke to him." He replied, "I did not speak to him, but I saw the Prophet (ﷺ) when a blind man came to him complaining of his failing eyesight," and he mentioned to him the substance of the previous narration.

Finally, *"ya Muhammad"* is the speech of Prophet Jesus (ﷺ) to the Prophet after Jesus' descent, according to an authentic hadith on the authority of Abu Hurayra:

> I heard the Prophet say: "By the One in Whose hand is Abu al-Qasim's soul, Jesus son of Mary (ﷺ) shall descend as a just and wise ruler. He shall destroy the cross, slay the swine, eradicate discord and grudges, and money shall be offered to him but he will not accept it. Then he shall stand at my grave side and say, '*Ya Muhammad!*' and I will answer him."[105]

---

104 Authenticated by Bayhaqi, Abu Nuaym in the *Marifa*, Mundhiri (*Targhib* 1:473-474), Haythami, and Tabarani in the *Kabir* (9:17-18) and the *Saghir* (1:184/201-202) on the authority of Uthman ibn Hunayf's nephew Abu Imama ibn Sahl ibn Hunayf.

105 Abu Yala relates it with a sound (*sahih*) chain in his *Musnad* (Dar al-Mamun ed. 1407/1987) 11:462; Ibn Hajar al-Asqalani cites it in *al-Matalib al-aliya* (Kuwait,

It is not necessary for the person greeting the Prophet (ﷺ) to be standing at the Prophet's graveside, since the Prophet (ﷺ) also said:

> Whoever invokes blessings on me at my grave, I hear him, and whoever invokes blessings on me from afar, I am informed about it.[106]

The following report of Ibn Abi Fudayk, one of the early scholars of Madina and one of the Shafii shaykhs, applies not only to the Prophet's visitors in Madina, but to every person who invokes blessings on the Prophet (ﷺ) with the words *ya Muhammad* from afar as if he were standing in front of him.

> I heard one of the authorities whom I have met say, "It has reached us that whoever stands at the Prophet's grave and recites, "Allah and His angels send blessings on the Prophet (ﷺ) . . ." (33:56) and then says, "May Allah bless you, O Muhammad" (*sallallahu alayka ya Muhammad*) seventy times, an angel will call him saying, May Allah bless you, O So-and-so; none of your needs will be left unfulfilled."[107]

Bukhari, Nawawi, and Shawkani all relate the narrations of Ibn Umar and Ibn Abbas whereby they would call out *ya Muhammad* whenever they had a cramp in their leg.[108] Regardless of the grade of authenticity of these narrations, it is significant that Bukhari, Nawawi, and Shawkani never raised such a disturbing notion as to say that calling out "O Muhammad" amounted to *shirk*.[109]

1393/1973) 4:23, in the chapter entitled: "Concerning the Prophet's life in his grave" and #4574. Haythami says in *Majma al-zawaid* (8:5), Chapter entitled: "Isa ibn Maryam's Descent": "Its sub-narrators are the men of sound *(sahih)* hadith."

106 Abu al-Shaykh cites it in *Kitab al-salat ala al-nabi (Jala al-afham* p. 22), and Ibn Hajar says in *Fath al-bari* (6:379): "Abu al-Shaykh cites it with a good chain *(sanad jayyid)*." Bayhaqi mentions it in *Hayat al-anbiya* and *Shuab al-iman* (2:218 #1583) with *ublightuhu* in the end.

107 Ibn Jamaa related it in *Hidayat al-salik* 3:1382-1383, Ibn al-Jawzi in *Muthir al-gharam* p. 487, Qadi Iyad in *al-Shifa*, and Bayhaqi in *Shuab al-iman* (#4169).

108 In Bukhari's *Adab al-mufrad,* in Nawawi's *Adhkar,* and in Shawkani's *Tuhfat al-dhakirin.* Chapters entitled: "What one says if he feels a cramp in his leg."

109 See Nawawi's *Adhkar*: 1970 Riyadh edition: p. 27; 1988 Taif edition: p. 383; 1992 Makka edition: p. 370; Bukhari's *Adab al-mufrad*; 1990 Abd al-Baqi Beirut edition: p. 286; 1994 Albani edition entitled *Daif al-adab al-mufrad*: p. 87. The latter gives as a reference: *Takhrij al-kalim al-tayyib* (235)," date? Beirut: Alam al-kitab: p. 324, date? Beirut: Dar al-kutub al-ilmiyya: p.142. Shawkani's *Tuhfat al-dhakirin*, 1970 Beirut: Dar al-kutub al-ilmiyya: p. 206-207.

In conclusion, it is advised that Muslims who meet objections to saying *"ya rasul Allah"* stand firm in the knowledge that this act is well-grounded in the *Sharia* and that it is the objectors who are in the wrong.

1.5. CONCLUSION: MAY ONE NOT OBJECT TO THE COMMEMORATION OF THE PROPHET'S BIRTHDAY (*MAWLID*)

From evidence in Quran and *sunna*, and from the scholars of the major schools, it is clear that commemorating the *mawlid* is not only permissible but meritorious and praiseworthy. Let every Muslim who has questions about this topic not be intimidated by assertions like *"Mawlid* is like Christmas." Even Ibn Taymiyya, who wrote against the *mawlid*, admitted that it may be good to celebrate *mawlid*. He gave as his precedent for this concession the fact that Imam Ahmad accepted that a certain man spent a large sum of money decorating a copy of the Quran, although he considered it an innovation himself.

In the *Sharia*, nothing is declared forbidden (*haram*) unless the scholars are unanimous that the Quran and *sunna* declare it so, whether explicitly or indirectly. In the case of commemoration of the *mawlid*, not only does such unanimity not exist, but there is a majority who declare that it is an excellent action that merits reward.

2. VISITATION OF THE PROPHET (ﷺ) IN MADINA (*ZIYARA*)

Questions discussed in this chapter include, among others:

What do the scholars of the major schools say about traveling to visit the Prophet (ﷺ) in light of the "Salafi" prohibition of travel for the purpose of visiting the Prophet (ﷺ)?

What do the scholars of the major schools say about the continuous efforts of "Salafis" to eliminate the grave of the Prophet (ﷺ) from the Holy Mosque on the pretext that its inclusion was an innovation?

2.1. SOME FALSEHOODS OF THE "SALAFIS" CONCERNING THE PROPHET'S GRAVE AND HIS MOSQUE

The "Salafis" claim that since the Prophet's grave was not initially a part of the Prophet's mosque, its present location inside the mosque is an innovation. This is the position of Nasir al-Din Albani and those who follow him.

The response to such aberrant and discordant views is in the Prophet's hadith in *Sahih Muslim,* "The best of my Community are those of the century (*qarn*) wherein I was sent, then those that came after them." The blessed grave was incorporated into the mosque in the time of al-Walid ibn Abd al-Malik on the recommendation of his brother-in-law Umar ibn Abd al-Aziz. Both are *tabiin*, and the latter's standing in the Community then and now is second only to the first four rightly guided caliphs.

Let it be understood clearly that, in Islam, the primacy of the mosque of the Prophet (ﷺ) and the sanctity of Madina, its earth, flora, fauna, protected space, and the name itself, hinges on the fact that it is the city of the Prophet (ﷺ) because he emigrated and died there. The greatness of Madina and its mosque is due to no other reason.

Some of the "Salafis" say, "To visit the Prophet's Mosque is not obligatory, not even after performing the pilgrimage (*hajj*)." This is a contrived statement that typifies innovation, not the discourse of traditional Muslims. What the overwhelming majority of the books of jurisprudence say on the question is as follows: *ziyaratu qabr al-nabi sallallahu alayhi wa sallama mashruatun bi al-ijma wa hiya min afdal al-amal bi al-ijma* (The visit of the Prophet's grave is lawful by consensus, and it is among the most meritorious deeds by consensus).[1]

Some of the "Salafis" say, "It is not a sin not to visit the Prophet's mosque. It is recommended to visit it, but not mandatory such as the obligation of performing the pilgrimage (*hajj*)." Again these are contrived provisos that have an air of innovation about them. Also, the false comparison to the pilgrimage (*hajj*) is specious. The authors of such statements seem to confuse visiting the Prophet's mosque, which is recommended generally speaking, with visiting the Prophet (ﷺ) himself or the Prophet's grave, which is specifically recommended, as the authorities all attest. Imam Malik even stated that it should be said, "visit the Prophet" rather than "visit the Prophet's grave."

Some "Salafis" say, "One can perform all the rituals of the pilgrimage (*hajj*) and not visit the Prophet's mosque, and yet have the pilgrimage (*hajj*) accepted if Allah wills." This is clear and manifest innovation as it departs from the practice of the Salaf and Khalaf, for whom the question was whether to begin the pilgrimage (*hajj*) by visiting Madina or first going to Makka. Samhudi states that among the Salaf who considered that one should begin by visiting the Prophet (ﷺ) in Madina were Ilqima, al-Aswad, and Amr ibn Maymun.[2] He also states

---

1 Sources: Sadi Abu Habib, *Mawsuat al-ijma fi al-fiqh al-islami* 2:919; Nawawi, al-Majmu, *al-Idah fi manasik al-hajj* and *al-Adhkar*; Ibn Jamaa, *Hidayat al-salik* 3:1384f.; Ibn Hajar, *Fath al-bari* 3:51; Sakhawi, *al-Qawl al-badi* p. 160; Shawkani, *Nayl al-awtar* 5:97. etc.

2 Nawawi reports that Imam Ahmad said: "The best of the *tabiin* are Ibn al-Musayyib, then Ilqima and al-Aswad."

that Abu Hanifa said, in the *Fatawa* of Abu al-Layth al-Samarqandi, "The best for the pilgrim is to begin with Makka, and after he has finished his rituals, let him pass by Madina." Imam Ahmad said the same, and the reason he gave puts both of their opinions in perspective, "Let him go first to Makka lest something happen on the road that might prevent him from reaching it," in other words, to avoid any risk of not reaching Makka.

As for not going to Madina at all, it is unheard of. In fact, Ibn Abd al-Barr and al-Baladhuri relate that Abu Bakrah, Ziyad ibn Abih and others intended pilgrimage on a certain year but postponed it when they realized they would be unable to go to Madina as well! Abd al-Haqq al-Ishbili (d. 582) stated that the visit is an obligatory practice (*sunna wajiba*). As for the schools it differs between *wajib* (some Malikis and some Zahiris), near *wajib* (Hanafis), and *sunna manduba* (Shafiis and Hanbalis).[3]

In regard to visiting the Prophet's grave, it is permissible and praiseworthy in Islam according to the majority of the scholars of the major schools as established by the following excerpts. In his reference book for the jurisprudence of the recognized schools, Abd al-Rahman al-Jaziri writes at length about the many benefits of visiting the Prophet's grave and of the importance of the visit.[4] He says that it is among the great actions that Islam, the pure religion, encourages. He also says that it is not a secret that visiting the Prophet's grave is more beneficial to those endowed with understanding (*ulu al-albab*) than any other experience. He cites many recommended acts for the visit, and proper manners (*adab*):

Let the visitor imagine the Prophet's magnificent and generous form, as if he is sleeping in his grave, knowing him (the visitor) and hearing his words. Only then does he say, "Peace be upon you, O Messenger of Allah" . . . and the visitor conveys to the Prophet (ﷺ) the greetings of those who asked him to send *salam* to the Prophet (ﷺ), so he says, "Peace be upon you, O Messenger of Allah, from [name of person] the son of [name of parent] who seeks *shafaa* (intercession) with you to your

---

3 Sources: Samhudi, *Khulasat al-wafa* p. 101; Nawawi, *al-Taqrib wa al-taysir* p. 98-99; Shawkani, *Nayl al-awtar* 5:94, 97.

4 Abd al-Rahman al-Jaziri, *al-Fiqh ala al-Madhahib al-arbaa* (p. 711-715).

Lord, therefore ask for his *shafaa* for all believers . . ."

Among the fallacies of those who oppose visiting the graves of the Prophet (⁕) and the saints is their interpretation of the saying of Ali ibn Abi Talib, "The Messenger of Allah commanded me that I omit no honored tomb but to level it, no statue but to efface it." In response to their error, the meaning of the words "honored tomb" here is "a tomb that is worshiped." After Islam, and the prohibition of idolatry, such worship is precluded. This is proven by the fact that the Prophet (⁕) marked one grave with a rock with his own hand to identify it so that he might visit it later.

Abu Dawud narrates in his *Sunan*, book of *Janaiz*:

> When Uthman ibn Mazun died, he was brought out on his bier and buried. The Prophet (⁕) ordered a man to bring him a stone, but he was unable to carry it (due to its great size and weight). The Prophet (⁕) got up and going over to it rolled up his sleeves. The narrator Kathir told that al-Muttalib remarked, 'The one who told me about the Messenger of Allah said, I still seem to see the whiteness of the forearms of the Messenger of Allah when he rolled up his sleeves. He then carried it and placed it at his head saying, "I am marking my brother's grave with it, and I shall bury beside him those of my family who die."

Another proof is the fact that the *sunna* is to build the grave up slightly into a convex mound or a flat top. Scholars have seen in this a principle for supporting a superstructure over the grave, and evidence supporting the practice of visiting graves the praiseworthiness of which is established by other sound evidence.

Another fallacy is the "Salafi" misinterpretation of the hadiths "May Allah curse the Jews and Christians who have taken the tombs of their prophets for mosques," and "Those who were before you used to take tombs as mosques. Do not do that. Do not take tombs as mosques, for I have forbidden you that." They misconstrue these hadith as evidence against the inclusion of the Prophet's grave inside his mosque by the Salaf.

Scholars of the major schools have explained the words "take their graves for mosques" to mean "take their graves as directions for their prayers." This is confirmed by the hadith mentioning the pictures; when they mentioned the church in Ethiopia to the Prophet (ﷺ) and related to him the beautiful things and pictures in it, he said, "Those people, when some upright man among them dies, they build a mosque on his grave and fashion those pictures. Those people are the worst of creation before Allah on the Day of Resurrection." Allah's curse therefore is on those who worship the prophets and saints whether they are buried or represented on pictures, not on those who visit them in search of blessings.

No Muslims have made the Prophet's grave a mosque, since none of them pray to it. The orientation of Aisha's room in relation to the Prophet's mosque was arranged deliberately in order to respect the Prophet's prohibition. A stronger proof yet is the fact that Allah answers the supplication of the Prophet (ﷺ), and the Prophet (ﷺ) asked of Him, "O Allah, do not allow my grave to be taken as an idol that is worshiped after me." This is the basis of the hadith, "Allah's wrath is great against the nation that took the graves of their prophets as idols."

It is particularly wrong to ascribe *shirk* to Muslims who visit the graves of prophets and the pious. The Prophet (ﷺ) asked Allah not to allow his Community to relapse into idol-worship, and it is a tenet of mainstream Islam that the supplication (*dua*) of the Prophet (ﷺ) is *mustajab* or fulfilled. Furthermore, the Sharia forbids interpreting in the worst sense acts that are subject to more than one interpretation, which is exactly what is being done by those who cast the worst aspersions on Muslims who come to the grave of prophets and saints do.

2.2. SHAYKH ALAWI AL-MALIKI'S EXCELLENT WORDS ON TRAVELING TO VISIT THE PROPHET (ﷺ)

The following is translated from Shaykh Muhammad ibn Alawi al-Maliki al-Hasani's *Mafahim yajib an tusahhah*:[5]

---

5 Shaykh Muhammad ibn Alawi al-Maliki al-Hasani, *Mafahim yajib an tusah-hah*, "The Necessary Correction of Certain Preconceptions." Dubai: Hashr ibn Ahmad Dalmook, 4th ed. 1407/1986.

Some people—may Allah reform them and guide them to the straight path—look at the grave of the honored Prophet (ﷺ) from the mere perspective that it is a grave like any other. It is no wonder that all sorts of wrong imaginings and bad thoughts occur in their minds and hearts with regard to the Muslims who do visit the Prophet (ﷺ) and travel for that purpose and stand at his grave reciting invocations (*dua*).

Such people may be heard objecting, "It is forbidden to travel to his grave," and "it is forbidden to recite invocations at his grave." Indeed they will push their denial to the point that they say, "Supplication (*dua*) at his grave is idolatry (*shirk*) or unbelief (*kufr*)," or "Whoever says that the grave is the most blessed spot in the earth including the Kabah, has committed *shirk* and is misguided (*dalal*)." And this wholesale blind and thoughtless condemnation of others with the charges of unbelief (*kufr*) and misguidance (*dalal*) contravenes the way of the Pious Predecessors (*salaf al-salih*, pious early generations).

No two people can be found who will not agree on what is meant when we (Muslims) speak of the noble grave or the visit to it or its preference or travelling to it or invoking Allah and asking Him in front of the grave. There is no qualm nor divergence about the meaning of all this among Muslims. Clearly, the meaning of what is sought after is the inhabitant of the grave himself: the master of all prophets and the best of all of Allah's creations, the greatest Prophet (ﷺ) and the most noble Messenger (ﷺ).

2.3. THE PRAISEWORTHINESS OF VISITING THE PROPHET'S BLESSED GRAVE

Imam Ghazali said, after mentioning the *hadith*, "Do not travel except to three mosques":

> The gist of the matter is that some *ulama* use it as evidence for prohibiting travel to places of religious visitation and pilgrimage. It is clear that this is not the case. On the contrary, visitation to graves is commanded by the hadith, "I have forbidden you in the past to visit graves, but now I tell you to visit them."

The hadith only mentions the prohibition of frequent visitation to other than the three Mosques because of the likeness of one mosque to another. Furthermore, there is no city in which there is no mosque. Hence, there is no need to travel to another mosque. As for places of religious visitation, the blessing (baraka) of visiting them varies to the measure of their rank with Allah."[6]

The following is an excerpt from a booklet by Shaykh Isa ibn Abd Allah ibn Mani al-Humayri, Director of the Dirat al-awqaf in Dubai, United Arab Emirates:[7]

2.3.1. THE HADITH SUPPORTING THE GENERAL ORDER TO VISIT GRAVES

There are many hadith to that effect which have reached the grade of highest authenticity (tawatur). See: *Nazm al-mutanathir fi al-hadith al-mutawatir*. One of the common *mutawatir* narrations is, "I had forbidden you from visiting graves, but now I tell you to visit them for they remind you of the hereafter." Muslim, Ahmad and al-Tahawi from Burayda ibn al-Hasib.

Another narration according to al-Nasai also from Burayda, *"Faman arada an yazur al-qubur fal yazur . . ."* (whoever wants to visit the graves, let him do so, and do not prohibit it)" *[wa la taqulu hajran]*. This is a general narration which makes visiting permitted whether a journey was intended for it or not. This hadith is definitely not restricted to one person or one circumstance but is a general order in nature.[8]

This general order is evidence that the Legislator is recommending movement by the word *"ziyara"* (visitation) which in Arabic implies traveling from one place to another by undertaking a journey.

If people claim that Ibn Taymiyya in his answer to Akhnai said, "The order to visit graves does not entail travel," I answer, The hadith is general without any condition. If *ziyara* implies

---

6 Imam Ghazali, *Ihya ulum al-din.*

7 Shaykh Isa ibn Abd Allah ibn Mani al-Humayri, *Al-ilam bi istihbab shadd al-rihal li ziyarati qabr khayr al-anam alayhi al-salat wa al-salam* (The notification concerning the recommendation of travelling to visit the grave of the best of creation blessings and peace be upon him).

8 See next section for the hadith on visiting graves.

a journey, there is no way for us legally to prohibit that journey! Further, the higher reference in case of difference of opinion, is the Law *(al-shar)*, and the Legislator called the journeying "*ziyara.*"

"*Inna rajulan zara akhan lahu fi qariyatin ukhra . . .*" "A man visited a close brother of him in another village, so Allah ordered an angel to meet him on the way and ask him, 'Where are you going?' He answered, 'I intend to visit a brother of mine in the next village.' He asked him, 'Is there any business between you and him?' He replied, 'None except love of Allah.' He said, Know that I am a messenger from your Lord to tell you that Allah loves You both as you both love each other for His sake." Narrated by Muslim in his *Sahih* 4:1988.

The Legislator here made *ziyara* entail both travel and non-travel. To limit the *ziyara* to something not entailing travel is an abuse of the meaning of the word and a deviation from the fundamentals of the Law, and Allah knows best.

Ibn Rajab al-Hanbali, disciple of Ibn Taymiyya once told *al-Hafiz* al-Iraqi on a trip, "I am intending to pray in the mosque of Prophet Abraham (ﷺ)." Al-Iraqi said, "As for myself I am intending to visit the grave of Prophet Abraham (ﷺ)." Ibn Rajab said, "Why your difference in intention?" al-Iraqi said, "You have contradicted the *sunna* of the Prophet (ﷺ) who said, 'Do not intend to journey except to three mosques,' and you have intended to visit a fourth. As for me, I am following his *sunna* according to the hadith: 'Visit the graves'"–i.e. all of the graves, not excluding those of the prophets.

2.3.2. TRAVELING TO VISIT THE PROPHET'S GRAVE

Ibn Abd al-Barr said, It is allowed among people to visit graves in general, and it is obligatory *(wajib)* to travel to the grave of the Prophet (ﷺ): *wajib shadd al matiyy ila qabrihi.*

Abu al-Hasanat al-Lucknawi said in his *Ibraz al-ghayy fi shifa al-ayy* [The exposure of deviation for the healing of the sick], "Until Ibn Taymiyya, not a single scholar ever questioned even in the slightest the permissibility of visiting the Prophet's grave. Rather, all scholars unanimously supported the ruling that it was one of the best acts of worship *(afdal al-ibadat)* and highest acts of obedience *(arfa al-taaat)*. The only difference was whether it was *wajib* (Malikis) or near the *wajib* (Hanafis) or merely recommended–*mandub* (Shafiis and Hanbalis). The first who broke the unanimity is Ibn Taymiyya."

Ijma in *shadd al-rihal* (traveling) to visit the noble grave is of the highest grades of *ijma* among the religious scholars. Level after level of both the religious scholars and the commonality, century after century, across the disciplines–all agree on this. This is for both the grave and the mosque. To make a difference between the grave and the mosque of the Prophet (﷽) is decisively null and void.

The hadith *"La tushaddu al-rihal illa li thalath* (mounts are not to be saddled except to go to three (mosques))," does not indicate that it is forbidden to visit the noble grave. Ibn Taymiyya's inference that this kind of trip (traveling to visit the grave) is a disobedience and the prescribed prayer *(salat)* must not be shortened during it, is patently incorrect. Ibn Hajar said in the *Fath,* "This is one of the ugliest matters reported from Ibn Taymiyya."

Hafiz al-Iraqi said in *al-Ajwiba al-makkiyya* and *Tarh al-tathrib* (6:43):

There are several answers to this:

1 Either he means: absolutely no travel except to these three places. And this is completely false. The nature of an exception must be the same as that of the things forbidden. If the exception concerns the mosques *(masajid)*, the prohibition must concern the mosques *(masajid)*. This rule is followed by Imam Ahmad as quoted in *Sharh al-kawkab al-munir* by Ibn al-Najjar al-Hanbali, al-Kharqi in the *Mukhtasar,* Ibn Badran, al-Ghazali in *al-Mankhul,* and Abu Ishaq al-Shirazi in *al-Luma.*

2 Therefore the proper significance must be, "Do not travel to any mosque *(masjid)* other than these three mosques *(masajid)*. This is confirmed by the hadith related by Shahr Ibn Hawshab formulating the legal ruling retained by the religious scholars: *"La yanbaghi lil musafiri an yashudda rihalahu ila masjidin yabtaghi fihi al-salat ghayra al-masjidi al-haram wal-masjid al-aqsa wa masjidi hadha* (the traveller must not saddle the mounts in order to go to pray a certain prayer in a

mosque except in the Holy Mosque [in Makka], or the Farthest
Mosque [al-Aqsa in Jerusalem], or my mosque [in Madina])."
Cf. Ahmad in the *Musnad* (3:64, 3:93) Abu Yala in the *Musnad*
(2:489). Ibn Hajar said in *Fath al-bari* (3:65): "Shahr's narration is good despite some weakness." Dhahabi said, "Shahr is
trustworthy."

3 Subki in *Shifa al-siqam,* p. 121, said, "There are two reasons for traveling: a certain cause (seeking knowledge, visiting
parents), or the place of destination itself (Makka, Madina,
Quds). There is no question about the first one. As for the limitation on the latter in the hadith, although it has to do with
the Prophet's mosque, the limitation does not rule concerning
the grave of the Prophet (ﷺ). Therefore even if the mosque of
Madina were not mentioned in that hadith, we would still not
be concerned by the order in relation to visiting the Prophet's
grave."

4 The true meaning of the hadith can be seen in the light of
other authentic hadiths praising the travel to the mosque in
Quba:

> If they knew what was in Quba (the mosque), they
> would have travelled there at the highest speed (rid-
> ing the camel to death) [*sahih*].

> If the masjid of Quba was at the top of the skies,
> we would have ridden our camels to death in order to
> attain it" (Umar ibn al-Khattab) [*hasan*].

Abu Hurayra used to travel to visit the Quba mosque. If he
understood the hadith *la tushadd al-rihal* as a categorical prohibition (*tahrim*) he would not have gone. See Ibn Battal,
Nawawi (*Sharh sahih Muslim* 9:106), Ibn Qudama in *al-
Mughni* (2:103-104), al-Khattabi in *Maalim al-sunan,* (2:443),
Ahmad (3:336), Bazzar in *Kashf al-astar* (2:4), Tahawi in
Mushkil al-athar (1:241), Ibn Abi Shayba in his *Musannaf*
(2:373), Ibn Hajar in *Fath al-bari* (3:69), and Abd al-Razzaq in
the *Musannaf* (5:133).

In conclusion, al-Khattabi said, the position of Nawawi and
Ibn Qudama and Ibn Battal is that there is no prohibition

(*tahrim*) of an act of travel in the hadith. Rather it is an emphasis on the importance of traveling to these three mosques in particular, and the emphasis becomes an obligation in case of a vow (*nadhr*), which is not the case for a vow to pray in any *masjid* other than these three.

2.4. HADITH ON VISITING GRAVES

Whoever wishes to visit the graves, let him visit them, for they remind one of the next world.[9]

Pay visits to your dead and give them your salutations, for in them there lies a lesson for you.[10]

Visit the graves, and you will be reminded of the afterlife.[11]

Visit the graves for they soften the heart."[12]

The Prophet (ﷺ) placed a stone on top of the grave of Uthman ibn Mazun and said, "By this I shall know where the grave of my brother Uthman is.[13]

No man visits the grave of his brother and sits by him except his brother enjoys his company until he rises."[14]
Do not visit the graves of the disbelievers except weeping profusely. If you are not weeping, do not visit them lest something of what touched them touches you.[15]

I forbade you in the past to visit graves, but now I tell you to visit them. (For visiting graves promotes

9 It is related in Muslim, Abu Dawud, Tirmidhi, Ibn Majah, and al-Nisai through various chains.
10 Related by Ibn Abi al-Dunya, Ahmad 3:38, 5:356, and Tabarani in his *Kabir*. Al-Iraqi said: "Its chain is fair (*hasan*)." Haythami mentions it in *Majma al-zawaid* (3:58 #348) with the words: "to your brothers" instead of "to your dead."
11 Al-Hakim related it (1:377, 4:330) with a good chain (*jayyid*) according to al-Iraqi.
12 Tabarani mentions it in his *Kabir* and Haythami in *Majma al-zawaid* (#152).
13 Abu Dawud and others narrated it.
14 See Appendix 1 for Ibn Qayyam's views. Cited by Ibn Abi al-Dunya in *Kitab al-qubur*, Ibn Abd al-Barr in *al-Tamhid*, Suyuti in *Sharh al-sudur* p. 202, Ghazali in the book on the Remembrance of Death in his *Ihya*, and Zabidi in his *Commentary on the Ihya* 10:367. Al-Iraqi said: It was declared sound (*sahih*) by Abd al-Haqq al-Ishbili.
15 Muslim related it.

renunciation of this World and remembrance of the Hereafter)."[16]

Abd Allah ibn Umar said, The Prophet (ﷺ) took hold of my shirt, or of me, and said, "Abd Allah! be like a stranger or a traveller passing by, and count your-self as one of the inhabitants of the graves."[17]

2.5. TRANSLATING THE HADITH "DO NOT MAKE MY GRAVE AN *ID*"

This section concerns the proper translation of the well-known hadith from Abu Hurayra that the Prophet (ﷺ) said, "Do not make my grave an *id*."[18] Some translate it falsely to read, "Do not make my grave a place to gather as for visita-tion."

It should be pointed out that the translation of the word *id*" as "place to gather as for visitation" or even simply "place" is inaccurate. One never translates, for example, *id al-adha* and *id al-fitr* as the "place of sacrifice" and the "place of breaking fast." The translation of any word in the hadith should be as lit-eral as possible, and additional or explanatory meanings should be placed in brackets, not the other way around. The lit-eral meaning of *id* is "anniversary festival," because *id* denotes two things:

1 A time that returns *(=aada)* annually

2 A time one observes with festive activities *(=ayyada)*.

A further connotation is of gathering, and only then does the word *id* suggest a "place"-which the above mistranslation arbitrarily gave as the primary meaning. The hadith would be literally translated: "Do not make my grave an anniversary fes-tival."

Since this rendering associates a time to an object, which is impossible, it becomes clear that the proper meaning is: "Do not make (the visit to) my grave an anniversary festival."

This is understood as expressing the Prophet's insistence that believers visit him frequently, rather than visit him occa-

16 Muslim (*Janaiz*, penultimate chapter; *Adahi* 37); Abu Dawud (*Janaiz* 77; *Ashriba* 7); Tirmidhi (*Janaiz* 7, 60); Nasai (*Janaiz* 100; *Dahaya* 39; *Ashriba* 40); Ibn Majah (*Janaiz* 47); Ahmad (1:145, 452; 3:38, 63, 66, 237, 250; 5:350, 355-357, 359, 361).

17 Tirmidhi (*Zuhd* 25); Ibn Majah (*Zuhd* 3); Ahmad (2:41); al-Hakim.

18 Abu Dawud relates it with a sound chain.

sionally, as suggested in the mistranslation quoted at the top. The mistranslation imposes on the hadith the exact reverse of its intended meaning!

"Visit me often and at all times" is the explanation preferred by *hafiz* al-Sakhawi, the student of Imam al-hadith Ibn Hajar.[19] He writes:

> The author of *Silah al-mumin* said, 'It is probable that the intent (*murad*) of the Prophet's saying, "Do not make my grave an *id*, is emphasis and encouragement (*al-hathth*) on the frequency of visiting him and not treating his visit like an anniversary festival which does not occur in the year other than at two times.

This meaning is supported by his saying, "Do not make your houses graves," that is, do not abandon prayer in your houses and thus turn them into places similar to the graves where one does not pray." There is no agreement on this. It seems that the Prophet (ﷺ) was pointing to what he said in the other hadith concerning the prohibition of taking his grave as a place of prostration (*masjid*), or else that his intent was from the perspective of gathering. We have already seen something to that effect in the hadith of this chapter. Some of the commentators of the *Masabih* [Baghawi's *Masabih al-sunna*] have said, "The Prophet's saying is an abridged form of the sense, 'Do not make the visit to my grave an anniversary festival,' and its meaning is the prohibition of (formally) gathering for the purpose of his visit in the way that people gather together to celebrate *id*. The Jews and Christians used to gather for the visit of their prophets' graves and busy themselves with entertainment and music, so the Prophet (ﷺ) forbade his Community from doing that."

It was also said that it is probable that the Prophet's prohibition was intended to prevent hardship (*raf al-mashaqqa*) for his Community, and also because it was disliked that they commit excess in overly honoring his grave. I say: The emphasis and encouragement on visiting his noble grave is mentioned in numerous hadith, and it would suffice to show this if there was

---

19 Al-Sakhawi, in his chapter entitled "On the meaning of the *hadith*: Do not make my grave an *id*" in *al-Qawl al-badi fi al-salat ala al-habib al-shafi* (Beirut 1987/1407) p. 159-160.

only the hadith whereby the truthful Prophet (ﷺ) confirmed by Allah promises that his intercession among other things becomes guaranteed for whoever visits him, and the Imams are in complete agreement from the time directly after his passing until our own time that this is among the best acts of drawing near to Allah. Shaykh al-Islam (Taqi al-Din) al-Subki said in his book *Shifa al-siqam,* "A large number of imams have inferred from the hadith, "No one greets me except Allah has returned my soul to me so that I can return his *salam"* [Abu Dawud with a sound chain] the legal desirability *(istihbab)* of visiting the grave of the Prophet (ﷺ)." I say, This is a sound inference because when the visitor greets the Prophet (ﷺ) his reply is given from near, and this is a benefit much sought-after which Allah has made easily available for us to return again and again to the very beginning of that blessing.

2.6. AL-HAFIZ AL-QADI IYAD AL-MALIKI ON VISITATION (*ZIYARA*)

Qadi Iyad devoted a section of his book, *al-Shifa*, to visiting the Prophet (ﷺ).[20] The following are excerpts from that chapter:

> Visiting his grave is part of the *sunna* and is both excellent and desirable. Ibn Umar said that the Prophet (ﷺ) said, "My intercession is assured for all who visit me." The *ziyara* to his grave is a *sunna* of the *sunna*s of Muslims (*sunna min sunan al-muslim-in*) over which there is consensus (*mujma alayha*)." (Qari comments, "Of those that state that there is a consensus are al-Nawawi and Ibn al-Humam, [and it is more than *sunna*] rather it was said that it is necessary (*qila innaha wajiba*) and a great benefit (*fadi-la*) that is highly desirable (*murghabun fiha*).")
>
> Imam Malik disliked people saying, "We visited the grave of the Prophet (ﷺ)." People have disagreed about the meaning of this statement. It is said that he disliked it because of the Prophet's saying, 'Allah curses women who visit graves' [Ahmad, Tirmidhi, Ibn Hibban]. People related that the Prophet (ﷺ) then

---

20 Qadi Iyad, *al-Shifa,* under the Chapter entitled: "On the visit to the Prophet's grave, the excellence of those who visit it and how he should be greeted." Adapted from the translation of Qadi Iyad al-Maliki's *al-Shifa* by Aisha Bewley, Madinah Press, p. 265-271.

said, 'I forbade you to visit graves, but now you can visit them' [Muslim]. The Prophet (ﷺ) also said, 'Anyone who visits my grave . . .' [*man zara qabri*] and he himself used the word 'visit' . . .

Abu Imran al-Fasi said, "Malik disliked anyone saying, "the circumambulation (*tawaf*) of the visit," or, "we visited the grave of the Prophet (ﷺ)," because people normally use that for visits between themselves, and he did not like to put the Prophet (ﷺ) on the same level as other people. He liked that the Prophet (ﷺ) be distinguished by one's saying, We bade peace to the Prophet (ﷺ), as opposed to saying, We visited his grave; and also because visiting graves is 'permitted' (*jaiz*) among ordinary people, whereas it is 'necessary' to travel to his grave (*WAJIB shadd al-rihal ila qabrihi*). Here he means a kind of necessity (*wujubiyya*) equating recommendation, encouragement, and confirmation that it is important, not one of absolute obligation (*fard*)."

I think the best interpretation is that Malik forbade and disliked the practice of connecting the word "grave" with the Prophet (ﷺ). He did not dislike the people saying, "We visited the Prophet (ﷺ)." This is because of the Prophet's statement, "O Allah, do not make my grave an idol to be worshiped after me. Allah was angry with people who took the graves of their prophets as mosques." So he [Malik] omitted the word "grave" in order to cut off the means and close the door to this wrong action. Allah knows best.

Ishaq ibn Ibrahim, the *faqih*, said that when someone goes on *hajj*, he should go to Madina with the intention of praying in the mosque of the Messenger of Allah, seeking the blessing of seeing his Meadow [*rawda*], his pulpit [*minbar*], his grave, the place where he sat, the places his hands touched and the places where his feet walked and the post on which he used to lean, where Gabriel descended to him with the revelation, and the places connected with the Companions and the Imams of the Muslims who lived there. He should have consideration for all these things.

Ibn Abi Fudayk said that he heard someone state, "We have heard that all who stop at the Prophet's grave should recite the *ayah*, "*Allah and His angels bless the Prophet . . .*" (33:56) and then say, "May Allah bless you, Muhammad." If someone says this seventy times, an angel will call to him, "May Allah bless you!" and all his needs will be taken care of."

Yazid ibn Abi Said al-Mahri said that he went to Umar ibn Abd al-Aziz and when Umar bade him farewell, he said, "I would like you to do something for me. When you reach Madina and see the grave of the Prophet (ﷺ) greet him for me with peace." Another said, "He used to send such greetings in his letters from Sham."

In *al-Mabsut*, Malik says, "I do not think people should stand at the grave of the Prophet (ﷺ), but should greet and then depart," . . . and "It is not necessary for the people of Madina who enter and leave the mosque to stand at the grave. That is for strangers," . . . and "There is no harm in someone who comes from a journey or leaves on a journey standing at the grave of the Prophet (ﷺ)," . . .

Ibn al-Qasim said, "When the people of Madina left or entered Madina, I saw that they used to come to the grave and give the greeting . . . That is what is considered the correct thing to do."

Al-Baji said, "There is a difference between the people of Madina and strangers because strangers have a specific intention for doing so [visiting the grave] whereas the Madinans live there and do not intend to go there for the sake of the grave and the greeting." End of Qadi Iyad's words.

In the Chapter entitled, "The *adab* of entering the Mosque of the Prophet (ﷺ) and its excellence, the excellence of the prayer in it and in the mosque of Makka, the Prophet's grave and *minbar*, and the excellence of living in Madina and Makka," the same author says, "There is no dispute that the place of his grave is the best place on earth."

2.7. IBN QUNFUDH AL-QUSANTINI AL-MALIKI ON *ZIYARA*

Ibn Qunfudh (d. 810 H) says the following:[21]

21 Ibn Qunfudh, in his book *Wasilat al-islam bi al-nabi alayhi al-salat wa al-salam* [The Means to Islam With the Prophet, blessings and peace upon him] (Beirut: Dar al-gharb al-islami, 1404/1984) p. 144-145.

The visit to his grave, blessings and peace upon him, is a *sunna* from among the *sunna*s of prophets, and an excellent action which is highly desirable. The Prophet (ﷺ) said: "Whoso visits my grave, my intercession for him becomes guaranteed,"[22] and "Whoever [performs the pilgrimage and then] visits me after my death, it is as if he visited me in my life."[23] His visit is a greatly profitable matter for seeking blessings by standing at his grave, and by praying in his mosque.

The order of priority is to send blessings upon him before greeting the mosque (*tahiyyat al-masjid*) and before approaching to greet him. It is permissible to say, "So-and-so sends his greetings to you." Ibn Wahb relates from Imam Malik, "When one greets the Prophet (ﷺ), let him face the grave not the *qibla*, and let him not touch the grave with his hand nor raise his voice. The Prophet (ﷺ) said, "A prayer in this mosque of mine [in Madina] is better than a thousand prayers in any other, except the Holy Mosque [in Makka]" (Muslim). Its meaning is that prayer in the Prophet's mosque is better than that in the Holy Mosque, but not by one thousand times."[24]

There is also in the hadith, "Between my grave and my pulpit lies a grove from the groves of Paradise" (Bukhari and Muslim) and, "Madina is a

---

22 The grading of this hadith (*hasan*) has been detailed above.

23 Daraqutni, Abu al-Shaykh, Tabarani, Ibn al-Jawzi in *Muthir al-azm al-sakin ila ashraf al-amakin*, Ibn al-Najjar in *al-durra al-thamina fi akhbar al-madina*, Ibn Adi, Ibn Asakir, al-Subki in *Shifa al-siqam* (p. 17-23), Said ibn Mansur in his *Sunan*, and Bayhaqi in *al-Sunan al-kubra* (5:246), Book of *Hajj*, Chapter on visiting the Prophet's grave, through Ibn Umar. Ibn Adi, Ibn Asakir, and Bayhaqi declared it weak because of Hafs ibn Sulayman. However: Tabarani relates it through other than Hafs in *al-Kabir* and *al-Awsat*; Mulla Qari says in *Sharh al-shifa* (Beirut: Dar al-kutub al-ilmiyya ed. 2:149): "The hadith on this chapter are numerous and their narrations are well-known, among them Ali's narration traced back to the Prophet: "Whoever visits my grave after my death it is as if he visited me in my life" and "Whoever does not visit my grave has slighted me." It has been inferred from this that the Prophet's visitation is obligatory upon those who are able to visit him." Sakhawi relates in *al-Maqasid al-hasana* (p. 410 #1125) that Dhahabi says: "Its chains strengthen each other and none of them contains a liar. Among its best is the hadith: "Whoever visits me after my death it is as if he visited me in my life;" Ahmad ibn Hanbal declared Hafs a good *(salih)* and acceptable *(ma bihi bas)* narrator as cited in Subki p. 22; Subki shows (p. 20-21) that there are two possible Hafs ibn Sulayman one of which Ibn Hibban declared reliable and the other weak.

24 The reason why one does not raise his voice in front of the Prophet's grave is because he is in the Prophet's presence, and Allah said: "*Lo! they who subdue their voices in the presence of the Messenger of Allah, those are they whose hearts Allah hath proven unto righteousness. Theirs will be forgiveness and immense reward*" (49:3). This is its meaning according to the school of Imam Malik. Imam Nawawi said in his com-

great good for them, if they but knew!" (Malik, al-
Bazzar with a sound chain, Tabarani with a fair
chain, and Ahmad in the *Musnad*) and, "Whoever is
able to die in Madina let him die there, for verily I
intercede for him who dies there".[25] The scholars differ concerning which is better, Makka or Madina.
Allah the Exalted said, *"Lo! the first sanctuary
appointed for mankind was that at Bakka, a blessed
place, a guidance to the peoples; wherein are plain
memorials (of Allah's guidance); the place where
Abraham stood up to pray; and whosoever entereth it
is safe"* (3:96-97). The experts of Quranic commentary
said that "he is safe" means safe from the fire.

2.8. IMAM MALIK'S PREFERENCE OF MADINA OVER MAKKA

Abu Hurayra related that the Prophet (ﷺ) said, "One
prayer in this mosque of mine is better than a thousand
prayers in any other, except the Sacred Mosque (in Makka)."[26]

Imam Nawawi, in his commentary on *Sahih Muslim*, said:

The scholars have differed regarding the meaning

mentary on this hadith: According to Shafii and the majority of the scholars the meaning of "except the Holy Mosque" is that prayer in the Holy Mosque is better than prayer
in the Prophet's Mosque. According to Malik and those who agree with him, its meaning is that prayer in the Prophet's mosque is better, but not by one thousand times.
Qadi Iyad said: The scholars are unanimous that the site of his grave is the best spot
on earth and that Makka and Madina are the best spots on earth, but they differ as to
which of these two is better apart from the site of his grave. Umar, some others of the
Companions, Malik, and most of the people of Madina say that Madina is better. The
people of Makka and Kufa, al-Shafi, Ibn Wahb al-Maliki and Ibn Habib al-Maliki hold
that Makka is preferable.

I say: What our companions adduced as evidence for their position about the
preference of Makka is the hadith of Abd Allah ibn Adi ibn al-Hamra whereby he
heard the Prophet say as he stood on top of his mount in Makka: "By Allah, verily
you are the best of Allah's earth and the most beloved of Allah's earth to Him, and
had I not been brought out from you I would have never come out. Tirmidhi and
Nisai narrated it and the former said it is *hasan sahih* [Ibn Hibban and Bayhaqi also
narrated it]. Abd Allah ibn al-Zubayr related that the Prophet said: "One prayer in
this mosque of mine is better than a thousand in any other except the Holy Mosque,
and one prayer in the Holy Mosque is better than a hundred in mine." A fair (*hasan*)
hadith narrated by Ahmad ibn Hanbal in his *Musnad*, Bayhaqi, and others with a
fair chain. And Allah knows best. (Nawawi, *Sharh sahih Muslim* (Beirut: Dar al-
Qalam ed.) vol. 9/10 p. 172-173.)

25 The first part of the hadith is narrated by Ahmad, Ibn Majah, Ibn Hibban,
and Tirmidhi who said it is *hasan sahih gharib*. The *hadith* with both its first and
second part is related by Tabarani with a fair (*hasan*) chain.

26 Muslim narrated it through ten chains in his *Sahih*.

of the above exception in the same way that they have differed concerning Makka and Madina: which of the two is better? The way of Shafii and the vast majority of the scholars is that Makka is better than Madina and that the mosque in Makka is better than the mosque in Madina. The opposite is true for Malik and a group of scholars.

According to Shafii and the vast majority, the meaning of the exception is: "except the Holy Mosque (in Makka), for prayer in it is better than in my mosque." According to Malik and those who agree with him, however, the meaning of the exception is, "except the Holy Mosque (in Makka), for prayer in my mosque is better than there, but not by a thousand times."

Nawawi goes on to quote the hadith of Abd Allah Ibn al-Zubayr stating that the Prophet (ﷺ) said, "One prayer in this mosque of mine is better than a thousand prayers in any other except the Holy Mosque (in Makka), and one prayer in the Holy Mosque (in Makka) is better than one hundred prayers in my mosque." Nawawi comments, "A fair (*hasan*) hadith, narrated by Ahmad ibn Hanbal in his *Musnad*, Bayhaqi, and others with a fair chain, and Allah knows best."[27]

Regarding the hadith, "One prayer in this mosque of mine is better than a thousand prayers in any other, except the Sacred Mosque (in Makka)," Qadi Iyad al-Maliki said:

> The scholars have differed regarding the meaning of the above exception in the same way that they have differed concerning the greater excellence of Makka and Madina. Malik considers, according to the narrations of Ashhab [ibn Abd al-Aziz], Ibn Nafi the companion of Malik, and a large group of others among his companions: that the meaning of the hadith whereby prayer in the Prophet's mosque is better than that one thousand in any other mosque except the Holy Mosque (in Makka), is that prayer in the Prophet's mosque is better than that in the Holy Mosque (in Makka), but not by a thousand times. They use as proof what has been related from Umar ibn al-Khattab ["in *Musnad al-Humaydi*"–Ali al-Qari]

27 Nawawi, *Sharh sahih Muslim*, Khalil al-Mays ed., Beirut: Dar al-Qalam, 9/10:172.

whereby prayer in the Sacred Mosque (in Makka) is better than a hundred prayers in other mosques in any other. It follows from this that the excellence of the Prophet's mosque (over Makka) is nine hundred times greater, and a thousand times greater than all other mosques. This is based on the preferability of Madina over Makka to which we have referred, and is the position of Umar ibn al-Khattab, Malik, and the majority of the people of Madina.[28]

Al-Shawkani in *Nayl al-Awtar* says:

> The position of Umar and some of the Companions and Malik and the majority of the people of Madina is that Madina is better.[29]

In his commentary on Qadi Iyad, Imam Ali al-Qari al-Hanafi writes:

> There is no doubt that Makka, among the highly venerated sanctuaries, is preferable to Madina itself, except for the mound of the Prophet's grave, which is mercy and tranquillity, for it is better than the Kabah or rather, better than the Throne itself according to a group of the scholars.[30]

Yahya ibn Sad related that the Prophet (ﷺ) said, "There is no place on earth which I would prefer my grave to be rather than here (meaning Madina). He repeated it three times."[31]

2.9. IMAM MALIK'S ADDITIONAL NARRATIONS ON THE MERITS OF MADINA IN HIS *AL-MUWATTA*

2.9.1. THE PROPHET'S SUPPLICATION (*DUA*) FOR MADINA AND ITS PEOPLE

Yahya ibn Yahya related to me from Ishaq ibn Abd Allah ibn Abi Talha al-Ansari from Anas ibn

---

28 Qadi Iyad, *al-Shifa*, ed. Al-Bajawi (2:681). in *al-Shifa*, chapter entitled "The Etiquette of Entering the Mosque of the Prophet and Its Excellence."

29 Shawkani, *Nayl al-awtar*, Dar al-kutub al-ilmiyya (5:28).

30 Al-Qari, *Sharh al-Shifa*, Dar al-kutub al-ilmiyya (2:162).

31 Malik narrated it in *al-Muwatta*.

Malik that the Messenger of Allah, may Allah bless him and grant him peace, said, "O Allah! Bless them in their measure, and bless them in their *sa* and *mudd*." He meant the people of Madina.[32]

2.9.2. On Residing in Madina and Leaving It

Yahya related to me from Malik from Qattan ibn Wahb ibn Umayr ibn al-Ajda that Yuhannas, the freedman of al-Zubayr ibn al-Awamm informed him that he was sitting with Abd Allah ibn Umar during the sedition (at the time of al-Hajjaj ibn Yusuf). A female freedwoman of his came and greeted him. She said, "I want to leave, Abu Abd al-Rahman. The time is harsh for us." Abd Allah ibn Umar said to her, "Sit down, O you with little knowledge, for I have heard the Messenger of Allah, may Allah bless him and grant him peace, say, "No one will be patient in hunger and hardship in it (Madina) except that I will be a witness or intercede for him on the Day of Rising."[33]

Malik related to me that Yahya ibn Said said, 'I heard Abu al-Hubab Said ibn Yasar say that he heard Abu Hurayra say that he heard the Messenger of Allah, may Allah bless him and grant him peace, say, "I was ordered to a town which will eat up towns. They used to say Yathrib, but it is Madina. It removes the bad people like the blacksmith's furnace removes impurities from the iron."[34]

Malik related to me from Hisham ibn Urwa from his father that the Messenger of Allah, may Allah bless him and grant him peace, said, "No one leaves Madina preferring to live elsewhere, but that Allah will give it better than him in place of him.'[35]

Malik related to me from Hisham ibn Urwa from his father from Abdullah ibn al-Zubayr that Sufyan ibn Abi Zuhayr said, I heard the Messenger of Allah, may Allah bless him and grant him peace, say, "Yemen will be conquered and the people will be attracted to it, taking their families and whoever obeys them. Madina would have been better for them, had they but known. Al-Sham will be conquered and

32 *Ibid*. Book 45, Number 45.1.1.
33 *Ibid*. Number 45.2.3.
34 *Ibid*. Number 45.2.5.
35 *Ibid*. Number 45.2.6.

people will be attracted to it, taking their families and whoever obeys them. Madina would have been better for them, had they but known. Iraq will be conquered and people will be attracted to it, taking their families and whoever obeys them. Madina would have been better for them, had they but known."[36]

Malik related to me that he had heard that when Umar ibn Abd al-Aziz left Madina, he turned towards it and wept. Then he said, "O Muzahim! Do you fear that we might be among those that Madina casts off?"[37]

2.9.3. THE MAKING OF MADINA SACROSANCT (*HARAM*)

Yahya related to me from Malik from Amr, the freedman of al-Muttalib from Anas ibn Malik that the Messenger of Allah, may Allah bless him and grant him peace, saw Uhud and said, "This is a mountain which loves us and we love it. O Allah! Abraham (ﷺ) made Makka a *haram*, and I will make what is between the two tracts of black stones (in Madina) a *haram*."[38]

2.9.4. THE EPIDEMIC OF MADINA

Yahya related to me from Malik from Hisham ibn Urwa from his father that Aisha, *umm al-muminin* said, When the Messenger of Allah, may Allah bless him and grant him peace, came to Madina, Abu Bakr and Bilal came down with a fever. I visited them and said, "Father, how are you? Bilal, how are you?" She continued: When Abu Bakr's fever worsened he would say, "Every man is visited among his family in the early morning and death is nearer to him than the strap of his sandal."

When the fever left Bilal, he raised his voice and said, "Will I spend another night in the valley of Makka with the *idhkhir* and the *jalil* (fragrant herbs) around me. Will I go one day to the waters of Majinna? Will Shama and Tafil (two mountains or springs near Makka) ever appear to me again?"

---

36 *Ibid*. Number 45.2.7.
37 *Ibid*. Number 45.2.9.
38 *Ibid*. Number 45.3.10.

Aisha continued, I went to the Messenger of Allah, may Allah bless him and grant him peace, and informed him. He said, "O Allah! Make us love Madina as much as we love Makka or even more. Make it sound and bless us in its *sa* and its *mudd* (units of measure used in Madina). Remove its fever and put it in al-Juhfa (a town seven travelling-units from Madina, and three travelling-units from Makka)." [39]

Yahya related to me from Malik from Nuaym ibn Abd Allah al-Mujmir that Abu Hurayra said, The Messenger of Allah, may Allah bless him and grant him peace, said, "There are angels at the entries of Madina, and neither plague nor the Dajjal will enter it." [40]

2.9.5. THE EXPULSION OF THE JEWS FROM MADINA

Yahya related to me from Malik from Ismail ibn Abi Hakim that he heard Umar ibn Abd al-Aziz say, One of the last things that the Messenger of Allah, may Allah bless him and grant him peace, said was, "May Allah fight the Jews and the Christians. They took the graves of their prophets as places of prostration. Two religions shall not co-exist in the land of the Arabs." [41]

Yahya related to me from Malik from Ibn Shihab al-Zuhri that the Messenger of Allah, may Allah bless him and grant him peace, said, "Two religions shall not co-exist in the Arabian Peninsula."

Malik said that Ibn Shihab said, Umar ibn al-Khattab searched for information about that until he was absolutely convinced that the Messenger of Allah, may Allah bless him and grant him peace, had said, "Two religions shall not co-exist in the Arabian Peninsula," and he therefore expelled the Jews from Khaybar. [42]

2.10. THE PROPHET'S GRAVE IS THE HOLIEST SITE ON EARTH

Qadi Iyad expresses the consensus of Muslims that the site

39 *Ibid*. Number 45.4.14.
40 *Ibid*. Number 45.4.16.
41 *Ibid*. Number 45.5.17.
42 *Ibid*. Number 45.5.18.

of the Prophet's grave is the holiest site on earth.[43] This particular consensus has been questioned by Ibn Taymiyya and
Shawkani,[44] however, it is established that some of the major
scholars of all Four Schools agree to this view whether or not it
is a consensus. Among these are the following:

Hanafis: Ali al-Qari in his *Sharh al-shifa*

Malikis: Qadi Iyad in *al-Shifa*. He cited *ijma* on this question.

Shafiis: Nawawi in his *Sharh sahih Muslim* 6:101 and *al-
Majmu sharh al-muhadhdhab* 7:444. He reported Iyad's statement and did not contradict it.

Hanbalis: Ibn Aqil as quoted by Ibn Qayyim in *Badai al-fawaid*

Also: Sadi Abu Habib, *Mawsuat al-ijma fi al-fiqh al-islami*
2:919.

2.11. AL-SHAYKH ABD AL-QADIR AL-JILANI AL-HASANI AL-HANBALI ON *ZIYARA*

Shaykh Abd al-Qadir al-Jilani writes the following in his
book *al-Ghunya li talibi tariq al-haqq azza wa jall*:

2.11.1. ENTERING MADINA THE ILLUMINATED

If Allah blesses the pilgrim with prosperity and he
is able to come to Madina, then what is desirable for
him is that he come to the mosque of the Prophet (ﷺ)
and say upon entering it: "*allahumma salli ala
muhammadin wa ala ali muhammad, waftah li
abwab rahmatik, wa kaffi anni abwab adhabik, al-
hamdu lillah rabb al-alamin.* (O Allah, send blessings
upon Muhammad and upon the family of Muhammad,
and open for me the gates of your mercy, and close for
me the gates of your punishment, all praise belongs to
Allah!)."

Then let him come to the grave of the Prophet (ﷺ)
and stand in its proximity so that he will be between
the grave and the *qibla*, and let him stand so that the
facade of the *qibla* will be behind him and the grave
in front of him exactly facing his face, and the *minbar*
to his left . . . Let him then say:

Peace upon you, O Prophet!

O Allah, send blessings upon Muhammad and
upon the family of Muhammad as you have sent bless-

---

43 Qadi Iyad, *al-Shifa*, in the chapter on visiting the Prophet.
44 Ibn Taymiyya's *al-Ziyara* and Shawkani's *Nayl al-awtar*.

ings upon Ibrahim, praised and glorified are You!

O Allah, bestow upon our master Muhammad the Means (al-wasila) and the Priority (al-fadila) and the high rank (al-daraja al-rafia), and raise him to the exalted station (al-maqam al-mahmud) which You have promised him!

O Allah, send blessings upon the spirit of Muhammad among all spirits, and upon his body among all bodies, just as he has conveyed Your Message and recited Your Signs and fought according to Your command and striven in Your path and commanded that You be obeyed and forbade that You be disobeyed and opposed those who opposed You and befriended those who befriended You and served You until death came to him.

O Allah, You said to Your Prophet in Your Book, '*If they had only, when they were unjust to themselves, come unto thee and asked Allah's forgiveness, and the Messenger had asked forgiveness for them, they would have found Allah indeed Oft-Returning, Most Merciful*' (4:64), and I have come to Your House[45] in repentance from my sins and seeking forgiveness, therefore I ask You that you make forgiveness guaranteed for me as you have made it guaranteed for those who came to him in his lifetime acknowledging their sins, so that their Prophet invoked You on their behalf and You forgave them.

O Allah! I am turning to You with Your Prophet, upon him Your peace, the Prophet of mercy. O Messenger of Allah! I am turning with you to my Lord so that He will forgive me my sins. O Allah, I am asking You for his sake (bi haqqihi) that You forgive me and grant me mercy.

O Allah, grant to Muhammad that he be the first of the intercessors, the most successful of those who ask, and the most honorable of the first and the last. O Allah, just as we believed in him without seeing him; and just as we confirmed him without meeting him: enter us where he entered and raise us in his group and bring us to his Pond and quench us with his cup of a satisfying, pure, fresh, whole drink after which we shall never thirst, and keep us forever away from disappointment, betrayal, deviation, negation, and doubt, and make us not of those You are angered

---

45 See the explanation of these words in the next section.

against, nor of the misguided, but place us among the people of his intercession."

Then let him step to his left and say, "Peace be upon both of you, O Companions of Allah's Messenger, and Allah's mercy and His blessings. Peace be upon you, O Abu Bakr the Most-Truthful. Peace be upon you, O Umar the Distinguisher. O Allah, reward them with abundant good on behalf of their Prophet and all Islam, and forgive us and our brothers who preceded us in the faith, and do not place in our hearts rancor towards the believers, O Allah! for You are Most Kind, Merciful." Then let him pray two *rakat* and sit. It is desirable that he pray between the grave and the pulpit in the Rawda; and, if he so desires, that he rub the pulpit to take its blessing (*wa in ahabba an yatamassah bi al-minbar tabarrukan bih*); and that he pray in the mosque of Quba; and that he go visit the graves of the martyrs and make abundant invocations there.

Then, if he wants to leave Madina, let him come to the Prophet's mosque, approach the grave, greet the Prophet, and do exactly as he did before, then bid him farewell and similarly greet his two Companions and bid them farewell. Then let him say, "O Allah, don't make this the last of my visits to the grave of Your Prophet, and if you cause me to die, then make me die loving him and his *sunna. Amin*, O Most Merciful of the merciful!" Then he may leave in peace, by Allah's will.[46]

2.11.2. EXPLANATION OF JILANI'S SUPPLICATION, "I HAVE COME TO YOUR HOUSE"

The mention of "coming to Your House" in the supplication (*dua*) recommended by Shaykh Abd al-Qadir Jilani to the visitor to the Prophet's grave stresses the importance of place as an efficient intermediary in one's supplication (*dua*). Such places include the three holy mosques, the homes and mosques associated with the prophets and friends of Allah, etc.

Therefore the importance and blessings (*baraka*) of the saints (friends of Allah, *awliya*) do not disappear after their

---

46 Al-Jilani, *al-Ghunya*, ed. Farj Tawfiq al-Walid (Baghdad: Maktabat al-sharq al-jadida, n.d.) 1:89-93. in the section on entering Madina, at the end of the section on the pilgrimage.

passing and the termination of their deeds, but continue in the places associated with them. This is referred to in the verse of Zakariyya's visit to Mary, who was not a prophet but a friend of Allah, when he noted the importance of her chamber, an importance based on her own piety and good deeds. Zakariyya therefore emphasized that place by going back to it and making his supplication there and nowhere else.

> *Right graciously did her Lord accept her; He made her grow in purity and beauty: to the care of Zakariyya was she assigned. Every time he entered her chamber to see her, he found her supplied with sustenance. He said, "O Mary! Whence comes this to you?" She said, "From Allah: for Allah provides sustenance to whom He pleases without measure." There did Zakariyya pray to his Lord saying, "O my Lord, grant unto me a progeny that is pure: for Thou art He that heareth prayer." While he was standing in prayer in the chamber, the angels called unto him, "Allah doth give thee glad tidings of Yahya, confirming the truth of a Word from Allah and besides, noble, chaste, and a prophet–of the goodly company of the righteous"* (3:37-39).

The Virgin Mary's purity had made her chamber itself a holy place. Zakariyya saw this and used that place as a means of supplication (*dua*). His supplication (*dua*) was accepted immediately as he was still standing in that place. This is the reason why al-Jilani emphasized the importance of the place and recommended that the verse of intercession be read by the visitor upon arrival at the Prophet's grave.

This is similar to the report on *tawassul* (see *tawassul*) of Abu Musa al-Ashari placing his cheek against the surface of the grave, thus showing the importance of the place for its *baraka*. It is similar again to the story of al-Utbi, cited in this chapter, in which the visitor mentions the spot of the grave itself as a place of blessing, rather than merely saying that he was visiting the Prophet (ﷺ).

In the same way, supplication (*dua*) is accepted in the chamber of any friend of Allah around the world, by virtue of the good deeds, piety, and sincerity of that person even after his or her passing away, simply because he or she inhabited that place. Similarly, Abu Bakr and Umar asked permission to be buried near the Prophet (ﷺ), seeking the immense blessings (*baraka*) of the place.

This is further confirmed by Aisha's words when she allowed Umar to be buried near the Prophet (ﷺ) in her place; "I wanted to be buried there (near the Prophet (ﷺ)) but I did not want people to treat me as holy."[47] This demonstrates that she knew the place to be holy but, out of humility, reserved the privilege of that holiness for Abu Bakr and Umar rather than for herself.

2.12. AL-HAFIZ ABU AL-FARAJ IBN AL-JAWZI AL-HANBALI ON *ZIYARA*

Ibn al-Jawzi writes in *Muthir al-gharam al-sakin ila ashraf al-amakin:*[48]

2.12.1. CHAPTER ON VISITING THE GRAVE OF THE PROPHET (ﷺ)

He who visits the grave of Allah's Messenger should stand while visiting him in the most respectful manner possible, as if he were with him in his lifetime. Ibn Umar narrates that Allah's Messenger said, "He who performs pilgrimage then visits my grave after my death, is like those who visited me during my lifetime."[49] Ibn Umar narrates, Allah's Messenger said, "He who visits my grave becomes eligible for my intercession."[50] Anas narrates, Allah's Messenger said, "He who visits me in Madina counting on his visit to me (*muhtasiban*), I will be his witness and

---

47 Narrated by Bukhari.

48 Ibn al-Jawzi: *Muthir al-gharam al-sakin ila ashraf al-amakin* (Cairo: Dar al-hadith, 1415/1995) p. 486-498.

49 Bayhaqi, *Sunan* 5:246 and *Shuab* (#4154); al-Asbahani, *al-Targhib* (#1080), Ibn Asakir, *Mukhtasar tarikh dimashq* 2:406; Daylami, *al-Firdaws* (#5709), Ibn al-Najjar, *Akhbar al-Madina* p. 144; al-Daraqutni, *Sunan* 2:278; Tabarani, *al-Kabir*, *al-Awsat*. Bayhaqi in the *Shuab* (#4155) said: "Only Hafs ibn Sulayman narrates it and he is weak." However, al-Haythami mentions in his *Majma al-zawaid* (4:2) that Ahmad declared him reliable although others said he was weak. See Dhahabi's *Mizan* #2121.

50 See section of Nawawi's *Idah fi manasik al-hajj*.

intercessor on the Day of Judgment."[51]

Ibn Abi Mulayka said, "Whoever wants to stand facing the Prophet (ﷺ), let him position himself where the lamp which is located in the *qibla* at the grave is over his head." There is another mark that is more easily recognizable than the lamp, it is a brass nail in the room's wall. When someone stands besides it, the lamp would be over his head.

Ibn Abi Fudayk said, "I heard some people who lived during the same era, we heard that anyone who stands at the Prophet's grave and recites this verse, *inna Allaha wa malaikatahu yusalluna ala al-nabi* (33:56) and then says *salla Allahu alaika ya Muhammad* seventy times, an angel will call out to him, "May Allah send blessings on you, O So-and-so! No need of yours will go from hence unfulfilled."[52]

It was related to us [with its chain of transmission] that Kab al-Ahbar said, "Every dawn, seventy thousand angels descend and encircle the grave, flapping their wings, and invoking blessings on the Prophet (ﷺ) until it is evening time, whereupon they ascend, and an equal number descend and do the same. And this is so until the earth breaks open, whereupon he will come out among seventy thousand angels supporting him.[53]

Umar ibn Abd al-Aziz used to send his courier from Sham with the message, "Convey my greetings to Allah's Messenger."[54]

2.12.2. CHAPTER ON HIS COMMUNITY'S GREETING REACHING HIM

Abd Allah ibn Masud said, Allah's Messenger said, "Allah has angels that roam the earth bringing me the greetings of my nation."[55] Abu Hurayra said, "No one sends me salam except Allah has returned

---

51 Al-Mundhiri, *al-Targhib wa al-tarhib* 2:224; al-Bayhaqi, *Shuab al-iman* (#4157), Ibn Asakir, *Mukhtasar tarikh dimashq* 2:406; *Tanzih al-sharia* 2:176; Suyuti, *al-Laali al-masnua* 2:72; *Tadhkirat al-mawduat* (#75). Weak because of Sulayman ibn Yazid al-Kabi, however, he was declared trustworthy (*thiqa*) by Ibn Hibban.

52 Bayhaqi, *Shuab al-iman* #4169.

53 Ibn Asakir, *Mukhtasar tarikh dimashq* 2:407; Suyuti from Ibn Mubarak in *al-Khasais al-kubra*; Ibn Abi al-Dunya 2:376; Ibn al-Najjar p. 145; al-Bayhaqi, *Shuab al-iman* (#4170) from Wahb ibn Munabbih.

54 Bayhaqi in *Shuab al-iman* (#4166), al-Samhudi, *Wafa al-wafa* p. 1357, Ibn Jamaa in *Hidayat al-salik*.

55 Ahmad, *Musnad* 1:378, 441, 452; Ibn Hibban, *Sahih* (#2393); al-Darimi, *Sunan* 2:58; al-Nisai, *Sunan* 3:43; al-Hakim, *Mustadrak* 2:421, (*sahih*), and Dhahabi confirmed it, cf. *Siyar alam al-nubala* 17:106; Ibn al-Najjar, *Akhbar al-madina* p. 144.

my soul to me so that I can return his salam."[56]

2.12.3. CHAPTER ON SOME SAYINGS THAT WERE RETAINED FROM THE VISITORS TO HIS GRAVE AND STATES THEY HAD EXPERIENCED

Abu Nasir told us [with his chain of transmission] that Ali said, "When Allah's Messenger was buried, Fatima came and stood in front of his grave, took a handful of soil, put it on her eyes, cried and recited:
The one who breathes from the soil of Ahmad
Will never breathe trouble all his life long
If the troubles that have been poured on me
Were poured on days, they would turn into nights.[57]

Muhammad ibn Hibban said, I heard Ibrahim ibn Shayban saying, "I performed pilgrimage one year, so I came to Madina and approached the grave of the Prophet (ﷺ) and said Salam to him. I heard from inside the room, "Wa alayka al-salam."[58]

Abu Hazim [Salama ibn Dinar] said, 'I heard Said ibn al-Musayyib say, "During the nights of the heat wave there were no people in the Prophet's mosque except myself. The people of Sham would enter in groups and say, "Look at this crazy old man!" and whenever the time of prayer came, I would hear adhan coming from the Prophet's grave. I would step forward, call iqama and pray, and there would be no one in the masjid but me'."[59]

Muhammad ibn Harb al-Hilali said, 'I entered Madina, and came to the grave of Allah's Messenger. An Arab came to visit him and said, "O best of the prophets, Allah has revealed to you a truthful book and said in it, 'If they had only, when they were unjust to themselves, come unto thee and asked Allah's for-

---

56 The explanation of this hadith is in the section on *mawlid* above. Abu Hurayra in Abu Dawud (*Manasik* #2039) with a sound chain; Ibn Asakir, *Mukhtasar tarikh dimashq* 2:407; Ahmad, *Musnad* 2:527; Abu Nuaym, *Akhbar asbahan* 2:353; Ibn al-Najjar, *Akhbar al-madina* p. 145; Bayhaqi, *Shuab al-iman* #4161; Haythami, *Majma al-zawaid* 10:162; Ibn Kathir, *Tafsir* 6:464; al-Mundhiri, *al-Targhib wa al-tarhib* 2:499; *Talkhis al-kabir* 2:267.

57 Ibn Qudama, *al-Riqqa* p. 62; Ibn Najjar, *Akhbar al-madina* p. 125; Samhudi, *Wafa al-wafa* p. 1045 cites Ibn Asakir's *Tarikh dimashq*; Ibn al-Jawzi, *al-Wafa* 2:804.

58 Abu Nuaym, *al-Targhib* (#102), Ibn Najjar, *Akhbar al-madina* p. 146.

59 Suyuti, *al-Khasais al-kubra* (2:490) from Abu Nuaym.

giveness, and the Messenger had asked forgiveness for them, they would have found Allah indeed Oft-Returning, Most Merciful' (4:64), so I have come to you asking forgiveness for my sin, seeking your intercession with my Lord." Then he began to recite poetry:

O best of those whose bones are buried in the deep
    earth,
And from whose fragrance the depth
    and the height have become sweet,
May I be the ransom for a grave which thou
    inhabit,
And in which are found purity, bounty and
    munificence!

Then he left, and I dozed and saw the Prophet (ﷺ) in my sleep. He said to me, "Run after the Arab and give him glad tidings that Allah has forgiven him through my intercession."[60]

Abu al-Khayr al-Aqta said, "I entered the city of Allah's Messenger and I was in material need. I stayed five days without eating anything. I came toward the grave and said salam to the Prophet (ﷺ) and to Abu Bakr and to Umar, then said, "I am your guest tonight, O Allah's Messenger!" I then stepped aside and slept behind the minbar. I saw the Prophet (ﷺ) in my dream, with Abu Bakr to his right, Umar to his left, and Ali in front of him. Ali shook me and said, "Get up, *Rasulullah* is coming." I got up and kissed him between his eyes; he gave me a loaf of bread, I ate half of it; when I woke up I found half a loaf in my hand."[61]

2.13. SHAYKH AL-ISLAM AL-HAFIZ AL-IMAM MUHYI AL-DIN AL-NAWAWI AL-SHAFII ON VISITATION (*ZIYARA*)

Imam Nawawi writes in his *al-Idah fi manasik al-hajj*:[62]

Chapter 6: On Visiting the Grave of our Master, the Messenger of Allah (ﷺ)

In this chapter are discussed the recommended

---

60 See above.

61 Ibn al-Jawzi, *Sifat al-safwa* 4:236; Ibn al-Najjar, *Akhbar al-Madina* p. 148; al-Qushayri, *al-Risala* p. 195; Samhudi, *Wafa al-wafa* p. 1380.

62 Imam Nawawi, *al-Idah fi manasik al-hajj* (Damascus: Dar ibn Khaldun, n.d.) p. 140-150. See also identical passages in Nawawi's *Adhkar* (many editions) and his

and discouraged actions of those who perform the pilgrimage (hajj).

The first of the issues concerns those who perform the pilgrimage (hajj) and visitation (umra). When they leave Makka, they should go towards the city of Allah's Messenger to visit his burial ground (turba). It is one of the most important of those actions that bring one towards Allah, and a most important effort. Al-Bazzar and al-Daraqutni narrated on the authority of Ibn Umar that Allah's Messenger said "Whoever visits my grave, my intercession becomes guaranteed for him."[63]

The second point concerns preferred or recommended actions for the visitor to have intention to do when visiting Allah's Messenger. His intention should be to draw closer to Allah by travelling to his mosque and praying in it.

Third, it is also recommended that when the visitor is in transit he should increase his recitation of greetings and blessings on the Prophet (ﷺ), and that when he sees the trees of Madina, its blessed sanctuary, or any landmark in Madina, he should increase his recitations of greetings and blessings; he should ask that Allah accept his visit and grant him benefit for visiting.

Fourth, it is recommended that the pilgrim perform the greater ablution (ghusl) before entering Madina and put on his cleanest clothes. He should visualize in his heart the honor of Madina, the best place in the world after Makka according to some scholars; others consider Madina to be the best place in the world without exception. What makes it so honorable is the presence of Allah's Prophet (ﷺ), the best of all creation.

Fifth, the pilgrim should attune himself to the feeling of the greatness of Allah's Messenger; his heart should be full of his presence, as if he is seeing him.

Sixth, when he arrives at the door of his mosque, let him say the things he says when entering Makka; he should enter with his right foot and leave with his left, as he should when entering and leaving any mosque. As he approaches the holy rawda, which is

Majmu (8:212f.).
   63 Hadith hasan: see above, section on Intercession.

the place between the Prophet's grave and his pulpit,
he prays the prayer of greeting the mosque (*tahiyyat
al-masjid*) near the *minbar*, in the standing place of
Allah's Messenger. In the book of Madina the distance
between the *minbar* and the *maqam* or standing
place, where he used to pray until his death, is four-
teen arm-lengths and one hand span, and the distance between the *minbar* and the grave is fifty-three
arm lengths and a span, and Allah knows best.

Seventh, after he prays the *tahiyya* in the *rawda*
(or anywhere else in the mosque), in thankfulness to
Allah for this bounty, and asking Him for the completion of his mission and for the acceptance of his visit,
he should face the wall of the holy grave, with the
qibla behind him, looking to the lower part of the
grave's wall, lowering his gaze in a state of awe and
reverence, emptying his heart of worldly concerns
and focusing on the reverent nature of his situation
and the status of the one in whose presence he is.
Then he gives greetings in a voice neither too loud nor
too soft, but with moderation; he says the following:

> *al-salamu alayka ya rasul Allah*
> *al-salamu alayka ya nabi Allah*
> *al-salamu alayka ya khiyarat Allah*
> *al-salamu alayka ya khayr Allah*
> *al-salamu alayka ya habib Allah*
> *al-salamu alayka ya nadhir*
> *al-salamu alayka ya bashir*
> *al-salamu alayka ya tuhr*
> *al-salamu alayka ya tahir*
> *al-salamu alayka ya nabi al-rahma*
> *al-salamu alayka ya nabi al-imma*
> *al-salamu alayka ya Abu Qasim*
> *al-salamu alayka ya rasul rabb al-alamin*
> *al-salamu alayka ya sayyid al-mursalin wa ya*
>   *khatam al-nabiyyin*
> *al-salamu alayka ya khayr al-khalaiqi ajmain*
> *al-salamu alayka ya qaid al-ghurri al-muhajjalin*
> *al-salamu alayka wa ala alika wa ahli baytika wa*
>   *azwajika wa dhurriyyatika wa ashabika*
>   *ajmain*
> *al-salamu alayka wa ala sair al-anbiyai wa jamii*

ibad Allah al-salihin
jazak Allahu ya rasulallahi anna afdala ma jaza
nabiyyan wa rasulan an ummatihi
wa sallallahu alayka wa sallama kulla ma
dhakaraka al-dhakirun wa ghafala an
dhikrika al-ghafilun
afdala wa akmala wa atyaba ma salla wa salla
ma ala ahadin min al-khalqi ajmain
ashhadu an la ilaha illallahu wahdahu la
sharika lah
wa ashhadu annaka abduhu wa rasuluhu wa
khiyaratuhu min khalqihi
wa ashhadu annaka qad ballaghta al-risala wa
addayta al-amana wa nasahta al-umma wa
jahadta fillahi haqqa jihadih
Allahumma atihi al-wasilata wa al-fadilata wa
ibathhu maqaman mahmudan al-ladhi waad
tah
wa atihi nihayata ma yanbaghi an yasaluhu al-
sailun
Allahumma salli ala sayyidina Muhammadin
abdika wa rasulika al-nabiyyi al-ummi wa
ala ali sayyidina Muhammadin wa azwajihi
wa dhurriyyatih
kama sallayta ala sayyidina Ibrahima wa ala ali
sayyidina Ibrahima
wa barik ala sayyidina Muhammadin al-nabiyyi
al-ummi wa ala ali sayyidina Muhammadin
wa azwajihi wa dhurriyyatih
kama barakta ala sayyidina Ibrahima wa ala ali
sayyidina Ibrahima fi al-alamina innaka
hamidun majid.

Translation:
Peace be upon you O Messenger of Allah
Peace be upon you O Prophet of Allah
Peace be upon you O Elect of Allah
Peace be upon you O Goodness of Allah
Peace be upon you O Beloved of Allah
Peace be upon you O Warner
Peace be upon you O Bearer of Glad Tidings
Peace be upon you O Purity
Peace be upon you O Pure One

Peace be upon you O Prophet of Mercy

Peace be upon you O Prophet of the Community

Peace be upon you O Father of Qasim

Peace be upon you O Messenger of the Lord of the
Worlds

Peace be upon you O Master of Messengers and
Seal of Prophets

Peace be upon you O Best of All Creatures

Peace be upon you O Leader of the Bright-faced
ones

Peace be upon you and upon your Family, the
people of your house, your wives, your
children, and all your Companions

Peace be upon you and upon all the prophets and
Allah's righteous servants

May Allah reward you, O Messenger of Allah,
with the best reward a prophet or a
messenger ever received on behalf of his
Community

Blessings and peace of Allah upon you every time
one remembers you and every time one fails
to remember you

With the best, most perfect, and choicest of
blessings and peace ever bestowed upon any
one in creation

I bear witness that there is no deity but Allah
alone, without partner

And I bear witness that you are His servant, His
Messenger, His elect among all creatures

And I bear witness that you have conveyed the
Message and fulfilled the trust and counseled
the Community and striven for Allah with the
most truthful striving

O Allah! Grant him the Means and the Excellent
Gift and raise him to the Exalted Station You
have promised him

And grant him the goal of what those who beseech
You, do beseech for him

O Allah! Send blessings on our master
Muhammad Your servant and Messenger, the
Unlettered Prophet, and upon the Family of
our master Muhammad, his wives and his
children

As you have sent blessings on our master Ibrahim and on the Family of our master Abraham (ﷺ).

And send benedictions on our master Muhammad Your servant and messenger, the Unlettered Prophet, and upon the Family of our master Muhammad, his wives and his children

As you have sent benedictions on our master Ibrahim and on the Family of our master Ibrahim in the worlds, for You are truly the most praiseworthy and noble.

As for him who cannot memorize all of this or who does not have the time to recite it, it is enough to recite a part of it, as a minimum the words *al-salamu alayka ya rasul Allah*.

Then, if someone has asked him to convey salams to Allah's Messenger, let him say *al-salamu alayka ya rasul Allah min fulan ibn fulan* (Greetings to you, O Messenger of Allah, from so-and-so, the son of so-and-so), or some such greeting, after which he steps an arm's length to the right and sends salams to Abu Bakr because he stands at the shoulder of Allah's Messenger; then he says *al-salamu alayka ya Aba Bakrin safiyya rasulillahi wa thaniyahu fi al-ghari, jazakallahu an ummat al-nabiyyi khayran*, (Greetings to you, O Abu Bakr, the intimate friend of Allah's Messenger and his second in the Cave! May Allah grant you the best reward on behalf of the Prophet's community). Then he steps an arm's length to the left of his original position, to the space before Umar, saying: "*Al-salamu alayka ya umara aazz allahu bika al-islam, jazak allahu an ummati muhammadin khayran* (Greetings to you O Umar, Allah has strengthened Islam through you, may Allah reward you well on behalf of the nation of Muhammad)." Then he returns to his original position, directly in front of Allah's Messenger, and he uses the Prophet as his means with regard to himself (*fa yatawassalu bihi fi haqqi nafsihi*), and seeks his intercession before his Exalted and Mighty Lord (*wa yatashaffau bihi ila rabbihi subhanahu wa taala*), and one of the best things that he can say is what has been narrated by our colleagues on al-Utbi's authority, and they admired what he said:

As I was sitting by the grave of the Prophet, a Bedouin Arab came and said, "Peace be upon you, O Messenger of Allah! I have heard Allah saying, *'If they had only, when they were unjust to themselves, come unto thee and asked Allah's forgiveness, and the Messenger had asked forgiveness for them, they would have found Allah indeed Oft-Returning, Most Merciful'* (4:64), so I have come to you asking forgiveness for my sin, seeking your intercession with my Lord." Then he began to recite poetry:

O best of those whose bones are buried in the deep
    earth,
And from whose fragrance the depth and the
    height have become sweet,
May I be the ransom for a grave which thou
    inhabit,
And in which are found purity, bounty and
    munificence!

Then he left, and I dozed and saw the Prophet in my sleep. He said to me, "O Utbi, run after the Bedouin and give him glad tidings that Allah has forgiven him."[64]

The pilgrim should next advance to the head of the grave and stand between the grave and the pillar that is there, facing the *qibla* [without turning his back on the grave]. Let him praise and glorify Allah and supplicate for himself regarding what concerns him and what he loves, for his parents, and for whomever he likes among his relatives, revered teachers, brothers, and Muslims in general; then he comes to the *rawda* and increases his supplication and prayer. It established in the two *Sahih*s in a narration from Abu Hurayra that the Prophet said, "Between my grave and my *minbar* lies one of the gardens of paradise, and my *minbar* overlooks my pool (*hawd*). Let him stand by the *minbar* to make supplication.

Eighth: It is impermissible (*la yajuz*) to circumambulate the grave of the Prophet, and it is reprehensible (*makruh*) to stand so close to the grave that one's entire front or back is in direct contact with it. This is according to the opinion of al-Halimi and others. Also reprehensible is rubbing the grave with one's

64 See above.

hand or kissing it.[65] The good etiquette is to stay a distance from it, as one would from a living person. This is what the religious scholars have said, and we should not be misled by such actions of common people that are in violation of these good manners; we should only follow the prescriptions of the scholars, without paying attention to the behavior of the common people. The respected master, Abu Ali al-Fudayl ibn Iyad spoke to the effect that one must follow the paths of guidance and not be distracted that so few travel them, and to beware the paths of misguidance that are well-travelled by those who will perish. Therefore, he who thinks that rubbing and such brings more *baraka* is misled by his ignorance and heedlessness, because *baraka* is in what is in accordance with the Sharia and the sayings of the scholars; how then can benefit be obtained through opposition to what is right?

Ninth: Throughout his stay in Madina he must perform all of his prayers in the Prophet's *masjid*, and must form the intention of making retreat (*itikaf*) in it.

Tenth: It is desirable that he go daily to the cemetery of Baqi, especially on Friday; he should first say salams to the Prophet. When he arrives at Baqi, he says: *al-salamu alaykum dara qawmin muminina wa inna insha Allahu bikum lahiqun, Allahumma ighfir li ahli baqi al-gharqad, Allahumma ighfir lana wa lahum.* Then he visits the visible graves there, such as that of Ibrahim, Uthman, al-Abbas, al-Hasan the son of Ali, Ali the son of Al-Hussein, Muhammad ibn Ali, Jafar ibn Muhammad, and others. The last stop would be the grave of Safiyya, the Aunt of Allah's Messenger; it has been established in numerous

---

65 For Imam Ahmad's permission to touch the grave and kiss it, and Dhahabi's words of endorsement to this effect in his *Mujam al-shuyukh* Vol. 1 p. 73 #58, see above: "[The Companions] saw the Prophet with their very eyes when he was alive, enjoyed his presence directly, kissed his very hand, nearly fought with each other over the remnants of his ablution water, shared his purified hair on the day of the greater pilgrimage, and even if he spat it would virtually not fall except in someones hand so that he could pass it over his face. Since we have not had the tremendous fortune of sharing in this, we throw ourselves on his grave as a mark of commitment, reverence, and acceptance, even to kiss it. Don't you see what Thabit al-Bunani did when he kissed the hand of Anas ibn Malik and placed it on his face saying: "This is the hand that touched the hand of Allah's Messenger?" Muslims are not moved to these matters except by their excessive love for the Prophet, as they are ordered to love Allah and the Prophet more than they love their own lives, their children, all human beings, their property, and paradise and its maidens."

sound hadiths that there is merit in the graves of the Baqi and in visiting them.[66]

Eleventh: It is recommended to visit the graves of the martyrs of Uhud, the best day being Thursday, and to begin with Hamza, starting early in the morning after the dawn prayer in the mosque of the Prophet, so as to allow time to return to the mosque before the noon prescribed prayer.

Twelfth: It is definitely recommended to come to the mosque of Quba, preferably on a Saturday, with the intention of drawing closer to Allah by visiting it and praying in it, due to the authentic hadith in the book of Tirmidhi and others from Usayb ibn Hudhayr, that a prayer in the mosque of Quba is like *umra*; and in the two *Sahih*s Ibn Umar is related to say that Allah's Messenger used to come to the Quba mosque both riding and walking to pray in it two *rakat*, and in an authentic narration he used to come to it every Saturday. It is recommended to visit the well of Aris, which is located by the mosque of Quba, and drink from its water and perform ablution with it.

Thirteenth: It is desirable that one visit all the sites of significance in Islam. There are approximately thirty such places, and they are known to the inhabitants of Madina. The pilgrim should visit as many as he can. He should also come to and drink from the wells where Allah's Messenger used to perform ablution and wash. There are seven such wells.

Fourteenth: The pilgrim must maintain reverence toward this city throughout his stay there, keeping in his heart that it is the place chosen as the place of Allah's Messenger's emigration and residence, and the place where he was buried; he must visualize the Prophet's coming and going in the city and his walking in its streets.

---

66 The "Salafis"/Wahhabis have destroyed all these graves, so that they are no longer known when someone wishes to make the visitation according to the prescriptions of the *sunna* in Imam Nawawi's definition, so that the Baqi now appears like a desert, where none of the graves can be recognized. In the time of the Prophet, those buried people were few and it was easy to recognize where they were. In later times, however, because the cemetery became filled with Muslims, the importance of signs to determine where the Companions are buried became even greater than in the past, just as it is important to maintain the mark of the site of the Prophet's grave. That is why Muslims have kept these signs protected from the vicissitudes of time and change, until the advent of Wahhabis and "Salafis" on the scene. Nevertheless it is important to keep up these signs, more now than in the past, for the reasons Nawawi mentioned.

Fifteenth: Taking up residence in Madina [especially for study] is desirable on the same conditions that were previously mentioned with reference to Makka. The desirability of this practice has been established in *Sahih Muslim*, Ibn Umar and Abu Hurayra related that the Prophet said, "He who perseveres through the difficulties and hardships of Madina, I will be a witness or an intercessor for him on the Day of Judgment."[67]

Sixteenth: It is recommended that the believer fast in Madina whenever it is possible and as much as possible, and to give *sadaqa* as much as possible to the Prophet's *jiran* (people performing *mujawara* i.e. living in Madina in order to keep the *sunna*), because it is a way of being faithful to the Prophet.

Seventeenth: He is not to carry with him any of the pottery made from the soil and stones of the *haram* of Madina, nor the pitchers nor others of the utensils made from it, as has been stated with regard to the *haram* of Makka.

Eighteenth: Hunting at the *haram* of Madina is forbidden, and it is also forbidden to remove from the trees of the *haram*; these rules have been discussed in reference to the *haram* of Makka. The boundary of the *haram* of Madina is what has been narrated by Bukhari and Muslim in their two authentic books from Ali ibn Abi Talib from the Prophet, "The *haram* of Madina is between Ayr and Thawr [a hill behind Uhud]"; and in the two authentic books from the hadith of Abu Hurayrah who said, "If I see the deer grazing or drinking in Madina I would never interfere with them." The Prophet also said, "What is between her two tracts of black stones [i.e. city limits]," and so it has been narrated by a group of Companions in the *Sahih*.

Nineteenth: If he wants to travel from Madina and go back to his country or another country, it is desirable to say farewell to the mosque by performing two *rakat* and making supplication for any matter about which he is concerned; he has to come to the grave and say something similar to the supplications mentioned at the beginning and says, "Oh Allah, do

---

67 Ibn Hajar al-Haytami added in his commentary on Nawawi: "Ahmad, Tirmidhi, and others related that the Prophet said: "Whoever can die in Madina, let him die in it, for I shall intercede for him who dies in it." The hadith on the merit of living and dying in Madina are numerous."

not make this the last time that I come to the *haram* of Your Messenger; make easy my return to the two Sacred Sanctuaries, and bestow upon me forgiveness and security in this life and in the hereafter, and grant us safe return with Your bounty." He leaves facing away from the tomb.

Twentieth: Important matters regarding the Prophet's mosque: It has been narrated in *Sahih Bukhari* from Ibn Umar that he said, "In the time of Allah's Messenger the mosque was built with sun-dried clay bricks, its roof was made of palm branches, the pillars were of palm wood. Abu Bakr did not add to it anything; Umar added to it and built it the way that it used to be during the time of the Prophet with bricks and palm branches and palm-wood pillars. Uthman, in turn, changed it, adding considerably to it, and he built up its walls with engraved stone and freestone, put up pillars of engraved stone, and a roof of teak [Indian oak]." It is incumbent to keep prescribed prayer (*salat*) in the mosque that used to exist during the time of Allah's Messenger. For the previously mentioned sound hadith, "A prayer in this, my mosque, is better than a thousand prayers in any other mosque" applies only to what was in place in his own time.[68] If one prays in congregation, stepping forward to the first row, and those rows immediately behind it, is best. Let him pay attention to what I have warned about. In the two *Sahih* books on the authority of Abu Hurayra the Prophet said, "My minbar overlooks my pool." Al-Khattabi said that the meaning of this hadith is that he who keeps the prayers at my *minbar* shall be given water from the Prophet's pool on the Day of Judgment. The other hadith in the *Sahih* has already been mentioned, "Between my grave and the *minbar*, lies one of the gardens of paradise."

Twenty-first: Some of the common people claimed that Allah's Messenger said, "Whoever visits me and my father Ibrahim in the same year, I guarantee paradise for him," and this is false; it is not from Allah's Messenger and it is not mentioned in any books of hadith. Rather, it is a fabrication of some corrupt individuals. The visit of the Friend of the Merciful is not

---

68 Ibn Hajar al-Haytami says: "There is divergence among the scholars concerning this. However, there is no sound hadith from the Prophet differing from what Nawawi said."

disapproved. What is rejected is only what the common people have narrated and there is no relation between the visit of the Khalil and *hajj*; the visit of the Khalil is a separate act of devotion. Likewise, the saying of some of the common people whereby if they perform the *hajj* and complement it by visiting Jerusalem, they are thereby completing the pilgrimage; this is false. While visiting Jerusalem is desirable, it is not related to *hajj*. And Allah knows best.

Twenty-second: If one swears an oath to visit the Prophet's Mosque or Jerusalem, there are two points of view according to al-Shafii; the more correct one is that it is desirable to go, but not obligatory.

And Allah knows best.

2.14 "SALAFI" CORRUPTION OF THE TEXT OF NAWAWI'S *ADHKAR*

The following is translated from a booklet by Shaykh Hassan ibn Ali al-Saqqaf entitled, *al-Ighatha bi adillat al-istighatha* (Help with the proof-texts of seeking help):[69]

> This is the untampered text of Imam Nawawi in the Book of Pilgrimage which is part of his larger book *Kitab al-Adhkar* according to the original manuscript, published editions, and Ibn Allan's commentary on the *Adhkar*:
>
> **Concerning the visit to the grave (*qabr*) of the Prophet and the invocations pertaining thereto:**
> Know that it is incumbent (*yanbaghi*) upon every pilgrim to go and visit the Prophet, whether this visit is on his way or not. Indeed, the visit of the Prophet is among the most important of the acts that draw one near to Allah (*qurubat*) and of the most gainful of errands and of the most excellent of quests. Once one turns his steps to visit the Prophet, let him invoke abundant blessings on him while on the way. As soon as his sight reaches the trees of Madina [he invokes even more blessings] . . .

---

69 Shaykh Hassan ibn Ali al-Saqqaf, *al-Ighatha bi adillat al-istighatha*, published in Amman at Maktabat al-Imam Nawawi (1410/1990) page 17.

Below is the corrupt (*munharif*) text of the same passage of Imam Nawawi's book, as it stands mutilated by the hand of the *mutamaslif* Abd al-Qadir al-Arnaut . . . in the edition of Dar al-Huda, Riyadh, 1409/1989 sponsored by the Supervisory Board for Publications, which is presided by the Saudi Authority for Scholarly Research and *Ifta*, p. 295:

Concerning the visit of the mosque (*masjid*) of the Prophet:

Know that it is recommended (*yustahabb*) that whoever wants to visit the mosque of the Prophet invoke abundant blessings on him while on the way there. As soon as his sight reaches the trees of Madina . . .[70]

Observe how this "Salafi" editor distorted Imam Nawawi's text, omitting two important sentences:

"It is incumbent (*yanbaghi*) upon every pilgrim to go and visit the Prophet, whether this visit is on his way or not. Indeed, the visit of the Prophet is among the most important of the acts that draw one near to Allah (*qurubat*) and of the most gainful of errands and of the most excellent of quests."

Al-Arnaut then replaced them with, "It is recommended (*yustahabb*) that whoever wants to visit the mosque of the Prophet . . ."!

Saqqaf continues: Then the said "Salafi" editor took a further liberty by completely eliminating the account of al-Utbi told by al-Nawawi [at the end of this section], because it contradicts his impure spring [the "Salafi" School]. Is this scholarly trustworthiness? He could have commented on it and denied it, as some of his ["Salafi"] brothers have done in other editions. He did not have to commit such corruption of the text, such disgraceful tampering which leads Muslims to doubt in the great texts of our heritage that are printed and disseminated among all.[71]

---

70 Nawawi, *Kitab al-adhkar*, ed. Abd al-Qadir al-Arnaut. Dar al-huda, Riyadh, 1409/1989 p. 5.
71 *Ibid*.

2.15. THE OPINION PROHIBITING TRAVEL TO VISIT THE PROPHET (ﷺ) IS NULL AND VOID

Mulla Ali al-Qari said in his commentary on *al-Shifa*:

> What al-Shubi and al-Nakhi claimed about hatred of visiting graves is out of the pale (*shadhdh*) and not to be depended upon (*la yuawwal alayh*) as it contradicts the consensus of everyone else (*limukhalaftihi ijma ghayrihima*). Ibn Taymiyya exceeded proper bounds (*farrata*) from among the Hanbalis by prohibiting traveling to visit the Prophet (ﷺ). Others have also exaggerated by saying that whoever denies the visitation is an act bringing one closer to Allah that is obligatory knowledge in the religion, is ruled upon to be a disbeliever (*kafir*). Perhaps the latter is closer to correctness (than what Ibn Taymiyya claimed), because to prohibit that upon which the scholars have formed consensus is disbelief because it exceeds the allowable prohibiting that is agreed upon in this topic.

The objections of the scholars to Ibn Taymiyya's view are well-known. Ibn Hajar said, in *Fath al-bari*:

> Ibn Taymiyya said, This kind of trip (traveling to visit the grave of the Prophet (ﷺ)) is a disobedience and *salat* must not be shortened during it. And this is one of the ugliest matters reported from Ibn Taymiyya.[72]

The "Salafi" scholar Bin Baz commented on the above, saying: "No! it is not ugly, and Ibn Taymiyya was right." [73] The vast majority of the scholars obviously think otherwise.

In *Nayl al-awtar*, Shawkani writes:

> The sayings of the people of knowledge have differed on it [travelling to visit the Prophet (ﷺ)]. The vast majority (*al-jumhur*) have said that it is recom-

---

72 Ibn Hajar, *Fath al-Bari*, 3:85 1989 ed.
73 Bin Baz, in his few notes on *Fath al-bari* (3:85 1989 ed.).

mended. Some of the Malikis and some of the Zahiris said that it is necessary (*wajib*), and the Hanafis said it is close to being necessary, while Ibn Taymiyya al-Hanbali said that it is not lawful (*ghayr mashru*), and in this he was followed by some of the Hanbalis. He ascribed this view to Malik, al-Juwayni, and Qadi-Iyad . . . The gist of his words is that not one of the hadiths related to the *ziyara* is fair (*hasan*) or sound (*sahih*), but all are weak and forged, or rejected and without foundation.[74]

Abu al-Hasanat al-Lucknawi commented on these statements:[75]

> Do not listen to the saying that is far from the truth by one of the eminent people of our time in his article entitled *Rihlat al-siddiq ila al-bayt al-atiq* whereby "not one of the hadiths related to the *ziyara* is fair (*hasan*) or sound (*sahih*), but all are weak and forged, or rejected and without foundation." I wonder that he can even ascribe the claim that they are weak, to Imam Malik, Qadi Iyad, and others, for this is an invention attributed to them. For example, his saying: "Shaykh al-Islam Ibn Taymiyya said that it is not in the Law, and in this he was followed by some of the Hanbalis, and he related this from Malik, al-Juwayni, and Qadi Iyad." This is all an utter fabrication, for neither Malik, nor Juwayni, nor Iyad ever considered it unlawful to visit the grave of the Prophet (ﷺ). They were not of those whose learning exceeded their intelligence so that they would say with their mouth what Ibn Taymiyya said.[76]

Lucknawi's strong words are reminiscent of Mulla Ali al-Qari's statement, already quoted, whereby "Ibn Taymiyya exceeded proper bounds from among the Hanbalis by prohibiting traveling to visit the Prophet (ﷺ)."
Shawkani concludes:

---

74 Shawkani, *Nayl al-awtar* 3:94-97.

75 Abu al-Hasanat al-Lucknawi, *Zafr al-amani sharh mukhtasar al-sayyid al-sharif al-Jurjani fi mustalah al-hadith* edited by Abd al-Fattah Abu Ghudda (Aleppo and Beirut: Maktab al-matbuat al-islamiyya, 3rd ed. 1416, p. 422 n.).

76 A reference to al-Subki's unflattering remark about Ibn Taymiyya, "his learning exceeded his intelligence."

And it has been answered to one who related from Malik the saying of hating the visiting of the Prophet's grave, that he only said it to preclude wrongdoing, and it has been said he hated saying the phrase *al-ziyara* (the visit), because whoever wishes to visit does it, and whoever wishes to leave it is free also, whereas the visit to his grave, blessings and peace upon him, is from the necessary *sunnas* (*min al-sunan al-wajiba*). Abd al-Haqq [Ibn al-Kharrat al-Ishbili] held this also. And also those who say that it is part of the Law have adduced as evidence the persistence of Muslims who proceed to *hajj* at all times, regardless of the varied countries of origin and the different *madhhabs*, in coming to Madina with the goal (*qasd*) of visiting him, and they consider this to be among the best of actions. And it has not been narrated that anyone has forbidden that for them, and so it is a consensus.

2.16. EDICT (*FATWA*) OF FORTY-FIVE SCHOLARS OF MAKKA, MADINA, EGYPT, SYRIA, AND INDIA ON THE PRAISEWORTHINESS OF TRAVELING TO VISIT THE PROPHET (ﷺ)

A century ago, eleven major Sunni scholars in India issued an edict (*fatwa*) on the lawfulness of travelling with the explicit intention of visiting the Prophet (ﷺ), in response to the question:

> What do you say concerning traveling to visit the leader of creation, blessings and peace upon him and upon his Family and Companions? Which do you prefer for the traveller at the time of undertaking travel: to intend to visit the Prophet (ﷺ), or to intend also to visit the mosque? For someone said, "One traveling to Madina must not intend other than the Mosque of the Prophet (ﷺ)."[77]

---

[77] The reply was reproduced in full in the book *al-Mufannad al-muhannad*, and Shaykh Muhammad ibn Alawi al-Maliki again reproduced it recently in his book *Shifa al-fuad bi ziyarati khayr al-ibad* (p. 83-88).

This *fatwa* was subsequently approved and co-signed by thirty-four additional scholars of Makka, Madina, Egypt, and Syria. Below is a list of these scholars, followed by excerpts from the edict (*fatwa*):

2.16.1. SCHOLARS FROM INDIA
Allama muhaddith Rashid Ahmad al-Gangohi (d. 1905 CE)
Allama muhaddith Khalil Ahmad al-Saharanfuri (d. 1927 CE)
Allama muhaddith Shaykh Mahmud al-Hasan al-Deobandi
Allama Shaykh Mir Ahmad Hasan al-Husayni
Allama muhaddith Shaykh Aziz al-Rahman al-Deobandi
Allama murshid Shaykh Ali Ashraf al-Tahanawi
Allama Shaykh Shah Abd al-Rahim al-Ranfuri
Shaykh al-Hajj al-Hakim Muhammad Hasan al-Deobandi
Mawlawi Qudrat Allah
Mawlawi Mufti Kifayat Allah
Allama Shaykh Muhammad Yahya Saharanfuri

2.16.2. SCHOLARS FROM MAKKA
Shaykh Muhammad Said ibn Muhammad al-Shafii the chief of
　　the scholars of Makka and the imam and *khatib* at the
　　Masjid al-Haram
Shaykh Ahmad Rashid Khan Nawab
Shaykh Muhammad Abid ibn Husayn al-Maliki
Shaykh Muhammad Ali ibn Husayn al-Maliki

2.16.3. SCHOLARS FROM MADINA
Al-faqih al-Sayyid Ahmad ibn Ismail al-Barzanji (d. 1919 CE)
Shaykh Ahmad al-Jazairi al-Maliki
Sayyid Muhammad Zaki al-Barzanji
Muhaddith al-Shaykh Umar Hamdan al-Mahrisi
Sharif Ahmad ibn al-Mamun al-Balghith
Shaykh Musa Kazim
Shaykh Mulla Muhammad Khan
Shaykh Khalil ibn Ibrahim
Shaykh Muhammad al-Aziz al-Wazir al-Tunisi
Shaykh Muhammad al-Susi al-Khayari
Hajj Ahmad ibn Muhammad Khayr al-Shanqiti

Shaykh Muhammad ibn Umar al-Fulani
Shaykh Ahmad ibn Ahmad Sad
Shaykh Muhammad Mansur ibn Numan
Shaykh Ahmad Bisati
Shaykh Muhammad Hasan Sindi
Shaykh Mahmud Abd al-Jawad

2.16.4. SCHOLARS FROM AL-AZHAR, EGYPT
Shaykh al-Azhar Shaykh Salim al-Bashri
Shaykh Muhammad Ibrahim al-Qayati

2.16.5. SCHOLARS FROM SYRIA
Al-faqih al-muhaddith Muhammad Abu al-Khayr Ibn Abidin
   al-Husayni
Shaykh Mustafa ibn Ahmad al-Shatti al-Hanbali (d. 1929)
Shaykh Mahmud Rashid al-Attar al-Dimashqi
Shaykh Muhammad al-Bushi al-Hamawi
Shaykh Muhammad Said al-Hamawi
Shaykh Ali ibn Muhammad al-Dallal al-Hamawi
Shaykh Muhammad Adib al-Hurani
Shaykh Abd al-Qadir al-Lababidi
Shaykh Muhammad Said Lutfi al-Hanafi
Shaykh Faris ibn Ahmad al-Shaqfa
Shaykh Mustafa al-Haddad al-Hamawi

2.17. TEXT OF THE *FATWA*

Bismillah al-Rahman al-Rahim . . .
First, let it be known, before we state our answer,
that by Allah's grace we, all our shaykhs–may Allah
be pleased with them–and the totality of our assembly
are, in the branches of the religion, strict imitators
(*muqallidun*) of the guide of mankind and the apex of
Muslim scholars, the greatest imam, Abu Hanifa al-
Numan; and, in beliefs and principles of the faith,
strict followers (*muttabiun*) of the principal imams
Abu al-Hasan al-Ashari and Abu Mansur al-Maturidi,
may Allah be well pleased with them; and that we are
strict adherents (*muntasibun*) to the following Sufi
ways: the most distinguished way of the Naqshbandi
masters, the most pure way of the Chishti masters,

and the most radiant way of the Suhrawardi masters.

Second, let it be known, that we do not here speak one word nor utter one syllable concerning the religion except that we stand upon authority for it with our proof from the Quran or *sunna*, or the consensus of the *umma*, or the saying of one of the major scholars of the schools of law. Nevertheless, we do not say that we are exempt from error and forgetfulness in writing and speaking, therefore, if it becomes apparent to us that we erred in something, whether in the principles or in the branches, then we are not ashamed to take it back and proclaim that we do so. How could it not be so when our own imams took back many of their positions, such as the most honorable imam of Allah's Sanctuary, our imam, al-Shafii, may Allah be well pleased with him, until there was little left except he had a new position concerning it? The Companions themselves took back some of their positions in the light of each other's opinions, as is known to those who pursue the sciences of hadith. Therefore, if one of our contemporary scholars asserts that we erred in some ruling, then if concerns the principles let him produce his evidence in the light of one of the imams of theology (*kalam*), and if it concerns the branches, then let him bring forth his evidence from the most conclusive position of one of the imams of the *madhhab*. If he so does, then nothing more is left for us except rightful acceptance with the heart and the tongue, and added to that, sincere gratitude . . .

IN REPLY TO THE QUESTION: According to us and our shaykhs, the visit to the grave of the master of Messengers–may my life be sacrificed for him – is among the greatest of the acts that draw near to Allah and those who earn the most reward and those most efficacious in obtaining a high rank. In fact, it is close to being a required act. This holds true even if its fulfillment comes by way of travelling and expenditure, and even if one forms the intention, at the time of departure, to visit the Prophet–upon him a thousand thousand salutations–and along with that intention he intends to visit his mosque and other blessed spots and noble graves.

Moreover, the most appropriate for him is as the

great savant Ibn al-Huham said: let him devote his
intention solely to the visit of his grave, then he will
obtain the visit of his mosque at the time he arrives
there, for in so doing he will show additional reverence and honor to him. This is according to the narration, "Whoever comes to me as a visitor driven by no
other need but my visit, it is incumbent upon me to be
his intercessor on the Day of Resurrection."[78] Hence
it is reported from the noble knower of Allah, al-Mulla
[Abd al-Rahman] Jami that he set apart the Visit
from the Pilgrimage, and that is more in keeping with
the *madhhab* of those who love the Prophet (ﷺ).

As for what the objectors say whereby the traveller to Madina–upon its dweller a thousand thousand
salutations–must not intend other than to visit the
noble mosque, on the basis of the hadith"Mounts are
not to be saddled except to go to three mosques," then
this is rejected because the hadith does not indicate
an absolute prohibition! Rather, if one endowed with
understanding and learning considers it carefully one
sees a proof in the text for permissibility. The factor
by which the three mosques are excepted from the
commonality of mosques or other places, is the special
merit that is attached to them: and that special merit
is present in the noble spot of the grave, for that noble
spot and enlightened expanse of space which contains
his limbs–blessings and peace upon him– is absolutely more meritorious even than the Kabah, the Throne,
and the *kursi*, as explicitly declared by our *fuqaha*.
And since the three mosques have been singled out for
their special merit, then it is definitely the case that
the blessed spot of his grave be singled out even more.

The sun of the pious scholars, our shaykh,
Mawlana Rashid Ahmad al-Gangohi has expounded
upon this matter in the same terms that we used, or
even more explicitly, in his treatise *Zubdat al-man-
asik fi fadl ziyarat al-madina al-munawwara*, which
has been printed several times. Also relevant to this
noble issue is the treatise of the shaykh of our
shaykhs, Mawlana Sadr al-Din al-Dihlawi–may Allah
sanctify his precious secret–in his treatise *Ahsan al-
maqal fi hadith la tushadd al-rihal* which came out in
print and became well-known, and in which he

---

78 Haytami said in *Majma al-zawaid,* "Tabarani narrates it in *al-Kabir* and *al-
Awsat* from Ibn Umar with a chain containing Maslama ibn Salim and he is weak."
al-Iraqi said in *al-Mughni an haml al-asfar*: "Ibn al-Sakan declared the hadith sound
(*sahih*)."

unleashed disaster on the heads of those who call themselves "*salafiyya.*" Let the reader consult these works. And Allah knows best.

3. THE PROPHET'S AND SAINTS' KNOWLEDGE OF THE UNSEEN (*ILM AL-GHAYB*)

Questions that are addressed in this chapter include:

What is the stand of the scholars of the recognized schools of law with respect to the Prophet's knowledge of the unseen?

Is there any narration in Bukhari or other *sahih* books stating that the Prophet (ﷺ) knew the unseen?

What is the unseen that the Prophet (ﷺ) can know and the unseen that he does not know, in light of the "Salafis" absolute denial of this knowledge?

Also, what is the belief of the major schools regarding the saints' knowledge of the permissible unseen?

3.1. THE PROPHET'S KNOWLEDGE OF THE UNSEEN

Knowledge of the unseen is one of Allah's prerogatives, exclusive to Him except insofar as He discloses it to His elect servants: *He discloses not His unseen (ghayb) to anyone, except only to such a messenger as He is well-pleased with* (72:26).

The *hafiz* Ibn Hajar al-Asqalani explained this verse saying:

> It follows from this verse that prophets can see some of the Unseen, and so do the saints (*wali*, pl. *awliya*) that follow each particular prophet also, as each takes from his prophet and is gifted (*yukram*)

with his knowledge. The difference between the two is that the prophet looks at this knowledge through all kinds of revelation, while the saint does not look upon it except in dreams or through inspiration, and Allah knows best.[1]

Al-Qurtubi confirms this:

The truthful, righteous Muslim (al-muslim al-sadiq al-salih) is he whose state matches that of prophets and thereby is bestowed (ukrima) some of the same kind of gifts they were given: that is to behold the unseen (wa huwa al-ittila ala al-ghayb). As for the disbeliever (al-kafir), the corrupt person (al-fasiq), and the contentious one who confuses matters for the listeners (al-mikhlat)–then no.[2]

It is incorrect and improper, therefore, to say that the Prophet did not know the unseen unless such a statement is qualified, as in saying, "He did not know that of the unseen which only Allah knows." Otherwise, it is incorrect to say that the Prophet (ﷺ) did not know the unseen. How could such a claim be true of any truthful prophet who brings news from His Lord, especially one who ascended above the seven heavens and the eight paradises to His Lord's presence, one who told of the events that attended creation, one who saw the events after resurrection, and one to whom the inimitable Quran was revealed. Allah said to him:

And We granted you knowledge of what you knew not, and the bounty of Allah for you has been infinite (4:113).

This is of the tidings of the Unseen which we reveal to you. You did not know it before this, nor your people (11:49).

Say: . . . Allah has already informed us of the true state of matters concerning you: It is your actions that Allah and His Apostle will observe . . . (9:94).

---

1 Ibn Hajar, Fath al-bari (1989 ed. 8:660) tafsir Surah Luqman, "Allah has knowl-edge of the Hour" (31:34).

2 Al-Qurtubi as quoted by Ibn Hajar in Fath al-bari (1989 ed.) 12:449.

> *And some of them hurt the Prophet and say, "He is*
> *all ear!" (i.e. gullible). Say, An ear of good for you: he*
> *believes in Allah, and believes the Believers, and is a*
> *Mercy to those of you who believe . . . (9:61).*

Imam al-Baydawi commented, "This verse is a warning
that, 'It is not due to his ignorance of your true position that
the Prophet (ﷺ) accepts what you say but out of leniency and
mercy for you.'"[3]

However, the Prophet (ﷺ) did not like to boast, and he
always stressed that certain matters of the unseen were exclusively Allah's domain; especially knowledge of the Last Hour,
and "the five things" mentioned at the end of *Surah Luqman*
(31:34). This is confirmed by the hadith:

> *Utiytu mafatihu kulli shayin illa al-khams.* "I
> have received the keys to everything (unseen) except
> the five (which Allah alone knows)."[4]

In similar fashion, Ibn Masud narrates, *Utiya mafatihu
kulli shayin ghayr al-khams.* "He has received the keys to
everything (unseen) except the five (which Allah alone
knows)."[5]

Ibn Hajar al-Asqalani also cites, without weakening them,
two very similar hadith in *Fath al-bari*:

*Utiya nabiyyukum ilmu kulli shayin siwa hadhihi al-
khams. Utiytu mafatih al-ghayb* (Your Prophet (ﷺ) has
received everything except these five: I have received the keys
of the unseen).[6]

These five things are:
Knowledge of what is in the wombs
Knowledge of when the Hour will rise
Knowledge of what one will gain tomorrow

---

3 Al-Baydawi, *Anwar al-tanzil* in *Majma al-tafasir* 3:149.

4 Narrated from Ibn Umar by Ahmad (2:85); Tabarani in the *Kabir* (12:361),
Haythami in *Majma al-zawaid* (8:263), Ibn Kathir in his *Tafsir* 6:355, and Suyuti in
his *Tafsir al-Durr al-manthur* (5:169). Haythami said: "The sub-narrators in Ahmad's
chain are the men of sound (*sahih*) narration."

5 Narrated from Ibn Masud by Ahmad and Ibn Adi. Haythami in *Majma al-
zawaid* (8:263) says: "The sub-narrators in both chains are the men of sound (*sahih*)
narration."

6 Ibn Hajar, *Fath al-bari* (Dar al-fikr ed. 1:124 and 8:514).

Knowledge of the land in which one will die
Knowledge of the time Allah will send rain.[7]

A man from Banu Amir, after asking the Prophet (ﷺ) certain questions, said, "Is there any knowledge left which you do not know?" whereupon the Prophet (ﷺ) said, *"Allah knows better than that, and there is a kind of unseen knowledge which Allah alone knows; With Him is knowledge of the Hour. He sends down the rain, He knows what is in the wombs, no soul knows what it will earn tomorrow, and no soul knows in what land it will die"* (31:34).[8]

This is confirmed by Ibn Mardawayh's narration that Ali said, in response to the verse, "On that day tidings will be darkened for them, *"Lam yuma ala nabiyyikum shayun illa khamsun min sarair al-ghayb* (Nothing was darkened for your Prophet (ﷺ) except five matters from the secrets of the unseen).[9]

In Tirmidhi *(hasan sahih)* and Baghawi in *Sharh al-sunna* on the authority of Muadh ibn Jabal:

> The Prophet (ﷺ) said, "My Lord came to me in the best image and asked me over what did the angels of the higher heaven vie, and I said I did not know, so He put His hand between my shoulders, and I felt its coolness in my innermost, and the knowledge of all things between the East and the West came to me."

Ali al-Qari wrote about this hadith:

> Whether the Prophet (ﷺ) saw his Lord during his sleep or whether Allah the Glorious and Exalted manifested Himself to him with a form (*bi al-tajalli al-suwari*), this type of manifestation is known among the masters of spiritual states and stations (*arbab al-hal wa al-maqam*), and it consists in being reminded of His qualities (*hayatihi*) and reflecting upon His vision (*ruyatihi*), which is the outcome of the perfec-

---

7 Hadith of Ibn Umar in Ahmad and Bukhari.

8 Ahmad narrated it and Ibn Kathir mentions it in his *Tafsir* for *Surah Luqman.* Al-Haythami said in *Majma al-zawaid* (#116): "Abu Dawud narrates part of it, and all of the sub-narrators in Ahmad's chain are trustworthy and they are Imams."

9 Cited in the chapter of *Surah Luqman* in *Kanz al-ummal*, as a commentary for the verse 28:66 in *Surah al-Qasas.*

tion of one's inner detachment (*takhliyatihi*) and self-adornment (*tahliyatihi*).[10]

And Allah knows best about the states of His prophets and intimate friends whom He has raised with His most excellent upbringing, and the mirrors of whose hearts He has polished with His most excellent polish, until they witnessed the Station of Divine Presence and Abiding (*maqam al-hudur wa al-baqa*), and they rid themselves of the rust of screens and extinction (*sada al-huzur wa al-fana*).

May Allah bestow on us their yearnings. May He make us taste their states and manners. May He make us die in the condition of loving them and raise us in their group.[11]

Al-Qari also said, in *al-Asrar al-marfua*:

Ibn Sadaqa said that Ibn Zara said, "The hadith of Ibn Abbas [about the Prophet (ﷺ) seeing His Lord] is sound (*sahih*), and no one denies it except a Mutazili" [!] . . . Ibn al-Humam answered, "This (representation) is the veil of form (*hijab al-sura*)." It seems that he meant by this that the entire goal can be visualized if it is interpreted as a formal manifestation (*tajalli suwari*), as it is incontrovertibly absurd to interpret it as a real or literal manifestation (*tajalli haqiqi*) . . . for Allah is exalted from possessing a body, a form (*sura*), and directions with regard to His essence . . . And if the hadith is shown to have something in its chain that indicates forgery, then fine; otherwise, the door of figurative interpretation is wide and imposes itself (*bab al-tawil wasiun muhattam*).[12]

The Prophet's "knowledge of all things between the East and the West" is confirmed by the famous narration from al-Bara ibn Azib:

At the time of the Battle of Ahzab or the battle of

---

10 Ali al-Qari, in the chapter on the Prophet's turban in his book *Jam al-wasail fi sharh al-shamail*, a commentary on Tirmidhi's *Shamail* or Characteristics of the Prophet.

11 Al-Qari, *Jam al-wasail* (Cairo, 1317 H) p. 209.

12 Al-Qari, *al-Asrar al-marfua* (#478, p. 126).

the Trench, the Prophet (ﷺ) went down to hit a rock with his pick, whereupon he said, *"Bismillah (In the Name of Allah)"* and shattered one third of the rock. Then he exclaimed, *"Allahu akbar (Allah is Greater)! I have been given the keys of Sham. By Allah, verily I can see her red palaces right from where I stand."* Then he said, *"Bismillah,"* and shattered another third and exclaimed: *"Allahu akbar! I have been given the keys of Persia. By Allah, I can see her cities and her white palace right from where I stand."* Then he said, *"Bismillah"* and shattered the remainder of the rock and exclaimed: *"Allahu akbar! I have been given the keys of Yemen. By Allah, I can see the gates of Sana right from where I stand."*[13]

Another version of the above is related from Salman al-Farsi. Ibn Hisham relates it in his *sira* through Ibn Ishaq:

Salman al-Farsi said, "I was digging in one corner of the trench at which time one rock gave me difficulty. Allah's Messenger came near me and saw my difficulty as I was digging. He came down and took the pick from my hands. Then he struck and a great spark flashed under the pick. He struck again and another spark flashed. He struck a third time and a third spark flashed. I said to him: My father and mother (be ransomed) for you, O Messenger of Allah! What is that I saw flashing under the pick as you were striking? He said: Did you see this, O Salman? I said: Yes! He said: The first time, Allah opened Yemen [in the south] for me; the second time, He opened Sham (in the north] and the West (al-*maghrib*) for me; and the third time, he opened the East (al-*mashriq*)."[14]

The above two narrations are confirmed by Abu Hurayra's words related by Ibn Hisham in his *Sira* directly after the above narration:

Ibn Ishaq said, A reliable source narrated to me

13 Graded *hasan* (fair). al-Haythami said: "Ahmad (4:303 #18718) narrated it and its chain contains Maymun Abu Abd Allah. Ibn Hibban declared him trustworthy while a group of others declared him weak. The remainder of its sub-narrators are trustworthy."

14 Ibn Hisham relates it in his *Sira* (Beirut, Dar al-wifaq ed. 3-4: 219) and also Ibn Kathir in *al-Bidaya* (4:99).

that Abu Hurayra used to say, when these countries were conquered in the time of Umar and in the time of Uthman and after Uthman, "Conquer what comes within your sight. By the One in Whose hand lies Abu Hurayra's soul, you do not conquer any city nor will you conquer any city until the Day of Resurrection except that Allah the Exalted gave Muhammad its keys beforehand."[15]

A further confirmation of the above is the hadith in Muslim:

The earth was collected together for me so that I was shown its Easts and Wests. And the kingdom of my Community will reach to the extent that it was brought together for me.

A further confirmation is the hadith in Bukhari:

Narrated Asma bint Abu Bakr, I went to Aisha during the solar eclipse. The people were standing (offering prayer) and she too, was standing and offering prayer. I asked, "What is wrong with the people?" She pointed towards the sky with her hand and said, "*Subhan Allah!*" I asked her, "Is there a sign?" She nodded with her head, meaning, yes. When Allah's Apostle finished (the prayer), he glorified and praised Allah and said, "There is not anything that I have not seen before but I have seen now at this place of mine, even paradise and hell. It has been revealed to me that you people will be put to trial nearly like the trial of al-Dajjal, in your graves. As for the true believer or a Muslim (the sub-narrator is not sure as to which of the two (words Asma had said) he will say, 'Muhammad came with clear signs from Allah, and we responded to him (accepted his teachings) and believed (what he said).' It will be said (to him), 'Sleep in peace; we have known that you were a true believer who believed with certainty.' As for a hypocrite or a doubtful person, (the sub-narrator is not sure as to which word Asma said) he will say, 'I do not know, but I heard the people saying something and so I said the same.'"[16]

15 Ibn Hisham, *Sira* 3-4:219.
16 Bukhari, Volume 9, Book 92, Number 390.

A further confirmation of the above is the hadith of Hudhayfa:[17]

> The Messenger of Allah gave us an address in which he did not leave out anything that would happen until the Last Hour came. Whoever remembered it remembered it and whoever forgot it forgot it. Many companions of mine have known it. When any of it came to pass, I would recognize it and remember it as a man remembers the face of a man who has gone away and which he recognizes when he sees him again." Then Hudhayfa said, "I do not know whether my companions may have forgotten or pretended to forget [i.e. to prevent *fitna*], but Allah's Messenger did not leave out the instigator of a single disaster that was going to happen until the end of the world. There were more than three hundred of them. He named them for us, each with his own name, the name of his father and his tribe.

A further confirmation is the hadith in Bukhari:

> . . .Then Allah's Messenger said, "By Him in Whose Hand my life is, paradise and hell were displayed before me across this wall while I was praying, and I never saw such good and evil as I have seen today."[18]

A further confirmation is the hadith of Abu al-Darda in Tabarani and Ahmad, which is sound (*sahih*), according to Haythami:[19]

> When the Messenger of Allah left us there was not a bird that flies in the sky but that he had given us some knowledge about it.

This profusion of the Prophet's knowledge of the unseen has been characterized by Allah as perspicuity and an ability to reveal knowledge of the unseen, in the two verses:

> *His sight swerved not, nor swept astray* (53:17)

---

17 In Bukhari and Muslim.
18 Bukhari, Volume 9, Book 92, Number 397.
19 Haythami, in *Majma al-zawaid*.

> He is not stingy of (his knowledge of) the unseen
> (81:24).

Nor is the Prophet's knowledge after his life in this world (*dunya*) lessened in any way. Rather, the contrary is true, as established in the following hadith:

> My life is a great good for you, you will relate about me and it will be related to you, and my death is a great good for you, your actions will be presented to me (in my grave) and if I see goodness I will praise Allah, and if I see other than that I will ask forgiveness of Him for you.[20]

Qadi Iyad, al-Qastallani, and other scholars of mainstream Islam included in their excellent books on the Prophet (ﷺ) extensive chapters that establish his knowledge of unseen and future events.[21]

Last but not least, Bukhari began the book of the Beginning of Creation in his *Sahih* with the following hadith:

> Narrated Umar: "One day the Prophet (ﷺ) stood up among us for a long period and informed us about the beginning of creation (and talked about everything in detail) until he mentioned how the people of Paradise will enter their places and the people of Hell will enter their places. Some remembered what he had said, and some forgot it."[22]

In light of the above evidence, statements such as that made by Muhammad ibn Abd al-Wahhab, at the end of his

---

20 Haythami says in *Majma al-zawaid* (9:24 #91), "al-Bazzar relates it and its sub-narrators are all sound *(rijaluhu rijal al-sahih)*." Qadi Iyad cites it in *al-Shifa* (1:56 of the Amman edition). Suyuti said in his *Manahil al-safa fi takhrij ahadith al-shifa* (Beirut 1988/1408) p. 31 (#8), "Ibn Abi Usama cites it in his *Musnad* from the hadith of Bakr ibn Abd Allah al-Muzani, and al-Bazzar from the hadith of Ibn Masud with a sound *(sahih)* chain." Ibn al-Jawzi mentions it through Bakr and then again through Anas ibn Malik in the penultimate chapter of the penultimate section of *al-Wafa*, and also mentions the version through Aws ibn Aws with a sound chain: "The actions of human beings are shown to me every Thursday on the night of (i.e. preceding) Friday." See also *Fath al-bari* 10:415, al-Mundhiri, *al-Targhib wa al-Tarhib* 3:343, and *Musnad Ahmad* 4:484.

21 Qadi Iyad, in his *al-Shifa fi marifat huquq al-mustafa* (The healing concerning the knowledge of the rights of the elect one) and Al-Qastallani, in his *al-Mawahib al-laduniyya bi al-minah al-muhammadiyya* (The gifts from Allah: the Muhammadan dispensations).

22 Bukhari, *Sahih*, Volume 4, Book 54, Number 414.

leaflet paradoxically entitled, "The Three Principles of Oneness," are misguided, and misguiding. He writes:

> One who claims to know something from knowledge of the unseen is a *taghut* or false deity![23]

This is utterly rejected as falsehood spoken against the Prophet (ﷺ) by those who would deny his status and the prerogatives of his rank as established by Allah in His speech, and in the sound hadith.

3.1.1. QADI IYAD AND ALI AL-QARI ON THE PROPHET'S KNOWLEDGE OF THE UNSEEN AND FUTURE EVENTS[24]

Qadi Iyad says, in his book *al-Shifa,* concerning the Prophet's knowledge of the unseen:

> The hadith on this subject are like a vast ocean whose depths cannot be plumbed and which does not cease to overflow. This is one aspect of his miracles which is definitely known. We have many hadith which have reached us by multiple paths of transmission (*tawatur*) regarding his familiarity with (*ittila*) the unseen.

Hudhayfa narrated:

> The Messenger of Allah gave us an address in which he did not leave out anything that would happen until the Last Hour came. Whoever remembered it remembered it and whoever forgot it forgot it. Many companions of mine have known it. When any of it came to pass, I would recognize it and remember it as a man remembers the face of a man who has gone away and which he recognizes when he sees him again.

Then Hudhayfa continued:

> I do not know whether my companions may have forgotten or pretended to forget [i.e. to prevent *fitna*;

---

23 Ibn Abd al-Wahhab, *al-Usul al-thalatha.*
24 The translation from Qadi Iyad is by Aisha Bint Abdurrahman Bewley with slight modifications, from the Madinah Press edition entitled *Muhammad Messenger of Allah: ash-Shifa of Qadi Iyad*, 2nd ed. (Granada: Madinah Press, 1992) p. 186-193.

Qari said: to turn to what is more important], but Allah's Messenger did not leave out the instigator of a single disaster that was going to happen until the end of the world. There were more than three hundred of them. He named them for us, each with his own name, the name of his father and his tribe.[25]

Abu Dharr said from Abu Darda, "When the Messenger of Allah left us there was not a bird that flies in the sky but that he had given us some knowledge about it."[26]

The compilers of the *Sahih*[27] and the Imams[28] have related what the Prophet (ﷺ) taught his Companions and family regarding his promises of victory over his enemies, the conquests of Makka, Jerusalem, the Yemen, Sham and Iraq, and the establishment of security between Hira, in Iraq, and Makka.

The Prophet (ﷺ) said that Madina would be raided and Khaybar would be conquered by Ali the next day. He foretold those parts of the world that Allah was going to open up to his Community and what they would be given of its flowers and fruits, such as the treasures of Chosroes and Caesar. He related what would happen among them with regard to sedition, disputes and sectarianism, acting as those before them had done, and splitting into seventy-three sects, only one of which would be saved. He said that they would spread out over the earth, that people would come who would wear one garment in the morning and another in the evening, and that dish after dish would be placed before them. They would embellish their houses as the Kabah is embellished. Then he said at the end of the hadith, "Today you are better than you will be on that day."

The Prophet (ﷺ) said that they would strut about on the earth and that the girls of Persia and Byzantium would serve them. Allah would withdraw their strength from them and the

25 Bukhari, Muslim, Abu Dawud.

26 Narrated in Tabarani and Ahmad with a sound (*sahih*) chain according to Haythami in *Majma al-zawaid*. Also narrated by Abu Yala and Ibn Mani.

27 Those who strictly bound themselves to the criteria of soundness in narrating *hadith*, such as Bukhari, Muslim, Ibn Hibban, Ibn Khuzayma, and al-Hakim in their well-known books.

28 Such as Malik, Ahmad, and the rest of the authors of the Six Books and others, i.e. those who did not strictly bind themselves to to the criteria of soundness in narrating *hadith*.

evil ones would overcome the good. They would fight the Turks and the Khazars and Byzantium. Chosroes and Persia would be obliterated so that there would be neither afterwards. Caesar would pass away and there would be no Caesar after him. He mentioned that Byzantium would continue generation after generation until the end of time. The noblest and best people would be taken away. When the time grew near, knowledge would be taken away, and sedition and bloodshed would appear. He said, "Woe to the Arabs for an evil that draws near!"

The earth was rolled up for him so that he could see its eastern and western extremities and the dominion of his Community was to reach what was rolled up for him. That is why it has extended from the east to the west, from the Indies in the east to the sea of Tangier, beyond which is no civilization. That was not given to any of the nations. Islam did not extend to the north and south in the same way.

He said, "The people of the west (ahl al-gharb) will know the truth until the Hour comes." Ibn al-Madini[29] believed that this refers to the Arabs because they are distinguished by drinking from a certain kind of leather bucket (al-gharb). Another believed that it refers to the people of the Maghrib.

In a hadith from Abu Umama, the Prophet (ﷺ) said, "A group of my Community will remain constant to the truth, conquering their enemy until the command of Allah comes to them while they are still in that condition." He was asked, "Messenger of Allah, where are they?" He replied, "In Jerusalem."[30]

He foretold the kingdom of the Umayyads and the rule of Muawiya, and counseled him saying that the Umayyads would

---

29 *Al-Imam al-hafiz* Abu al-Hasan Ali ibn Abd Allah al-Madini (pr. *ma-dEE-ni*). He narrated hadith from his father and from Hammad ibn Zayd and a large number of hadith masters. From him narrated Bukhari, Abu Dawud, al-Baghawi, Abu Yala. His shaykh Abd al-Rahman ibn Mahdi said: "Ali ibn al-Madini is the most knowledgeable of all human beings in the hadith of Allah's Messenger, especially concerning what Ibn Uyayna narrates. Do you blame me for loving Ali ibn al-Madini too much? By Allah, I learn more from him than he does from me." Yahya al-Qattan (al-Madini's shaykh and that of Ahmad ibn Hanbal) said the same about him. Bukhari said: "I did not think little of myself except before Ali (ibn al-Madini)." al-Nasai said: "It is as if Allah created him only for this science (hadith)." He died in Samarra. The name of Madini is related to the city of the Prophet. This was said by Ibn al-Athir. As for al-Jawhari, he said that the latter would be "Madani" (pr. *ma-da-nEE*) and that "Madini" was related to the city built by the caliph al-Mansur.

30 Ahmad and Tabarani from Abu Umama.

make the kingdom of Allah a dynasty. He said that the descendants of al-Abbas would emerge with black banners and would rule a far larger area than they then ruled.

He said that the Mahdi would appear, and he told about what the People of His House (*Ahl al-Bayt*), would experience, including their slaughter and exile.

The Prophet (ﷺ) foretold the murder of Ali and said that the most wretched of people would be his killer [this is Abd al-Rahman ibn Muljam] and that Ali would be the apportioner of the fire–his friends would enter the garden and his enemies the fire. Among those who would oppose him would be the *Kharijis* and the *Nasibiyya*[31] and a group who claimed to follow him among the Rafidis would reject him.

He said: "Uthman will be killed while reciting the Quran. Perhaps Allah will have him wearing a shirt [i.e. the caliphate]. They will want to remove it and his blood will fall on his utterance of Allah's words: '*Allah is enough for you against them*' (2:137).

He said that sedition would not appear as long as Umar was alive, al-Zubayr would fight against Ali, the dogs of al-Hawab[32] would bark at one of his wives and many would be killed around her and she would barely escape. They barked at Aisha when she went to Basra.

He said that Ammar would be killed by an unjust group and the companions of Muawiya killed him [at Siffin]. He said to Abdullah ibn Zubayr: "Woe to the people from you [i.e. they will be punished for killing him unjustly] and woe to you from the people [i.e. al-Hajjaj will attack you]!"

He said about Quzman [one of the worst hypocrites]: "He will be tested together with the Muslims although he is one of the people of the fire," and later Quzman committed suicide.

He said that a group which included Abu Hurayra, Samura ibn Jundub and Hudhayfa: "The last of you will die in a fire [in this world, not the next]." They kept asking about each other,

31 Fayruzabadi in the *Qamus*, Ibn Manzhur in *Lisan al-arab*, and al-Zabidi in *Taj al-arus* define the Nawasib as those who made a point of opposing Ali ibn Abi Talib, peace be upon him. They are part of the Khawarij, who are those Muslims (whether in past or recent times) who oppose one whom the majority of Muslims have taken as their leader.

32 A place between Basra and Makka where Aisha stayed when she was trying to intercede between Ali and Muawiya.

and Samura was the last of them to die when he was old and senile. He tried to warm himself over a fire and burned himself in it.

He said about Hanzala al-Ghasil (Washed-by-the-Angels): "Ask his wife about him. I saw the angels washing him." They asked her and she said: "He left (for jihad) in *janaba* (state of major ritual defilement after sexual intercourse) and died before he could do *ghusl* (major ablution)." Abu Said said: "We found his head dripping with water."

He said: "The caliphate is with Quraysh. This business will remain with Quryash as long as they establish the religion."

He said: "There will be one liar and one destroyer *(kadhd-hab wa mubir)* from Thaqif." It was thought that this referred to al-Hajjaj ibn Yusuf and al-Mukhtar ibn Ubayd.[33]

He said that Musaylima would be destroyed by Allah and that Fatima would be the first of his family to follow him to the grave (she died six months later).

He warned about the Great Apostasy *(al-ridda)* and said that the caliphate after him would last for thirty years and that it would then become a kingdom. This happened in the period of al-Hasan ibn Ali.

He said: "This business began as prophethood and mercy, then mercy and a caliphate, then a voracious kingdom and then arrogance and tyranny and corruption will enter the community."

He told of the existence of Uways al-Qarani and that there would be Amirs who would delay the prayer beyond its time.

In one hadith he says that there would be thirty liars in his community and four of them would be women. Another hadith says thirty liars, one of whom would be the Dajjal or Antichrist. They would all deny Allah and His Messenger.

He said: "The time is near when there will be a lot of non-Arabs among you who will consume your property and strike your necks. The Last Hour will not come until a man from Qahtan drives the people with his staff."

He also said: "The best of you are my generation, then those after them, and then those after them. After that, people will come who give testimony without being asked to do so, who will

---

33 Al-Hajjaj was a tyrant while al-Mukhtar was a Khariji.

be treacherous and are not trustworthy, who promise and do not fulfill. They will tend to be corpulent."

He said: "A time is only followed by one worse than it."

He also said: "My community will be destroyed at the hands of young men from Quraysh." One version from Abu Hurayra says: "If I had wanted to, I would have named them for you – the Banu so-and-so and the Banu so-and-so."

He told about the appearance of the Qadariyya and the Rafidis (those who curse the Companions and declare Sunnis to be disbelievers), and said that the last of this community would curse the first of it. The Helpers (ansar) would diminish until they became like the salt in food (i.e. rare). Their position would continue to dissipate until not a group of them remained. He said that they would meet with despotism after him.

He told about the Khawarij, describing them down to the malformed one among them, and said that their mark would be *tahliq* or shaved heads.[34]

He said that shepherds would become the leaders of the people and the naked barefoot ones would vie in constructing high buildings. Mothers would give birth to their mistresses.

He said that Quraysh and their confederates would not conquer him, but that he would conquer them.

He foretold "the Death"–a plague which occurred in the time of Umar and in which seventy thousand people perished – which would come after the conquest of Jerusalem and described what the houses of Basra would be like.

He said that they would ride in the sea like kings on thrones. He said that if the religion had been hung in the Pleiades, men from Persia would have obtained it.

A wind blew up during one of his raids and he said: "It blows for the death of a hypocrite." When they returned to Madina, they discovered it was true.

He told some people sitting with him: "The tooth of one of you in the fire will be greater in size than the mountain of Uhud." Abu Hurayra said: "The people eventually were all dead except for me and one other man. Then he was killed as

---

34 I.e. exaggeration in shaving the head. This was one of the marks of the Wahhabis as pointed out by Alawi ibn Ahmad al-Haddad and others. It is known that Ibn Abidin called the Wahhabis Kharijis in his *Hashiyat al-durr al-mukhtar*. It is also said that *tahliq* here means: "sitting in circles."

an apostate during the *ridda* in the battle of Yamama."

He told about the man who stole some pearls from a Jew and the jewels were found in that man's saddle-bag, and about the man who stole a cloak and it was found where he said it would be. He told about his she-camel when she had strayed and how she was tied to a tree with her halter. He told about the letter of Hatib (Ibn Abi Baltaa) to the people of Makka.

He told about the case where Safwan ibn Umayya persuaded Umayr ibn Wahb to go to the Prophet (ﷺ) and kill him. When Umayr arrived where the Prophet (ﷺ) was, intending to kill him, the Messenger of Allah told him about his business and secret, and Umayr became a Muslim.

He informed them about the money which his uncle, al-Abbas, had left concealed with Umm al-Fadl. Al-Abbas said: "No one except she and I knew where it was." So he became Muslim.

He informed them that he would kill Ubayy ibn Khalaf and that Utba ibn Abi Lahab would be eaten by one of Allah's beasts of prey. He knew about the deaths of the people of Badr and it happened as he said it would.

He said about al-Hasan: "This son of mine is a master *(sayyid)* and Allah will make peace between two groups through him."

He said to Sad (Ibn Abi Waqqas): "Perhaps you will survive until some people profit by you and others seek to harm you."

He told about the killing of the people of Muta on the very day they were slain, even though there was more than a month's distance between he and them.

The Negus died and he told them about it the very day he died although he was in his own land.

He informed Fayruz (the Persian minister) of the death of Chosroes on the very day that a messenger came to him bearing the news of his death. When Fayruz verified the story, he became Muslim.

One time when the Prophet (ﷺ) found Abu Dhar sleeping in the mosque in Madina he told him how he would be exiled. The Prophet (ﷺ) said to him: "How will it be when you are driven from it?" He said: "I will dwell in the *Masjid al-haram*." He asked: "And when you are driven from there?" The Prophet (ﷺ)

told him of his life alone and of his death alone.[35]

He said that the first of his wives to join him would be the one with the longest hand. It was Zaynab bint Jahsh because of the length of her hand in giving *sadaqa*.

He foretold the killing of al-Husayn at Taff [Karbala]. He took some earth [which Gabriel had shown him] from his hand and said: "His grave is in it."

He said about Zayd ibn Suhan: "One of his limbs will pre-

---

35 From Asma Bint Yazid: Abu Dhar (al-Ghifari) used to serve the Prophet and when he finished he would go to the mosque and sleep, and the mosque was his house. One time the Prophet came in and found Abu Dhar lying on the ground. He nudged him with his foot and Abu Dhar sat up. The Prophet said, "Sleeping?" He replied, "O Messenger of Allah, where else can I sleep? I have no house other than this." The Prophet said, "What will you do if they expel you from it?" He said, "I will repair to Syria, for verily Syria is the land of migration, the land of the Gathering (on the Day of Judgment), and the land of prophets. I shall be one of its dwellers." The Prophet said, "What will you do if they expel you from Syria?" He said, "I will come back here and make it my house and my dwelling." The Prophet said, "What if they expel you from it a second time?" He replied, "Then I will take up my sword and fight them off until I die." The Prophet looked displeased and he held him firmly and said, "Shall I tell you of a better way?" He said, "Yes, may my father and mother be ransomed for you, O Messenger of Allah!" The Prophet said, "Let them lead you whither they lead you, and let yourself be taken whither they take you, until you meet me again in that very state." Ahmad narrated it with one weak sub-narrator (Shahr ibn Hawshab), however, some have declared him reliable, e.g. Ibn Hajar in *Fath al-bari* 3:65 and *al-hafiz* al-Dhahabi.

The hadith of Abu Dhar's death and the prediction of its circumstances are narrated by Ibn Rahawayh, Ibn Abi Usama, and al-Bayhaqi: Umm Dhar (his wife) wept as he lay on his deathbed and upon his questioning she replied, "Why should I not weep seeing you die in a desert land and I have not even enough in my possession for my own shroud, nor yours?" He said, "Good tidings to you, and don't weep! for I heard the Prophet say to a large group as I was among them: One of you will die in a deserted land, with a handful of Muslims for witnesses. None of that large group remains and all of them died in a town surrounded by many. Therefore I am that one..."

From Ibn Masud: When the Prophet went out on the campaign of Tabuk, Abu Dhar lagged behind due to his old camel. They complained of it to the Prophet who said: "Leave him be, for perhaps there is good in it, and Allah will make him catch up with you." When Abu Dhar saw that his camel was too slow, he carried his own gear and continued on foot, following the traces of Allah's Messenger alone in the heat. When the Prophet saw him his eyes filled with tears and he said: "May Allah have mercy on Abu Dhar! He walks alone, and he shall die alone, and he shall be resurrected alone." Ibn Hajar mentions in *al-Isaba* that Ibn Ishaq narrated it with a weak chain.

It was so when he died in al-Rabdha, for there was no one with him except his wife and his young boy. After they washed him and shrouded him they waited by the side of the road for someone to help bury him. Abd Allah ibn Masud came with a following of the people of Iraq. When the boy saw them he jumped up to them and said: "This is Abu Dhar, the Companion of Allah's Messenger! Therefore, help us to bury him." Ibn Masud came down and wept saying: "Allah's Messenger told the truth."

Abu Dhar had heard from the Prophet that one must not hoard up provision for more than a certain time. During the caliphate of caliph Uthman, people became quite well-off. Abu Dhar used to come out and preach against this and say they were wrong

cede him to the garden." His hand was cut off in jihad.

to store up and save. The people complained to caliph Uthman. Whenever Abu Dhar met caliph Uthman, may Allah be well pleased with both of them, Abu Dhar would recite to him the verse: *On the day when it will (all) be heated in the fire, and their foreheads and their flanks and their backs will be branded therewith (and it will be said unto them): Here is that which ye hoarded for yourselves. Now taste of what ye used to hoard.* (9:35)

Finally he called Abu Dhar and told him to stop. When Abu Dhar refused, saying he must convey what was told to him, Uthman exiled him from Madina. Al-Qari says: Uthman exiled him to Syria, then he brought him back to Madina, then exiled him again to al-Rabdha, a village in ruins, where he stayed until his death.

Abu Dhar was evidently the strictest and most austere of the Companions in light of the hadith related from and about him. He was a Sufi-like Companion and is known as *al-zahid* or the Ascetic in the biographical dictionaries. He was extremely scrupulous and direct. The author of *Hayat al-sahaba* mentions Sufyan al-Thawri's relation that Abu Dhar used to stand by the Kabah and shout at the people: "Greed has killed you! You can never fulfill your greed!"

The following is illustrative of Abu Dhar's manner: Ahmad (1:63) relates on the authority of Abu Dhar that the latter came to ask something from Uthman ibn Affan and he had his staff in his hand. Uthman then asked, "O Kab, Abd al-Rahman [ibn Awf] has died and has left money behind. What is your opinion on it?" He replied, "If he paid Allah's dues with his money [i.e. his debts], then we may use it." Abu Dhar raised his staff and hit Kab with it. Then he said: I heard the Prophet say: "If this entire mountain of gold were mine to spend and it were accepted, I would not like to leave behind even six ounces of it." I adjure you by Allah, Uthman, did you hear it? Did you hear it? Did you hear it? Uthman said: "*Naam* (Yes)!"

This is the account of Abu Dhar's conversion in *Sahih Bukhari*: [English by Khan with slight modifications. Volume 5, Book 58, Number 201:] Narrated Ibn Abbas: When Abu Dhar received the news of the Advent of the Prophet he said to his brother, "Ride to this valley (of Makka) and try to find out the truth of the person who claims to be a prophet who is informed of the news of heaven. Listen to what he says and come back to me." So his brother set out, went to the Prophet, listened to some of his talks, returned to Abu Dhar and said to him. "I have seen him enjoining virtuous behavior and saying something that is not poetry." Abu Dhar said, "You have not satisfied me as to what I wanted." He then took his journey-food and carried a water-skin of his, containing some water till be reached Makka. He went to the mosque and searched for the Prophet and though he did not know him, he hated to ask anybody about him. When a part of the night had passed away, Ali saw him and knew that he was a stranger. So when Abu Dhar saw Ali, he followed him, and none of them asked his companion about anything, and when it was dawn, Abu Dhar took his journey food and his water-skin to the mosque and stayed there all the day long without being perceived by the Prophet, and when it was evening, he came back to his retiring place. Ali passed by him and said, "Has the man not known his dwelling place yet?" So Ali awakened him and took him with him and none of them spoke to the other about anything. When it was the third day. Ali did the same and Abu Dhar stayed with him. Then Ali said "Will you tell me what has brought you here?" Abu Dhar said, "If you give me a firm promise that you will guide me, then I will tell you." Ali promised him, and he informed Ali about the matter. Ali said, "It is true, and he is the Messenger of Allah. When you get up tomorrow morning, accompany me, and if I see any danger for you, I will stop as if to pass water, but if I go on, follow me and enter the place which I will enter." Abu Dhar did so, and followed Ali till he entered the place of the Prophet. Abu Dhar went in with Ali, listened to some of the Prophet's talks and embraced Islam on the spot. The Prophet said to him, "Go back to your people and inform them (about it) till you receive my order." Abu Dhar said, "By Him in Whose Hand my life is, I will proclaim my conversion loudly amongst them (i.e. the pagans)." So he went out, and when he reached the mosque, he said as loudly as possible, "I bear witness that there is no god except

He said about those who were with him on Mount Hira: "Be firm. On you is a Prophet (ﷺ), a true man, and a martyr." Ali, Umar, Uthman, Talha and al-Zubayr were killed and Sad was attacked.

He said to Suraqa: "How will it be when you wear the trousers of Chosroes?" When they were brought to Umar, Suraqa put them on and said: "Praise be to Allah who stripped Chosroes of them and put them on Suraqa."

The Prophet (ﷺ) said: "A city will be built between the Tigris and Dujayl and Qutrubull and al-Sara. The treasures of the earth will be brought to it which the earth will swallow up," clearly indicating Baghdad.

He said: "There will be a man called al-Walid in this Community and he will be worse for this Community than Pharaoh was for his."[36]

Allah, and Muhammad is the Messenger of Allah." The people got up and beat him painfully. Then al-Abbas came and knelt over him (to protect him) and said (to the people), "Woe to you! Don't you know that this man belongs to the tribe of Ghifar and your trade to Sham is through their way?" So he rescued him from them. Abu Dhar again did the same the next day. They beat him and took vengeance on him and again al-Abbas knelt over him.

Ibn Hajar says about him in *al-Isaba fi tamyiz al-sahaba*: The famous ascetic who spoke frankly . . . His full name was Jundub ibn Janada ibn Sakan; it was also said he was called Ibn Abd Allah, or Barir, or Burayr, or al-Sakan ibn Janada. . . He was tall, of dark complexion, and thin. . . Al-Tabarani cited the hadith from Abu al-Darda whereby the Prophet always looked for Abu Dhar when he was present, and missed him when he was absent. Ahmad mentioned the hadith whereby the Prophet said: "The one of you sitting closest to me on the Day of Rising is he who leaves this world in the same condition as on the day I left him." Abu Dhar added: "and, by Allah there is none among you except he has lusted for something in the world except I." Its sub-narrators are trustworthy except that the link [of the *tabii*] is missing, as I don't think Arrak ibn Malik narrated from Abu al-Darda. . .

Abu Dawud cited with a good chain Ali's saying: "Abu Dhar is a large vessel full of knowledge, and he became helpless about it." Abu Dawud and Ahmad narrated from Abd Allah ibn Umar that the Prophet said: "Neither dust has carried nor green has shaded one more frank of speech than Abu Dhar.". . . After he met the Prophet, Abu Dhar went to the Kabah and began shouting at the top of his lungs: "I bear witness that there is no god but Allah and that Muhammad is His servant and messenger!" whereupon the people pounced on him and beat him until he could not get up. Al-Abbas rescued him and said to the people: "Woe to you! He is from Ghifar, on the trade route to Damascus." Then Abu Dhar came back the next day and did the same, whereupon they beat him again and al-Abbas rescued him again. . .

He died in al-Rabdha in the year 31 or 32. The majority think the latter. It is said in a story related with a passable chain that Ibn Masud led the funeral prayer over him. Al-Madaini says the same and adds that Ibn Masud then returned to Madina and died shortly afterwards." End of Ibn Hajar's words in *al-Isaba*.

36 This is al-Walid ibn Yazid ibn Abd al-Malik.

He also said: "The Hour will not come until two parties fight each other with the same claim."[37]

He said to Umar about Suhayl ibn Amr: "Perhaps he will be in a position which will delight you, Umar." That happened. He stood up in Makka in a similar way to Abu Bakr on the day when they heard about the Prophet's death. He addressed them with a similar speech [i.e. similar to Abu Bakr's speech in Madina that day] and strengthened their insight.

When he sent Khalid to Ukaydar, he said: "You will send him hunting for wild cows," and he did.[38]

All these matters took place during his lifetime, and after his death, just as he had said they would.

He also told his Companions about their secrets and inward thoughts. He told them about the secrets of the hypocrites and their rejection and what they said about him and the believers, so that one of the hypocrites would say to his friend: "Be quiet! By Allah, if he does not have someone to inform him, the very stones of the plain would inform him." [These were Itab ibn Usayd and al-Harith ibn Hisham, both of whom became Muslims when the Prophet (ﷺ) subsequently told them that they had said this].

He described the magic which Labid ibn al-Asim used against him and how it was in the comb, the combings and the spade of the male palm and that he had thrown them into the well of Dharwan. It was found to be just as he had described it.

---

37 This was the battle of Siffin which took place around the caliphate. The people of Sham were sixty thousand of which twenty thousand died; while the people of Iraq were one hundred and twenty thousand of which forty thousand died.

38 Al-Bayhaqi narrates it. Ali al-Qari in his commentary on Qadi Iyad said: al-Khatib said, "He became Muslim." Others said, "He died as a Christian." Qari continues, "The contradiction is resolved by the fact that he became Muslim and then apostatized." Ibn Mindah and Abu Nuaym in their books entitled *Marifat al-Sahaba* (Knowledge of who the companions were) said he became a Muslim and gifted the Prophet a mantle of brocade *(hillatun siyara)* which the Prophet gave to Umar. Ibn al-Athir said (in his own dictionary of the Companions entitled *Usud al-ghaba*): "Concerning the approach and the gift they are right, but concerning his Islam they were mistaken, for there is no disagreement among the authors of biographies that he was not a Muslim [i.e. when he died]. He was a Christian when the Prophet approached him, then he went back to his stronghold and remained there until Khalid surrounded him in the time of Abu Bakr, and killed him as a Christian idolater for breaching his trust. Ibn al-Athir continues: al-Baladuri mentioned that Ukaydar came to the Prophet and then went back to Duma, also called Duma al-Jundul, a place between Hijaz and Syria, then, when the Prophet died, he apostatized. When Khalid marched from Iraq to Syria, he killed him."

He told Quraysh that the termites would eat what was in the paper which they issued against the Banu Hashim by which they cut off relations with them. He said that every mention of Allah would remain. It was found to be as he had said.

He described Jerusalem to the unbelievers when they did not believe what he had said as is related in the hadith of the Night Journey, describing it to them as someone who really knew it. He told them about their caravan which he had passed on his way and told them when it would arrive.

All of these things happened as he had said, including all that he told them regarding events which would take place and things whose beginnings had not yet even appeared, such as his words: "The flourishing of Jerusalem will prove the ruin of Yathrib. The ruin of Yathrib will result in the emergence of fierce fighting. The emergence of fierce fighting will encompass the conquest of Constantinople."

He mentioned the preconditions of the Hour, the signs of its arrival, the Rising and the Gathering, and told about what would happen to the good and those who deviated, the Garden and the fire and the events of the Rising.[39]

3.1.2. THE SIGHT OF THE PROPHET (ﷺ)[40]

The eyes of the Holy Prophet (ﷺ) were matchless in their outward beauty as well as in their vision and sight. Ibn Abbas in describing his beauteous eyesight states:

The Holy Prophet (ﷺ) could see equally well during the darkness of the night and the brightness of the day. (Bukhari).

Anas narrates: The Holy Prophet (ﷺ) said:

O people! I am your imam. Do not precede me in *ruku* and *sajda* because in addition to seeing what is in front of me I also see what is behind me. (Muslim)

Abu Hurayra similarly narrates the Prophet's words: "I swear on Allah Almighty, neither your *ruku* is hidden from me nor your *sajda* because I can see you behind my back as well." (Muslim and Bukhari)

The gist of the commentary which the great scholar Shaykh Abd al-Haqq Muhaddith Dihlawi has writ-

---

39 A whole volume could be devoted to this subject, but there is enough in what is indicated. Most of the hadith are in the *Sahih* volumes and have been mentioned by the Imams.

40 From *Soutul Islam* publications (Pretoria, South Africa).

ten on these traditions is as follows: "Only Allah Almighty exactly knows the truth [i.e. the extent] of his vision. In addition, every blessed limb also falls in this category [of piercing sight], because no one can fully understand what they were." They are without doubt beyond one's imagination and intellect. Any assumption falls short of their virtuosity. Allah Almighty has full Power to bestow vision to every part of the body, or grant this unique sight as His Favor and Grace on His beloved Messenger.

If by this sight is meant vision of the heart, then it is that knowledge which was bestowed upon him by Allah Almighty.

Some people tend to incorrectly rely on the inauthentic tradition whereby the Holy Prophet (ﷺ) said: "I do not know what is behind the wall." No origin is known (*la asl*) for such a hadith. Even if such an improbable saying were attributable to the Prophet (ﷺ), then its purpose would be to show personal humility and not to negate such knowledge. The meaning would then be: "I do not know that on my own, nor do I have such knowledge on my own," but as far as bestowed knowledge is concerned, i.e. knowledge given by Allah Almighty, the Holy Prophet (ﷺ) was fully equipped with it by his Creator.

The Holy Quran bears the testimony to this: *And We granted you knowledge of what you knew not, and the bounty of Allah for you has been infinite* (4:113).

3.1.3. CONCLUSION: THE PROPHET (ﷺ) "KNOWS" AND "CAN" BUT HE IS HUMBLE AND DOES NOT BOAST

The "Salafis" are often seen adducing the following verses among others in support of their view that the Prophet (ﷺ) is no more than an ordinary individual: *Say [O Prophet], I have no power to benefit myself nor to harm it, except that which Allah wills. Had I knowledge of the Unseen, I would have acquired much good, and adversity would not have touched me . . .* (7:188). *Say, I am but a man (or: a mortal) like yourselves* (18:110, 41:6). *And they say, We will not put faith in thee till thou cause a spring to gush forth . . . Or thou have a garden . . . and cause rivers to gush forth . . . Or thou cause the heaven to*

*fall . . . or bring Allah and the angels . . . have a house of gold;
ascend up into heaven . . . bring down for us a book . . . Say: My
Lord be glorified! Am I naught save a mortal messenger?"*
(17:90-93).

The "Salafis" quote such verses continually to try to prove
that the Prophet (ﷺ) was an ordinary person. They ignore the
last part of the verse that states: *Say, I am but a mortal like
yourselves, <u>but I receive revelation.</u>*

They also try to extend this doctrine of ordinariness to suggest that the saints are even more ordinary. Nuh Keller refers
to this way of thinking in his *Reliance of the Traveller* (p. 1112):

He (Yusuf al-Rifai) takes a keen interest in the problems of
Muslims today, and at a recent symposium in Amman with
Shaykh Abdullah Muhammad Ghimari and Shaykh Hassan
Saqqaf, he voiced his concern for the obstacles to the current
Islamic revival and world propagation of Islam that are being
put in its way by "fundamentalists" whose view of Allah is
anthropomorphic, view of the Prophet (ﷺ) is that he is over-
venerated and [overly] loved by Muslims, and view of Muslims
is that they are unbelievers or immersed in unlawful innovations.[41]

The scholars' explanation of the above verses is not that the
prophets declare their mortality as an expression of their ordinariness, but rather to express their dignity and humility, and
to destroy any claim to a nature other than human–i.e. god or
angel–that might be attributed to them.

These verses were also revealed in answer to some people
who asked the Prophet (ﷺ) for signs in a spirit of disbelief and
mockery. For instance, there was a group who claimed that
they would attest to his prophethood only if he performed for
them certain miracles, although it is established by the scholars of context for revelation (*asbab an-nuzul*) that the Prophet
(ﷺ) disliked being asked for miracles by unbelievers. To quote
these verses in an attempt to prove the supposed ordinariness
of the Prophet (ﷺ) is an aberrant practice, and a true under-
estimation of his rights and of Allah's generosity to him. The
Prophet (ﷺ) was certainly not limited as disbelievers claimed

41 Notice on Yusuf al-Rifai.

about prophets in the verse, *"They said, 'Ye are but mortals like unto us.'"* (36:15).

Finally, another reason for the disbelief toward the Prophet (ﷺ) was his humbleness. Ibn Abbas' explanation suffices for anyone who looks at the Prophet (ﷺ) with belief rather than skepticism; "Allah has taught modesty to His Prophet (ﷺ) Muhammad, lest he boast before His creation. He has therefore ordered him to be dignified and say, I am but a mortal man like you, except that I was chosen for Revelation."[42]

This section is concluded with an excerpt from Qadi Iyad's *al-Shifa* on the angelic nature of prophets:

Allah says, *"Muhammad is only a Messenger, and Messengers have passed away before him. Why, if he should die or be killed . . ."* (3:144) and *"The Messiah (Christ), son of Mary, is only a Messenger. Messengers have passed away before him and his mother was a truthful woman. They used to eat food"* (5:75) and *"We only sent Messengers before that ate food and walked in the markets"* (25:20) and *"Say, I am a mortal like you to whom revelation has been given."* (18:110).

Muhammad and all the prophets of mankind were sent to human beings. If it had not been for that, people would not have been able to meet them face-to-face, accept revelation from them, and speak with them.

Allah says, *"If We had made him an angel, We would have made him a man"* (6:9). That is to say, the angel would have taken the form of a man to whom they could speak since they would not be able to face an angel and speak with it if they saw it in its true form.

Allah says, *"Say, if there had been angels on the earth walking about in peace and quiet, We would have sent down upon them an angel as a messenger from heaven"* (17:95). That is to say, it is not possible in the *sunna* of Allah to send an angel except to one who is the same as it or one to whom Allah gives a special gift, chooses and makes strong enough to be able to face it, such as the prophets and messengers.

Prophets and messengers are intermediaries between Allah and His creation. They convey His commands and prohibitions, His warnings and threats to His creatures and they acquaint

---

42 Quoted by Qadi Iyad in *al-Shifa* and al-Khazin in his Commentary (18:110).

them with things they did not know regarding His commands, creation, majesty, power and His sovereignty. Their outward form, bodies and structure are characterized by the qualities of men as far as non-essential matters such as illnesses, death and passing away are concerned and they have human traits.

But their souls and inward parts have the highest possible human qualities, associated with the highest assembly, which are similar to angelic attributes, free of any possibility of alteration or evil. Generally speaking, the incapacities and weaknesses connected with being human cannot be associated with them. If their inward parts had been human in the same way as their outward, they would not have been able to receive revelation from the angels, see them, mix and sit with them in the way other mortals are unable to do.

If their bodies and outward parts had been marked by angelic attributes as opposed to human attributes, the mortals to whom they were sent would not have been able to speak with them as Allah has already said. Thus they have the aspect of men as far as their bodies and outward parts are concerned, and that of angels in respect of their souls and inward parts.

It is in this way that the Prophet (ﷺ) said, "If I had taken a close friend from my Community, I would have taken Abu Bakr as a friend, but it is the brotherhood of Islam. Rather your companion is the close friend of the Merciful."[43]

He said, "My eyes sleep and my heart does not sleep."[44]

He said, "I am not made the same as you but my Lord gives me food and drink."[45]

Their inward parts are disconnected from evil and free from imperfection and weakness.

This summary will certainly not be enough for all those who are concerned with this subject . . .[46]

3.2 THE SAINTS' UNVEILING
OF THE UNSEEN

Kashf, or unveiling, consists, according to al-Sharif al-Jurjani's definition, of "apprehending beyond the veil of ordinary phenomena, whether by vision or experience, the mean-

---

43 Narrated by Bukhari.
44 Narrated by Bukhari.
45 Narrated by Bukhari and Muslim.
46 From the translation of Qadi Iyad al-Maliki's *al-Shifa* by Aisha Bewley, Madinah Press, p. 277-278.

ings and realities that pertain to the unseen."[47] It is a kind of intuitive knowledge or discovery that is exemplified by Allah's friends, whose rank Allah extols with the affirmation: *Lo! Verily the Friends of Allah are those on whom fear comes not, nor do they grieve* (10:62).

Many sayings of the Prophet (ﷺ) discuss the various types and ranks of the saints.[48] These and other types of perfected individuals form the *khawass,* or elite of the pious, whom Allah also calls the *siddiqin* (saints, literally "very truthful ones"). They rank directly after the prophets and before the martyrs in the verse: *Whoso obey Allah and the Messenger, they are with those unto whom Allah has shown favor, of the prophets and the saints and the martyrs and the righteous. The best of company are they!* (4:69).

Their position in relation to Allah on the Day of Judgment is described as an object of desire for even the prophets, in the following sound hadith of the Prophet (ﷺ) related by Umar and others:[49]

When the Prophet (ﷺ) finished his prayer he turned to face the people and said, "O people! Listen to this, understand it, and know it. Allah has servants who are neither prophets nor martyrs and whom the prophets and martyrs yearn to be like, due to their seat and proximity in relation to Allah."

One of the Bedouin Arabs who came from among the most isolated of people twisted his hand at the prophet and said, "O Messenger of Allah! People from humankind who are neither prophets nor martyrs and yet the prophets and the martyrs yearn to be like them due to their seat and proximity in relation to Allah?! Describe them for us!"

The Prophet's face showed delight at the Bedouin's question and he said:

> They are of the strangers from this and that place. They frequent this or that tribe without belonging to them. They do not have family connections among

---

47 Al-Sharif al-Jurjani, *Kitab al-tarifat.*

48 As Suyuti has shown in his collection of these sayings in his *fatwa* already mentioned entitled: *al-Khabar al-dall ala wujud al-qutb wa al-awtad wa al-nujaba wa al-abdal* (The reports that indicate the existence of the pole, the pillars, the leaders, and the substitutes) in his *Hawi li al-fatawi.*

49 This is the narration of Abu Malik al-Ashari from the *Musnad* of Imam Ahmad.

themselves. They love one another for Allah's sake. They are of pure intent towards one another. On the Day of Resurrection Allah will place for them pedestals of light upon which He will make them sit, and He will turn their faces and clothes into light. On the Day of Resurrection the people will be terrified but not those. They are Allah's Friends upon whom fear comes not, nor do they grieve.[50]

Another famous description of the characteristics of *awliya* was given by Ali ibn Abi Talib, as related by Ibn al-Jawzi:

> They are the fewest in number, but the greatest in rank before Allah. Through them Allah preserves His proofs until they bequeath it to those like them (before passing on) and plant it firmly in their hearts. By them knowledge has taken by assault the reality of things, so that they found easy what those given to comfort found hard, and found intimacy in what the ignorant found desolate. They accompanied the world with bodies whose spirits were attached to the highest regard (*al-mahall al-ala*). Ah, ah! how one yearns to see them![51]

The saints may attain higher levels of knowledge than either ordinary humankind or *jinn*. The first and foremost of saints are the prophets themselves. It is firmly established in the Quran that Allah bestows powers on friends who are not prophets. For example, the saint (*wali*) who was with Prophet Solomon (ﷺ) and brought him the throne of Balqis (the Queen of Sheba) faster than the blink of an eye, was characterized as *"one who had knowledge of the Book:"*

> *One with whom was knowledge of the Scripture said, I will bring it thee (O Solomon) before thy gaze returneth unto thee . . .* (27:40)

---

50 Haythami in *Majma al-zawaid* says, "Ahmad relates it, and Tabarani relates something similar, and the men in its chain of transmission have been declared trustworthy." Also related through several chains by Abu Dawud, Ahmad, Baghawi in *Sharh al-sunna*, al-Hakim in the *Mustadrak*, Ibn Asakir, Ibn Abi al-Dunya in *Kitab al-ikhwan*, Ibn Jarir al-Tabari, Ibn Abi Hatim, Ibn Mardawayh, and others.

51 Ibn al-Jawzi, in the chapter devoted to *Sayyidina* Ali in *Sifat al-safwa*.

This reference is to Prophet Solomon's scribe, Asif ibn Barkhya who was, according to the *Tafsir Ibn Abbas* and the majority of the scholars, a non-prophet human being:

One with whom was knowledge of the Scripture": i.e. an angel . . . or Gabriel . . . or al-Khidr or Asif ibn Barkhya, Solomon's scribe, which is the most correct, and the majority (*jumhur*) agrees upon it . . .[52]

Similarly, al-Khidr, although considered by many to be a Prophet, possessed knowledge that Prophet Moses (ﷺ) did not have. He is characterized as *"one of Our slaves, unto whom We had given mercy from Us, and had taught knowledge from Our presence."* (18:65)

The word for both vision and true dream is *ruya*, which is mentioned in the Quran thus: *"Allah has fulfilled the vision (ruya) for His Messenger in very truth"* (48:27). The Prophet (ﷺ) said:

> The vision or dream (*al-ruya*) is one forty-sixth of prophecy.[53]

> When the Time draws near, almost no vision or dream of the believer will be false. The believer's dream is one forty-sixth of prophecy, and prophecy never lies.

> Whoever sees me in vision or dream sees me truly, for Satan cannot take on my form, and the believer's dream is one forty-sixth of prophecy.

> Among the greatest of lies is to ascribe to one's eyes the sight in a vision or dream of what one did not see.

> Nothing remains of prophecy except the glad tidings (*mubashshirat*). They asked him: What are they? He said, The good vision or dream. (*al-ruya al-saliha*).[54]

That *kashf* is an opening granted by Allah that is completely independent of one's own exertion or capacity for learning is clear from the Abu Hurayra's saying, "I have retained (*hafiztu*)

52 Nasafi, *Madarik al-tanzil* 27:40.
53 Bukhari and Muslim.
54 All four in Bukhari, Book of the Interpretation of Dreams.

from the Prophet (ﷺ) two large vessels of knowledge."[55] He used the term "vessels" to preclude the connotation of learning on his part, since liquid is not taught to the vessel, but poured in it. This indicates a state of passive receptivity that is independent of exertion or skill.

Another hadith, also in Bukhari, confirms that the Prophet (ﷺ) was literally pouring knowledge into Abu Hurayra rather than teaching it:

Narrated Abu Hurayra: I said, "O Allah's Apostle! I hear many narrations from you but I forget them." The Prophet (ﷺ) said, "Spread your covering sheet." I spread my sheet and he moved both his hands as if scooping something and emptied them in the sheet and said, "Wrap it around you." I wrapped it round my body, and I have never since forgotten a single hadith.[56]

Just as the true dream is a characteristic of the believer, so *kashf* is a characteristic of belief, according to the following hadith:

> From al-Harith ibn Malik al-Ansari (some chains have: al-Haritha ibn al-Naman al-Ansari): He passed by the Prophet (ﷺ) who asked him, "How are you this morning O Haritha [sic]?" He replied, "This morning I am a real believer." The Prophet (ﷺ) said, "Take care of what you say; what is the reality of your belief?" He said, "I have turned myself away from this world by keeping awake at night and by keeping myself thirsty by day; and I can almost see the Throne of my Lord in full sight; and I can almost see the people of the garden of paradise visiting each other; and I can almost see the people of the fire wailing to each other in it." The Prophet (ﷺ) said, "O Haritha, you do know; therefore cleave to it." Some versions add, "This is a believer, Allah has illumined his heart (*muminun nawwara Allahu qalbah*)."[57]

---

55 Bukhari narrates it in the book of knowledge of his *Sahih*.

56 English *Sahih Bukhari*, Volume 4, Book 56, Number 841.

57 Narrated by Tabarani in his *Mujam al-kabir*, al-Bazzar, Suyuti in his *Jami al-saghir*, al-Haythami in *Majma al-zawaid* in the "Chapter on the Reality of Belief and its Perfection" *(bab haqiqat al-iman wa kamalih)*, al-Askari, Ibn al-Mubarak in *Kitab al-zuhd*, Abd al-Razzaq through two chains, Ibn Mindah, Bayhaqi in *Shuab al-iman*, Ibn Asram in *Kitab al-istiqama*, Ibn Said, and Ibn Abi Shayba in his *Musannaf*. Abu Hanifa mentions it in his *al-Fiqh al-akbar*. Ibn Hajar in his *Isaba* lists its many chains and says that this is a *hadith mudal* (i.e. its chain is missing two or more sub-narra-

The Prophet (ﷺ) highlighted Umar's gift in this area in particular:

> In the nations before you were people who were spoken to (*muhaddathun*) though they were not prophets. If there is anyone in my Community, it is Umar ibn al-Khattab.[58]

This comment is elucidated by the two hadiths in Tirmidhi (which he graded *hasan*): "Allah has engraved truth on the tongue of Umar and his heart" and "If there were a prophet after me verily it would be Umar." Tirmidhi adds to the *muhaddath* narration that, according to Ibn Uyayna, "spoken to" means "made to understand" (*mufahhamun*). In his narration Muslim adds, "Ibn Wahb explained "spoken to" as meaning "inspired" (*mulhamun*)." This is the majority's opinion according to Ibn Hajar, who adds "spoken to" means "by the angels."[59] Nawawi said:

The scholars have differed concerning "spoken to." Ibn Wahb said it meant "inspired" (*mulhamun*). It was said also, "Those on the right, and when they give an opinion it is as if they were spoken to, and then they give their opinion. It was said also, "The angels speak to them . . ." Bukhari said, "Truth comes from their tongues." There is in this hadith a confirmation of the miracles of saints (*wa fihi ithbatu karamat al-awliya*).[60]

Ibn Hajar said:

> The one among [Muslims] who is "spoken to," if his existence is ascertained, what befalls him is not used as basis for a legal judgment, rather he is obliged to evaluate it with the Quran, and if it conforms to it or to the *sunna*, he acts upon it, otherwise he leaves it.[61]

One of the "Salafis" claimed that since the hadith states "If

---

tors) and *mawsul* (or: *muttasil*; i.e. it is linked back to a Companion through the authority of a *tabii*.

58 It is related by Bukhari, Muslim, Abu Dawud, Tirmidhi, and Ahmad.
59 Ibn Hajar, *Fath al-bari* (7:62:#3689).
60 Nawawi, *Sharh sahih Muslim Kitab* 44 Bab 2 #2398.
61 Ibn Hajar, *Fath al-bari* (1989 ed.) 7:62-63 #3689.

there is anyone in my *umma*, it is Umar," it must follow that at most the number of these inspired people is one. However, it is wrong to think that other Communities had many and this Community only one, as Ibn Hajar also stated in his commentary on that hadith. What is intended by the hadith is the perfection of *ilham* (inspiration) in Umar, not its total lack in other Muslims.

The exalted nature of the knowledge and power of the *awliya* is referred to in the verses: *Those who strive hard in Us, We shall most surely guide them in our Ways,* (29:69) *ittaqullah wa yuallimukumullah (be aware of Allah, and Allah Himself will teach you)* (2:282).

Also the hadith: *man amila bi ma alima warrathahullahu ilma ma lam yalam* (whoso acts upon what he knows, Allah will make him inherit a knowledge that he did not have.[62]

The master Bayazid al-Bistami cited this hadith in response to some naysayers in his time who asked him, "From where and from whom did you get this knowledge which you claim to have?"[63] The Shaykh al-Hakim al-Tirmidhi describes such striving as a kind of door that leads to nearness to Allah.[64] Shaykh Abd al-Qadir al-Jilani refers to the knowledge and power that result from it.

And fear Allah and He will teach you, then He will invest you with the power of controlling the universe with a clear permission which will have no obscurity in it . . . and He has done this with many of His prophets and saints and people especially favored from among the children of Adam.[65]

To receive such knowledge is called a gift (*karama*) for the saint and an act that disables opposition (*mujiza*) for the Prophet (ﷺ). The process of receiving it is similarly differentiated: revelation (*wahy*) for the latter and inspiration (*ilham*) or

---

62 Narrated from Anas by Abu Nuaym, *Hilyat al-awliya* 10:15. Cited in the Commentaries of Suyuti, *al-Durr al-manthur* (1:372) and Qurtubi (13:364), also by *al-hafiz* al-Zabidi in his *Ithaf al-sada al-muttaqin* 1:403. Shawkani included it in his collection of inauthentic hadith (*al-Fawaid* p. 289), however, al-Qari considers it authentic in his similar collection *al-Asrar al-marfua* p. 325.

63 Sharani, *al-Tabaqat al-kubra* (1343/1925) 1:66.

64 Shaykh al-Hakim al-Tirmidhi (Pronounced hakEEm. This is not the author of *al-Mustadrak ala al-sahihayn* whose name is pronounced hAAkim), in the second chapter of his *Adab al-muridin*.

65 Abd al-Qadir al-Jilani, in Discourse 16 of *Futuh al-ghayb*.

vision (*ruya*), disclosure (*kashf*), piercing sight (*firasa*) or glad tidings (*mubashshira*) from Allah, disclosure (*mukashafa*) mutual vision (*mushahada*) or divine conversation (*mukhataba*) for the former. Shaykh Abd al-Qadir al-Jilani said:

To saints (*awliya*) and substitute-saints (*abdal*) are disclosed such workings of Allah in the course of *kashf* and *mushahada* as overwhelm the reasoning power of man and shatter into pieces all habits and customs.[66]

Al-Siraj al-Tusi in his famous book *al-Luma* (The lights), a compilation of the sayings of the Sufis, mentions the following two definitions of the conditions of *kashf*:

Abu Muhammad al-Jurayri said, "Whoever does not work to fulfill what lies between him and Allah the Exalted by way of Godfear and vigilance, will never reach unveiling and contemplation." Al-Nuri said, "The uncoverings of the eyes are through eyesight, and the uncoverings of the hearts are through connection (*ittisal*)."[67]

One of the highest examples of such favor is undoubtedly the true vision of the Prophet (ﷺ). This is a reality established in the hadith of seeing the Prophet (ﷺ) in dream, and documented through the trustworthy from the Companions to the Successors and their Successors down to our day.[68] Al-Haytami's answer whereby it is possible for Allah's Friends to meet the Prophet (ﷺ) while awake in our time has already been mentioned.[69] They can also meet al-Khidr, according to Sakhawi, among others, who relates about Imam Nawawi:

It is well-known that he (Imam Nawawi) used to meet with al-Khidr and converse with him among many other *mukashafat*.[70]

The exalted nature of the saints' *firasa* is mentioned in the hadith where the Prophet (ﷺ) said, "*ittaqu firasat al-mumin fa innahu yara bi nurillah* (beware the vision of the believer, for he sees with the light of Allah). He then recited the verse,

66 *Ibid*, in Discourse 9.

67 Al-Siraj, *al-Lum* p. 422.

68 Some of these relations have been recorded in Suyuti's *fatwa Tanwir al-halak fi imkan ruyat al-nabi wa al malak* (The illumination of intense darkness through the possibility of seeing the Prophet and the angels) in his *Hawi li al-fatawi*.

69 Al-Haytami, *Fatawa hadithiyya* p. 297.

70 Al-Sakhawi, *Tarjimat shaykh al-islam qutb al-awliya Abi Zakariyya al-Nawawi*, p. 33.

"Therein lie portents for those who read the signs" (al-mutawas-simin 15:75).[71] Tirmidhi narrated this authentic hadith and said that some of the commentators have explained "Those who read the signs" as meaning those who possess vision *(al-muta-farrisin)*.[72] Al-Sakhawi mentions another authentic hadith that the Prophet (ﷺ) said, "Allah has servants who know (the truth about people) through reading the signs" *(tawassum)*.[73]

It is established in sound hadith that at the end of time every Muslim will be endowed with the ability to "read the signs," and recognize the *Dajjal,* or antichrist, as a disbeliever by reading the letters *K-F-R* over his forehead.[74]

It is related that the *firasa* of a pious shaykh was at the origin of Ibn Hajar al-Asqalani's decision to take up the study of jurisprudence rather than devote himself exclusively to hadith:

Ibn Hajar said: Muhibb al-Din al-Wahidi al-Maliki said to me, "Invest some of that energy of yours into jurisprudence *(fiqh)*, for I see by way of *firasa* that the scholars of this country (Egypt) are going to be depleted, and there will be need of you, so don't indulge yourself." And his word to me helped me greatly, and I still pray for him for that reason, may Allah have mercy on him.[75]

The following account of *firasa* is related about Imam al-Junayd al-Baghdadi:

> Abu Amr ibn Alwan relates, I went out one day to the market of al-Ruhba for something I needed. I saw a funeral procession and I followed it in order to pray with the others. I stood among the people until they buried the dead man. My eyes unwittingly fell on a woman who was unveiled. I lingered looking at her, then I held back and began to beg forgiveness of Allah the Exalted.
>
> On my way home an old woman told me, "My lord,

---

71 Tirmidhi *(gharib)* from Abu Said al-Khudri, and Tabarani from Abu Imama with a fair *(hasan)* chain according to al-Haythami in the chapter on *firasa* of *Majma al-zawaid*.

72 Tirmidhi, in the Book of the Commentary of the Quran in his *Sunan*.

73 Related from Anas with a fair chain by al-Bazzar, Tabarani, Abu Nuaym in *al-Tibb al-nabawi*, and from Ibn Said by Bukhari in his *Tarikh*, al-Askari in *al-Amthal*, Ibn Jarir al-Tabari in his *Tafsir* for 15:75, Ibn Abi Hatim, and Ibn Mardawayh.

74 Muslim, Book of *Fitan* (English vol. 4 p. 1515 #7009).

75 Related by al-Biqai, *Unwan al-zaman* p. 92.

why do I see your face all darkened?" I took a mirror
and behold, my face had turned dark. I examined my
conscience and searched: What calamity had befallen
unto me? I remembered the look I cast. Then I sat
alone somewhere and I began to ask Allah's forgiveness assiduously, and I asked to do with little for forty
days. (During that time,) the thought came to my
heart, "Visit your shaykh al-Junayd." I travelled to
Baghdad. When I reached the room where he lived, I
knocked at his door and heard him say, "Enter, O Aba
Amr, you sin in al-Ruhba and we ask forgiveness for
you here in Baghdad."[76]

The possessor of such gifts and powers of vision is of course
in no way exempted from the obligations of religion. Abu al-
Hasan al-Shadhili warned:

If your *kashf* opposes the Book and the *sunna*,
leave *kashf* and tell yourself: Allah has guaranteed
infallibility to the Book and the *sunna*, but He has not
guaranteed it for *kashf*.[77]

Similarly, Ibn Arabi said:

Someone in this Community who claims to be able
to guide others to Allah, but is remiss in but one rule
of the Sacred Law – even if he manifests miracles that
stagger the mind: . . . we do not even turn to look at
him, for such a person is not a shaykh, nor is he
speaking the truth, for no one is entrusted with the
secrets of Allah Most High save one in whom the ordi-
nances of the Sacred Law are preserved.[78]

Shaykh Abd al-Qadir Jilani says the same thing in the
Futuh. Their leader in this is the Sultan of the Knowers of
Allah, Bayazid al-Bistami, who said:

---

76 Narrated by Ibn al-Jawzi, *Sifat al-safwa* (Beirut: Dar al-kutub al-ilmiyya,
1409/1989) 1(2):271, in the chapter on al-Junayd (#296).
77 Al-Taftazani, *Madkhal ila al-tasawwuf* p. 240.
78 Quoted in Nabahani, *Jami karamat al-awliya* 1:3.

> If you see him fly in the air and walk on water do
> not be deluded by him, but see how he stands on the
> orders and the prohibitions.[79]

It is evident from the definition of the term *kashf* that it
refers to hidden knowledge of a tremendous nature, and that is
what Ibn Arabi meant by saying "the secrets of Allah Most
High." This is alluded to by the continuation of the hadith of
Abu Hurayra mentioned above:

> I have stored up from the Prophet (ﷺ) two large
> vessels of knowledge. One I have disseminated among
> the people; if I were to disseminate the other, they
> would cut my throat.

Imam Bukhari said, "The Knowers *(al-ulama)* are the
inheritors of the prophets; that is, they have inherited (their)
knowledge."[80] The first part of his statement is actually an
authentic hadith of the Prophet (ﷺ).[81] Thus it is beyond anyone's reach to put limitations on the gifts Allah bestows on His
Friends, except to give such gifts different name—*mujiza* or
karama—depending on whether the recipient is a prophet or a
saint. Nor is it impossible that some saints in the Prophet's
Community, like the Prophet (ﷺ) himself, know the Unseen,
except for what Allah hides from them and reserves for His
other creatures, like angels, or keeps to Himself, according to
His will.

The inheritance of the Prophet's knowledge by the great
scholars is illustrated by Abu Nuaym's assertion that it was
incumbent upon all Muslims to invoke Allah in their prayer for
Abu Hanifa, due to his preservation of the Prophet's *sunna* and
fiqh.[82] Another example is the following account about *Imam*
Malik, related by Ibn al-Jawzi:

> Abu Musab said, I went in to see Malik ibn Anas.
> He said to me, Look under my place of prayer or

79 Quoted in al-Qushayri, *Risala* (Cairo, 1319 ed.) p. 14, and in Ibn Taymiyya, *Fatawa* 11:466.

80 *Sahih Bukhari*, Book of Knowledge *(ilm)*, *Tarjimat al-bab* 11 (translation 1:59).

81 Ahmad (5:196), Tirmidhi, Darimi, Abu Dawud, Ibn Hibban, Ibn Majah, Bayhaqi in the *Shuab* and others.

82 Al-Khatib al-Baghdadi, *Tarikh baghdad* 13:344.

prayer-mat and see what is there. I looked and I
found a certain writing. He said, Read it. (I saw that)
it contained (the account of) a dream which one of his
brothers had seen and which concerned him. He said
(reciting what was written), "I saw the Prophet (ﷺ) in
my sleep. He was in his mosque and the people were
gathered around him, and he said, I have hidden for
you under my pulpit (*minbar*) something good–or,
knowledge–and I have ordered Malik to distribute it
to the people." Then Malik wept, so I got up and left.[83]

Observe the attitude of the saints towards meeting the
Prophet (ﷺ) in dreams and their strong belief in both the cred-
ibility and content of such dreams. This one explicitly states
that the Prophet (ﷺ) has kept something good hidden for his
Community (*umma*), and that he continues to give it through
one of the greatly learned religious scholars after his time.

Similarly, al-Daraqutni's (d. 385) statement on the unique
knowledge that he possessed shows the irreplaceable and
exclusive role of true scholars in Islam as custodians of the
Science *(al-ilm)*. Abu al-Fath ibn Abi al-Fawaris asked Ali ibn
Umar al-Daraqutni one day about a certain hadith, and he
answered him. Then he said to him, "O Abu al-Fath, there is
not, between the East and the West, anyone who knows this
other than myself."[84]

Imam Ahmad, also Ibn Abi al-Dunya, Abu Nuaym, Bayhaqi,
and Ibn Asakir all cited the following from Julays:

Wahb ibn Munabbih said: I saw the Prophet (ﷺ) in my
sleep, so I said, "*Ya rasul Allah*, where are the Substitutes
(budala) of your Community?" So he gestured with his hand
towards Sham. I said, "*Ya rasul Allah*, aren't there any in
Iraq?" He said, "Yes, Muhammad ibn Wasi, Hassan ibn Abi
Sinan, and Malik ibn Dinar, who walks among the people similarly to Abu Dhar in his time." [85]

The "Salafis" have claimed that *kashf* and inheritance from
the Prophet (ﷺ)—in any form other than memorization or
bookish learning— both contradict Allah's saying, "*Today I*

---

83 Ibn al-Jawzi, *Sifat al-safwa* (Beirut, 1989) 1:2:120. in the chapter entitled
"Layer Six of the People of Madina."

84 Cited by Salah Muhammad Uwayda, ed., Nawawi's *al-Taqrib wa al-taysir*
(Beirut: Dar al-kutub al-ilmiyya, 1407/1987) p. 15 n. 5.

85 Imam Ahmad, *Kitab al-zuhd.*

have perfected your religion, completed my favor upon you, and accepted for you Islam as religion," (5:3) and demean the Prophet's status as having perfectly conveyed the Message to the people. They also direct the same false claims to *ijtihad* or qualified independent reasoning, *ijma* or consensus of the scholars, and *qiyas* or analogy. This is shown by al-Zahawi in his refutation of the Wahhabi heresy:

> They (Wahhabis) denounce [the *ulama*] by saying that the Imams believe that the religion of Islam is deficient and that they complete it by "reasoning" like *ijma* and *qiyas*. For this, they cite the Quranic verse, "*Today I have completed your religion*" (5:3). They say we find whatever is necessary for life clearly stated in the Quran. So what need do we have for *qiyas*. The texts take in the whole of life's eventualities without need of derivation (*istinbat*) and analogy (*qiyas*) . . .[86]

The Mutazila sect did not believe in the miracles of the saints. Today some even claim "The saints are not known except to Allah, and there is no such thing as *kashf* in the Sharia," and "We only trust a person whom Allah or His Messenger ordered us to trust, but as for those claimed *awliya*, there is no specific evidence about them from Allah or His Messenger." This is said to justify withholding their respect for the pious.

These are all matters in which the "Salafis" and those who deny *kashf* reveal their Mutazili leanings. One of them said:

> The Sufi-doctrine of "miracles of saints" claims that the saints have control over it. Of course they say by Allah's will. (Also, the sect of the Shia believe in that!).

Observe how the speaker contradicted himself in his haste to reject miracles; on the one hand he asserts that "sufi-doctrine"–whatever that is–claims control over the elements. On the other hand he makes those who hold that doctrine ("they") say, "By Allah's will," which eradicates any claim of

86 Al-Zahawi, *The Doctrine of Ahl al-Sunna*, trans. Sh. Hisham Kabbani (Mountain View: ASFA, 1996) p. 51.

autonomous control. Observe also how he ascribes belief in gifts (*karama*) to the Shia, as if this sufficed to make it wrong when, in reality, belief in the gifts (*karama*) of saints is part of the Sunni creed!

In all of the above, the "Salafis" are roundly refuted by no less than Ibn Taymiyya, the most learned among the authorities they claim to follow and a self-proclaimed disciple of al-Jilani, whom he calls "my shaykh" and "my master."

3.2.1. IBN TAYMIYYA ON THE MIRACLES OF THE SAINTS (*AWLIYA*)

The putative imam of "Salafis," Ibn Taymiyya, said:

> It is established that the *awliya* possess spiritual communications (*mukhatabat*) and unveilings (*mukashafat*).[87]

Another of the Sunni principles is the faith in the *karama* of the saints, and in whatever Allah causes to happen at their hands of the suspension of the laws of nature in all kinds of knowledge and spiritual unveilings (*fi anwa al-ulum wa al-mukashafat*), and all kinds of powers and influences (*wa anwa al-qudra wa al-tathirat*) such as reported concerning the ancient Communities, (for example) in *al-kahf* and others, and as reported from the early beginnings of this Community regarding the Companions and the Followers and from every generation of Muslims after that, and these miracles will not cease to take place in this community until the Day of Resurrection (*wa hiya mawjudatun fiha ila yawm al-qiyama*)."[88]

The miracles of saints (*karama al-awliya*) are absolutely true and correct, by the acceptance of all mainstream Muslim scholars [i.e. as opposed to the Mutazila]. The Quran has pointed to them in different places as well as the authentic hadiths of the Prophet (ﷺ) and the reports transmitted from the Companions and the Successors through a large number of

---

87 Ibn Taymiyya, *al-Furqan bayna awliya al-shaytan wa awliya al-rahman,* 2nd ed. (Beirut: al-maktab al-islami, 1390/1970) p. 52.

88 Ibn Taymiyya, *al-Aqida al-wasitiyya* (Cairo: al-matbaa al-salafiyya, 1346) p. 33-34.

sources. Only the innovators such as the Mutazila and the Jahmiyya and their followers deny them.[89]

What is considered as a miracle related to knowledge is that sometimes the servant might hear something that others do not hear and see something that others do not see, whether in a wakeful or sleeping state of vision. And he can know something that others cannot know, through revelation or inspiration, or the dawning of necessary knowledge upon him, or truthful piercing sight *(firasa sadiqa)*, and such is called *kashf*, *mushahadat*, *mukashafat*, and *mukhatabat*.[90]

3.2.2. AL-HARAWI AL-ANSARI ON THE LEVELS OF *KASHF*

The *hafiz* al-Harawi al-Ansari, who is the model of "Salafis" in their fight against Asharis, wrote the following words about *kashf*:

> Regarding the word "finding" in the verses: *He will find Allah Forgiving, Merciful* (4:110) and *they would have found Allah Forgiving, Merciful* (4:64). . . *and he finds Allah* . . . (24:39), there are three meanings: first, it is the finding of knowledge emanating from the divine presence; it cuts off knowledge based on observations with the soundness of disclosure *(mukashafat)* from Allah to you.[91]

The renunciation *(zuhd)* of the privileged is to keep their aspiration *(himma)*, because Allah has kept them from depending on circumstances with the light of unveiling *(nur al-kashf)*.[92]

As for the claim by some "Salafis" that the saints *(awliya)* are not known, it demonstrates a lack of familiarity with Islam, as the sources of the religion are replete with their descriptions. Verses from the Quran, the hadith, and the sayings of the Companions concerning the characteristics of the *awliya* have already been quoted. Allah said, *"O those who have believed! Be*

---

89 Ibn Taymiyya, *Mukhtasar al-fatawa al-misriyya* (al-Madani Publishing House, 1400/1980) p. 603.

90 Ibn Taymiyya, *Majmua al-fatawa al-kubra* (1398 ed.) 11:313.

91 Al-Harawi al-Ansari, *Manazil al-sairin*, Station 96.

92 Al-Harawi al-Ansari, *Ilal al-maqamat*, Section 11 entitled: *Tariq al-khassa* (The way of the privileged).

conscious of Allah and stay with the truthful!" (9:119), and "Who comes against one of my saints, I declare war upon him!"[93] The Prophet (ﷺ) said, "There are some among Allah's servants who, when they swear by Allah, He vindicates them."[94] Does this all refer to unidentifiable beings who are known to Allah alone?

Ibn al-Jawzi went so far as to call the saints "the very purpose of existent beings."[95] If this is true how can they not be known or trusted? He said:

> The Friends of Allah and the Righteous are the very purpose of all that exists (*al-awliya wa al-salihun hum al-maqsud min al-kawn*), they are those who learned and practiced with the reality of knowledge . . . Those who practice what they know, do with little in the world, seek the next world, remain ready to leave from one to the other with wakeful eyes and good provision, as opposed to those renowned purely for their knowledge but not for shunning the world and practicing devotion.[96]

The "Salafis" also object to giving the title of *ghawth* or Arch-helper to Shaykh Abd al-Qadir al-Jilani, calling this practice innovation and *shirk*, and claiming that the title belongs only to Allah. When confronted with evidence from the sound hadith to the contrary, their claim is shown to be baseless:

> Bukhari narrates in his *Sahih* that our mother Hajar, when she was running in search of water between Safa and Marwa, heard a voice and said, "O you whose voice you have made me hear! If there is a *ghawth* (help/helper) with you (then help me)!" and an angel appeared at the spot of the spring of Zamzam.

Abu Yala, Ibn al-Sani, and Tabarani narrated that the Prophet (ﷺ) said, "If one of you loses something or seeks help or a helper *(ghawth)*, and he is in a land where there is no one to befriend, let him say, "O servants of Allah, help me! *(ya ibad*

---

93 Bukhari.
94 Bukhari and Muslim.
95 Ibn al-Jawzi, *Sifat al-safwa* (Beirut ed. 1989/1409).
96 *Ibid*, introduction p. 13, 17.

Allah, aghithuni), for verily Allah has servants whom one does not see."[97]

Ahmad relates in his *Musnad* that at the time of the greatest *fitna* of the Dajjal, when the Muslims will be at their weakest point, and just before Jesus son of Mary will descend at the time of the dawn prescribed prayer *(salat al-fajr),* people will hear a caller calling out three times, "O people, *al-ghawth* (the helper) has come to you!" (4:217).

The "Salafis" systematically ignore the authorities that fail to support their arguments and rely instead on whatever they can use to advance their position. They apply Muhammad ibn Abd al-Wahhab's aberrant statement already cited, "One who claims to know something from knowledge of the Unseen is a *taghut* or false deity,"[98] to saints but some of them fall short, in their selective logic, of applying it to prophets. By so doing they desert Ibn Abd al-Wahhab, for his statement evidently does not preclude anyone–prophet, angel, *jinn,* or any human being.

Even with respect to saints the supposed foundations of their assertions were exposed long ago by one of the scholars of the Community, Shaykh al-Islam Ibn Hajar al-Haytami. Would that they had only acquainted themselves with his *fatwa* on the matter and reflected upon it, instead of giving precedence to a less-qualified scholar. This *fatwa* is translated in full in *The Reliance of the Traveller,* from where it is quoted.

3.2.3. KNOWLEDGE OF THE UNSEEN
(IBN HAJAR HAYTAMI)

(Question) "Is someone who says, 'A believer knows the unseen *(al-ghayb),*' thereby considered an unbeliever, because of Allah Most High having said:

> *No one in the heavens or earth knows the unseen except Allah* (27:65)

> *[He is] the Knower of the unseen, and discloses not His unseen to anyone* . . . (72:26)

Or is such a person asked to further explain himself, in

---

97 Tabarani, in *al-Mujam al-kabir.* Haythami said in *Majma al-zawaid* (10:132), "The men in its chain of transmission have been declared reliable despite weakness in one of them."

98 Muhammad ibn Abd al-Wahhab, *Three Principles of Oneness.*

view of the possibility of knowing some details of the unseen?

(Answer:) "He is not unconditionally considered an unbeliever, because of the possibility of otherwise construing his words, for it is obligatory to ask whomever says something interpretable as either being or not being unbelief for further clarification, as has been stated. . .[99]

> If asked to explain and such a person answers, 'By saying, "A believer knows the unseen," I meant that Allah could impart certain details of the unseen to some of the friends of Allah (*awliya*)–this is accepted from him, since it is something logically possible and its occurrence has been documented, it being among the countless miracles (*karamat*) that have taken place over the ages. The possibility of such knowledge is amply attested to by what the Koran informs us about Khidr (Allah bless him and give him peace), and the account related of Abu Bakr Siddiq (Allah Most High be well pleased with him) that he told of his wife being pregnant with a boy, and thus it proved; or of 'Umar (Allah Most High be well pleased with him), who miraculously perceived[100] Sariya and his army who were in Persia, and while on the pulpit in Medina giving the Friday sermon, he said, 'O Sariya, the mountain!' warning them of the enemy ambush intending to exterminate the Muslims.[101] Or the rigorously authenticated hadith that the Prophet (ﷺ) (Allah bless him and give him peace) said of 'Umar (Allah Most High be well pleased with him), "He is of those who are spoken to [i.e. preternaturally inspired]."
>
>   . . .What we have mentioned about the above Quranic verse [on the unseen] has been explicitly stated by Nawawi in his *Fatawa*, where he says, 'It means that no one except Allah knows this independently and with full cognizance of all things knowable. As for [knowledge imparted through] inimitable prophetic miracles (*mujizat*) and divine favors (*karamat*) it is through Allah's giving them to know it that it is known; as is also the case with what is known

99 In Nawawi, *al-Rawda* and elsewhere.

100 I.e. the Muslim commander.

101 Abu Bakr ibn al-Arabi said of this incident, "It constitutes a tremendous rank and an evident gift from Allah, and it is present in all of the righteous incessantly until the Day of Resurrection." Ibn al-Arabi, *Aridat al-ahwadhi* 13:150.

through ordinary means' (*al-Fatawa al-hadithiyya*, 311-13).

(Muhammad Hamid): Allah Most Glorious is the All-Knower of things unseen and their inmost secrets, with primal, intrinsic, supernatural knowledge whose basis no one else has a share in. If any besides Him has awareness or knowledge, it is through their being made aware or given knowledge by Him Magnificent and Exalted. They are unable—being servants without capacity—to transcend their sphere or go beyond their limit to draw aside the veils from things unseen, and if not for His pouring something of the knowledge of these things upon their hearts, they would know nothing of it, little or much. Yet this knowledge is disparate in degree, and some of it higher than other of it and more certainly established.

The divine inspiration of it to prophet messengers is beyond doubt and above question, like the rising sun in its certitude and clarity, of which the Koran says: *[He is] the Knower of the unseen, and discloses not His unseen to anyone, save a messenger He approves: for him He places protectors before and behind"* (72:26-27).

"Protectors" meaning guards from among the angels, so that nothing of it is leaked to devils when it is being delivered to the Messenger (Allah bless him and give him peace), to safeguard its inimitability and it remain a unique prophetic sign (*mujiza*).

The miraculous perceptions (*kashf*) of the Friends of Allah (*awliya*) are a truth we do not deny, for Bukhari relates in his *Sahih* from Abu Hurayra (Allah Most High be well pleased with him) that the Prophet (ﷺ) said:

> In the nations before you were people who were spoken to [i.e. inspired] though they were not prophets. If there is anyone in my Community, it is Umar ibn Khattab.

Muslim relates in his *Sahih* from Aisha (Allah Most High be well pleased with her) that the Prophet (ﷺ) said:

> There used to be in the nations before you those

> who were spoken to. If there are any in my
> Community, Umar ibn Khattab is one of them.

But this intuition *(ilham)* does not equal the divine inspiration *(wahy)* of the prophets in strength [of certainty], because of the possibility that what is apprehended by the friend of Allah *(wali)* is merely the thoughts of his own mind. As it is sometimes admixed, and other things are mistaken for it, the possibility of error exists in it, and it cannot be a basis for establishing legal rulings or a criterion for works.

As for what astrologers and fortune-tellers say, there is no way it can be accepted, for sooth-saying was annulled when the Prophet (ﷺ) was sent and the heavens were safeguarded by stars, after which devils no longer had access to the heavens as they had had before, to eavesdrop on what angels were saying about the events on earth that Allah Most Glorious informed the angels of before *they happened* [15:17-18 and 72:8-10]. The Holy Quran is explicit that *"They [the devils] are prevented from hearing"* (26:212), and in a hadith: "Whoever goes to a 'psychic' *('arraf)* or fortune-teller and believes what he says has disbelieved in what has been revealed to Muhammad (ﷺ)."

The things that such people inform of that actually come to pass belong to the category of coincidence, which is not given the slightest value in Islam. All of which is on the topic of the unseen generally. As for the Final Hour, Allah Most High has veiled the knowledge of the time it will occur from all creatures entirely, and no one, archangel or prophetic messenger, knows when it will be, the Quranic verses and hadiths being intersubstantiative and in full agreement on this. Were I to list them it would be a lengthy matter, and what I have mentioned is adequate and sufficient for whomever the divine assistance reaches (*Rudud ala abatil wa rasail al-Shaykh Muhammad al-Hamid*, 2.61-63).

As Ghazali advised those who hear about *karama,* "Think good thoughts and do not harbor doubts in your heart".[102] Haytami also warned, in a situation identical to the story of Ghazali's brother, "Bad thoughts about them (Sufis or those who have *karama*) is the death of the heart."[103]

---

102 Al-Ghazali, *al-Munqidh min al-dalal*, Damascus 1956, p. 40.
103 Al-Haytami, *Fatawa hadithiyya*, al-Halabi ed. 1970, p. 331.

APPENDIX 1: IBN QAYYIM ON VISITING AND GREETING THE DECEASED AND THEIR INTERACTION WITH THE LIVING

An imam of today's "Salafis," Ibn Qayyim, in his *Kitab al-ruh*, elaborates on the dead's knowledge of the living, interaction with them and the permissibility of visitation, greeting, and praying for the deceased.

There points to this also, what has been the usage of men, formerly, and to the present time, of addressing the dead person in his grave. If the dead person did not hear that and benefit from it, there would be no use in doing it. Imam Ahmad was asked about it. He approved it and presented arguments for it based on usage.

HADITH ON ADDRESSING THE DEAD

... al-Tabarani related in his *Mujam* from a tradition of Abu Umama who said that the Messenger of Allah said, "'When one of you dies, and you smooth the earth over him, then let one of you stand at the head of his grave and say, 'O so and so, son of so and so (feminine),' twice for he sits up completely. Then let him say, 'O so and so, son of so an so (feminine),' for he is saying, 'Guide us aright, O you upon whom may Allah have mercy!' but you do not hear. Then say, 'Mention that which you held to when you left the world as a witness. There is no god but Allah, and Muhammad is the Messenger of Allah and that you accept Allah as your Lord, Islam as your religion, Muhammad as your Prophet and the Quran as your guide.' Then verily Munkar and Nakir will retreat and say, "That which causes us to sit with this one departed with us' because he has given an argument, and Allah is his Advocate without them.' A man asked, "O Messenger of Allah, but what if he does not know the name of the deceased's mother?" The Prophet said, "Let him relate him to his mother, Eve."

Although this tradition has not been established,

the continuity of its practice in other countries and
ages without objection is sufficient warrant for its
practice because Allah has never caused a custom to
persist, so that a people who encompass the eastern
and western parts of the earth, and who are the most
perfect of peoples in intelligence, and the most comprehensive of them in sciences, should agree to
address one who neither hears nor reasons, and
approve of that, without some mistrustful one of that
people disapproving of it. But, the first generations
established it for the last, and the last imitates the
first therein. So, were it not that the one addressed
hears, would that not have the status of address to
earth and wood and stone and the non-existent? And
although one alone might approve this, the learned
would be unanimously for its abhorrence and condemnation.

Abu Dawud related an *isnad* in his *Sunan* to
which there is no objection, that the Prophet attended
the funeral of a man and when the man was buried
the Prophet said, "Ask confirmation for your brother;
for he is now being questioned." So the Prophet
informed them that the man in the grave was being
questioned. Since he was being asked, then he could
hear the address. It is valid on the Prophet's authority that the dead person hears the beating of their san-
dals when they turn to leave.

INTERACTION BETWEEN THE
LIVING AND THE DEAD

Abd al-Haqq related on the authority of one of the
awliya (saints, friends of Allah) that a brother of one
of the saints died and he saw him in his sleep. The
saint asked, "O my brother, what was your state when
you were placed in your grave?" The saint's dead
brother said, "Someone kept coming to me with a
bright flame of fire. If it had not been that a petition-
er prayed for me I would have perished in the fire."

Shabib ibn Shayban said that his mother, on her
death bed, asked him, "O my son, when you bury me,
stand at my grave and say, 'O mother of Shabib,
repeat, "There is no god but Allah."'" So when I buried

her, I stood at her grave and said, "O mother of Shabib, repeat, 'there is no god but Allah.'" Then I departed. When night came I saw her in a dream. She said, "O my son, I was on the point of perishing in the fire but for the expression, 'There is no god but Allah' overtaking me. So you have observed by last wish, O my son.'"

Ibn Abu al-Dunya related concerning Tamadur, daughter of Sahl, wife of Ayyub ibn Uyayna, who said "I saw Sufyan ibn Uyayna in a dream and he said, 'May Allah recompense my brother Ayyub with good on my behalf, for he visits me often, and he was with me today.' Ayyub said, 'Yes, I was present at the cemetery today, and I went to his grave.'"

And it is valid on the authority of Hammad ibn Salama on the authority of Thabit on the authority of Shahr ibn Hawshab, Sab ibn Jathama and Awf that Sab and Awf had an agreement. Awf had said to Sab, "O my brother, whoever of us dies before his companion, let him appear to the other." Sab asked, "Is that possible!" Awf said that it was. Sab died and Awf saw him in a dream. Awf asked Sab, "O my brother, is that you?" Sab said, "Yes." Awf asked, "What happened to you [in the grave]?" Sab said, "I was forgiven after misfortunes." Awf said that he saw a black shining place on his neck and asked, "O my brother, what is this?" Sab said, "Ten dinars which I asked for as an advance from so and so, the Jewish man. The ten dinars are in my horn. Give them to him. And know, O my brother, that not a single event has taken place among my people since my death, without news of it reaching me, even the fact that a she-cat of ours died a few days ago. And know that my daughter will die within six days so be kind to her.'"

When I awoke in the morning I asked myself, "Truly this was real?" I went to Sab's people and they welcomed me complaining that they had not seen me since Sab's death. I made excuses like people do. Then I looked at the horn, took it down and emptied out what was in it. I found the purse with the ten dinars in it. I sent the ten dinars to the Jewish man with a note asking if Sab owed him anything. The Jewish man replied, "Allah have mercy on Sab. He was one of the best of the Companions of the Messenger of Allah. The dinars were his." I then asked Sab's family how they were and what had happened since Sab's death. They said, "Yes, a she-cat died a few days ago." I asked, "Where is Sab's daughter?" They replied, "She is playing." Then she was brought and I felt her. She was feverish! I said, "Be kind to her." And she died within six days.

This is of the discernment of Awf who was one of the Companions when he executed the will of al-Sab ibn Jathama after Sab's death. Awf knew the soundness of what had occured because of the accompanying circumstances of which he was told, that of the dinars being ten in number and in the horn. Then he asked the Jewish man and his statement agreed with what he had seen in his dream. Awf, being convinced of the soundness of the affair, gave the Jewish man the dinars.

This discernment is becoming only to the most discerning and most learned of men, who are the Companions of the Messenger of Allah. Perhaps the majority of the later people would deny it saying, "How is it lawful for Awf to transfer the dinars from the survivors of Sab (when they belong to his orphans and his heirs), to a Jewish man because of a dream."

A similar story of the discernment by which Allah distinguished them; rather than people in general, is the story of Thabit ibn Qays ibn Shammas. Abu Umar ibn Abd al-Barr and others related it. Abu Umar said, "Abd al-Warith ibn Sufyan told us that Qasim ibn Asbagh told us that Abu al-Zanba Rawh ibn al-Faraj told us that Said ibn Ufair and Abd al-Aziz Yahya al-Madani told us that Malik ibn Anas told us on the authority of Ibn Shihab on the authority of Ismail ibn Muhammad Thabit al-Ansari on the authority of Thabit ibn Qays ibn Shammas, that the Messenger of Allah said to him, "O Thabit, are you not willing to live worthy of praise, be killed a martyr, and enter the Garden?" Malik said, "Thabit ibn Qays died a martyr on the day of the battle of al-Yamama." Abu Umar said that Hisham ibn Ammar related on the authority of Sadaqa ibn Khalid that Abd al-Rahman ibn Yazid ibn Jabir told him that Ata al-Khurasani told him that the daughter of Thabit ibn Qays ibn Shammas told him that when the verse, *"O you who believe, do not raise your voices above the voice of the Prophet'* (49:2)," was revealed, her father entered his house and shut himself in a room. The Messenger of Allah missed her father and sent to him, asking how he was. Her father said, "I am a man mighty of voice. I fear that my work is useless." The Prophet said, "You are not of them; rather, you live well and you will die well." Then Allah revealed, *"Truly Allah dislikes every proud boaster"'* (31:17). So her father shut himself in his room and began to weep. The Messenger of Allah missed him and he sent to him. Her father said to him, "O Messenger of Allah, truly I love beauty, and I love to rule over my people." The Prophet said, "You are not of them; rather, you live worthy of praise. You will die a martyr, and enter the Garden."

She said, "When the day of the battle of al-Tamama came, he went forth with Khalid ibn al-Walid against Musayliman. When they met Thabit and Salim, client of Abu Hudhayfa, said to each other that they had not strived enough when they had been with the Messenger of Allah. Then each one dug a ditch for himself, and they stood fast and fought until they were killed. That day Thabit had worn a very fine coat of mail. One of the Muslims passed by him [as he lay dead] and took the coat of mail.

When another Muslim from the army had fallen asleep, Thabit came to him in a dream and said to him, "I give you a last command. Beware lest you say, 'This is dream,' and allow it to go unanswered. When I was killed yesterday, a man passed by me and took my coat of mail. [Thabit then proceeded to give a description of the man who stole his coat of mail was]. His place is that of the farthest of men. In his tent there is a horse prancing to the limits of its tether. The man inverted a wide-mouthed water jar to conceal the coat of mail and above the jar there is a camel-saddle. So go to Khalid and command him to send for my coat of mail and take it. And when you have come to the Khalifa at Madina, that is, Abu Bakr al-Siddiq, tell him that I have such and such debts, and so and so of my slaves is freed, and so and so also.' The man went to Khalid and told him. Khalid sent for the coat of mail. He brought it and told Abu Bakr of his dream, and Abu Bakr executed his last command." He said, "We do not know anyone whose command had been carried out after his death except Thabit ibn Qays."

This ends what Abu Umar related. Khalid and Abu Bakr al-Siddiq and the latter's companions agreed to carry out this dream, to take the coat of mail from him in whose hand it was, because of this dream. This is pure jurisprudence accepted by Abu Hanifa and Ahmad and Malik.

SHARIA PROOFS ON THE ACCEPTABILITY OF SUCH ACCOUNTS

Likewise, (the school of) Abu Hanifa accepts the statement of the claimant to a wall because of the faces of the bricks being toward his side, and because of the tying places of the ropes. And Allah made a law for the punishment of the wife by the oath of the husband, although the circumstantial evidence is in her favor, for truly that is one of the clearest indications of the truthfulness of the husband. And more perspicuous than that is the capital punishment of the one condemned in a dispute by the oath of the claimants, in spite of weak external circumstantial evidence. And Allah made a law of the acceptance of the statement of the claimants for the survivors of their dead one when he dies on a journey and gives his last command to two men who are not Muslims, and the heirs perceive the faithlessness of the two witnesses.

Two of them swear by Allah and they have a right to it (the silver vessel), and their oath is preferable to the oaths of the two witnesses. Allah revealed this at the end of affairs in *Surah al-Maidah* (and nothing has abrogated it. His Companions after him acted according to it. This is proof that judgment is passed on property on the basis of weak evidence. And if bloodshed is allowable by virtue of weak evidence in the oaths, then surely that judgment should be given on the basis of weak evidence (external circumstances) in regard to the property, is preferable and more suitable. And according to this governors executed justice in recovering stolen articles from thieves; so that many a one asks help of them whom he blames for that when something belonging to him has been stolen.

And Allah related concerning the witness who witnessed between Joseph the Truthful and the wife of al-Aziz (Potiphar), that he judged on the basis of circumstantial evidence against the truthfulness of Prophet Joseph, and declared the wife a liar. Allah did not disapprove of him for that, but related it about him, confirming him (12:30).

And the Prophet told about the Prophet of Allah, Solomon son of David, "He judged between two women who claimed a child, in favor of the younger, on the basis of the circumstantial evidence which appeared to him when he said, Bring me a knife, to divide the child between you." The older one said, "Yes, I am satisfied with that" because of the comfort in the loss of the son of her companion. But the other said, "Don't do it, he is her son." Soloman awarded him to the latter because of the pity and the mercy which arose in her heart, so that she generously bestowed him on the other that he might remain alive, and she might see him. This is one of the best and most equitable of judgments.

The law of Islam confirms what is similar to this, and testifies to its soundness. And behold judgment by means of physiognomy and the deduction of relationship by means of it, because of its reliance upon the circumstances of resemblance, despite their ambiguity and the concealment of them generally. The point is that the circumstances which arose in the dream of Awf ibn Malik and the story of Thabit ibn Qays, do not fall far short of these circumstances. Rather, they are stronger than simply the faces of the bricks, the tying places of the ropes, and the validity of the one claimant's right to the goods, rather than the other's, in the problem of the couple and the two workmen. This is clear, without doubt, and the inherent nature of people and their powers of reason testify to its soundness, and with Allah is help.

The intention is to answer the questioner. And truly when the dead one knows something like these particulars and their minutiae, then his knowledge of the living one's visiting him, and his greeting him and his prayer for him, is more fitting and reasonable.

GLOSSARY

ahkam: legal rulings.

ahl al-bida wa al-ahwa: the People of Unwarranted Innovations and Idle Desires.

ahl al-sunna wa al-jamaa: the Sunnis; the People of the Way of the Prophet and the Congregation of Muslims.[1]

*aqid*a pl. *aqad*: doctrine.

azaim: strict applications of the law. These are the modes of conduct signifying scrupulous determination to please one's Lord according to the model of the Prophet (ﷺ).

bida: blameworthy innovation.

faqih, pl. *fuqaha*: scholar of *fiqh* or jurisprudence; generally, "person of knowledge."

faqir, pl. *fuqara*: Sufi, lit. "poor one."

fatwa, pl. *fatawa*: legal opinion.

fiqh: jurisprudence.

fitna: dissension, confusion.

hadith: saying(s) of the Prophet, and the sciences thereof.

hafiz: hadith master, the highest rank of scholarship in hadith.

haqiqi: literal.

hashwiyya: uneducated anthropomorphists.

hijri: adjective from *hijra* applying to dates in the Muslim calendar.

hukm, pl. *ahkam*: legal ruling.

ibadat: worship, acts of worship.

ihsan: perfection of belief and practice.

ijtihad: personal effort of qualified legal reasoning.

isnad: chain of transmission in a hadith or report.

istinbat: derivation (of legal rulings).

jahmi: a follower of Jahm ibn Safwan (d. 128), who said: "Allah is the wind and everything else."[2]

jihad: struggle against disbelief by hand, tongue, and heart.

kalam: theology.

khalaf: "Followers," general name for all Muslims who lived after the first three centuries.

khawarij: "Outsiders," a sect who considered all Muslims who did not follow them, disbelievers. The Prophet said about them as related by Bukhari: "They will transfer the Quranic verses meant to refer to disbelievers and make them refer to believers." Ibn Abidin applied the name of khawarij to the Wahhabi movement.[3]

madhhab, pl. *madhahib*: a legal method or school of law in Islam. The major schools of law include the Hanafi, Maliki, Shafii, and Hanbali and Jafari.

majazi: figurative.

manhaj, *minhaj*: Way, or doctrinal and juridical method.

muamalat (pl.): plural name embracing all affairs between human beings as opposed to acts of worship *(ibadat)*.

muattila: those who commit *tatil*, i.e. divesting Allah of His attrib-

---

1 See the section entitled "Apostasies and Heresies" in our *Doctrine of Ahl al-Sunna Versus the "Salafi" Movement* p. 60-64.

2 See Bukhari, *Khalq af al al-ibad*, first chapter; Ibn Hajar, *Fath al-bari*, *Tawhid*, first chapter; and al-Baghdadi, *al-Farq bayn al-firaq*, chapter on the Jahmiyya.

3 al-Sayyid Muhammad Amin Ibn Abidin al-Hanafi, *Radd al-muhtar ala al-durr al-mukhtar*, *Kitab al-Iman*, *Bab al-bughat* [Answer to the Perplexed: A Commentary on "The Chosen Pearl," Book of Belief, Chapter on Rebels] (Cairo: Dar al-Tibaa al-Misriyya, 1272/1856) 3:309.

utes.

muhaddith: hadith scholar.

muhkamat: texts conveying firm and unequivocal meaning.

mujahid, pl. *mujahidin*: one who wages *jihad*.

mujassima (pl.): those who commit *tajsim*, attributing a body to Allah.

mujtahid: one who practices *ijtihad* or personal effort of qualified legal reasoning.

munafiq: a dissimulator of his disbelief.

mushabbiha (pl.): those who commit *tashbih*, likening Allah to creation.

mushrik, pl. *mushrikun*: one who associate partners to Allah.

mutakallim, pl. *mutakallimun*: expert in *kalam*.

mutashabihat (pl.): texts which admit of some uncertainty with regard to their interpretation.

mutazila: rationalist heresy of the third century.

sahih: sound (applied to the chain of transmission of a hadith).

salaf: the Predecessors, i.e. Muslims of the first three centuries.

salafi: what pertains to the "Salafi" movement, a modern heresy that rejects the principles of mainstream Islam

shafaa: intercession.

sharia: name embracing the principles and application of Islamic law.

suluk: rule of conduct, personal ethics.

tawil: figurative interpretation.

tafwid: committing the meaning to Allah.

tajsim: attributing a body to Allah

tajwid: Quran reading.

takyif: attributing modality to Allah's attributes.

tamthil: giving an example for Allah.

taqlid: following qualified legal reasoning.

tariqa: path, specifically the Sufi path.

tasawwuf: collective name for the schools and sciences of purification of the self.

tashbih: likening Allah to His Creation.

tatil: divesting Allah from His attributes.

tawassul: seeking a means.

tawhid: Islamic doctrine of monotheism.

tazkiyat al-nafs: purification of the self.

usul: principles.

wasila: means.

BIBLIOGRAPHY

Abbas, Abul, and Abul Qasim al-Azafi, *Kitab al-durr al-munazzam.*

Abidin, Ibn, *Hashiyat al-durr al-mukhtar.*

Abidin, Ibn, *Radd al-muhtar* (Kuitah, Pakistan ed.).

Adi, Ibn, *al-Kamil fi al-duafa.*

Ahmad, *Kitab al-zuhd.*

Ahmad, *Musnad.*

Albani, *Daif al-adab al-mufrad.*

Albani, *Silsilat al-ahadith al-sahiha.*

Amruni, Abd al-Hayy al- and Abd al-Karim Murad, *Hawla kitab al-hiwar ma al-Maliki.*

Ansari, Al-Harawi al-, *Ilal al-maqamat.*

Ansari, Al-Harawi al-, *Manazil al-sairin*, Station 96.

Arabi, Ibn al-, *Aridat al-ahwadhi.*

Arabi, Muhammad Nawawi ibn Umar ibn, *Fath al-samad al-alim ala Mawlid al-Shaykh ibn al-Qasim / al-Bulugh al-fawzi li-bayan alfaz Mawlid Ibn al-Jawzi* (Cairo: Tubia bi nafaqat Fada Muhammad al-Kashmiri al-Kutubi, 1328/1910).

Asakir, Ibn , *Tarikh Dimashq.*

Asakir, Ibn, *Mukhtasar Tarikh Dimashq.*

Asakir, Ibn, *Tanzih al-Sharia.*

Asbahani, Al-hafiz Abu Nuaym al-, *al-Targhib.*

Asbahani, Al-hafiz Abu Nuaym al-, *Hilyat al-awliya.*

Askari, al-, *al-Amthal.*

Asqalani, Ibn Hajar al-, *al-Durar al-kamina fi ayn al-Miat al-thamina.*

Asqalani, Ibn Hajar al-, *al-Matalib al-aliya* (Kuwait, 1393/1973).

Asqalani, Ibn Hajar al-, *Fath al-bari sharh sahih al-Bukhari.*

Asram, Ibn, *Kitab al-istiqama.*

Athir, Ibn al-, *Usud al-ghaba.*

Azafi, Abul Abbas al- and Abul Qasim al-Azafi, *Kitab ad-durr al-munazzam.* (unpublished).

Azraqi, Al-, *Akhbar Makka.*

Baghawi, *Sharh al-sunna.*

Baghdadi, *al-Farq bayn al-firaq.*

Battuta, Ibn, *Rihla.*

Baydawi, *Anwar al-tanzil* in *Majma al-tafasir.*

Bayhaqi, al-, *Hayat al-anbiya fi quburihim.*

Bayhaqi, *Dalail al-nubuwwa.*

Bayhaqi, *Hayat al-anbiya* and *Shuab al-iman.*

Bayhaqi, *Manaqib al-Shafii.*

Bayhaqi, *Shuab al-iman.*

Bayhaqi, *Sunan al-kubra.*

Bazzar, al-, *Musnad.*

Bewley, Aisha Bint Abdurrahman, trans. *Muhammad Messenger of Allah: ash-Shifa of Qadi Iyad*, 2nd ed. (Granada: Madinah Press, 1992).

Biqai, al-, *Unwan al-zaman.*

Bukhari, *Adab al-mufrad*. 1990 Abd al-Baqi Beirut edition.
Bukhari, *Khalq afal al-ibad*.
Bukhari, *Sahih*.
Dahlan, Ahmad ibn Zayni, *al-Sira al-nabawiyya wa al-athar al-muham-madiyya*.
Daraqutni, *Sunan*.
Darimi, *Musnad*.
Dawud, Abu, *Sunan*.
Daylami, *al-Firdaws*.
Dhahabi, *Mujam al-shuyukh*.
Dhahabi, *Siyar alam al-nubala*, ed. Shuayb Arnaut (Beirut: Muassasat al-Risalah, 1981).
Dimashqi, Hafiz Shamsuddin Muhammad ibn Nasir al-Din al-, *Mawrid al-sadi fi mawlid al-hadi*.
Diyarbakri, al-, *Tarikh al-Khamis*.
Dunya, Ibn Abi al-, *Kitab al-ikhwan*.
Fasi, al-, *Shifa al-gharam*.
Ghazali, *al-Munqidh min al-dalal*, Damascus 1956.
Ghazali, *Ihya ulum al-din*.
Guillaume, A. trans., *The Life of Muhammad: A Translation of Ishaqs Sirat Rasul Allah*.
Habib, Sadi Abu, *Mawsuat al-ijma fi al-fiqh al-islami*.
Hajar, Ibn, *al-Isaba fi tamyiz al-Sahaba*.
Hajar, Ibn, *Fath al-Bari* (Beirut: Dar al-kutub al-ilmiyya, 1410/1989).
Hajar, Ibn, *Fath al-Bari* (Cairo: al-Halabi, 1378 /1959).
Hajj, Ibn al-, *Kitab al-madkhal*.
Hakim, *Marifat ulum al-hadith*.
Hakim, *Mustadrak*.
Hanafi, al-Sayyid Muhammad Amin Ibn Abidin al-, *Radd al-muhtar ala al-durr al-mukhtar, Kitab al-Iman, Bab al-bughat*. (Cairo: Dar al-Tibaa al-Misriyya, 1272/1856).
Hanafi, Al-Tahanawi al-, *Kashshaf istilahat al-funun* (Beirut, 1966).
Hanafi, Al-Turkumani al-, *Kitab al-luma fi al-hawadith wa al-bida* (Stuttgart, 1986).
Hanafi, Ibn Zahira al-, *al-Jami al-latif fi fasl Makka wa ahliha*.
Hanbali, Al-hafiz Ibn Rajab al-, *Jami al-ulum wa al-hikam*.
Hanifa, Abu, *al-Fiqh al-akbar*.
Hasani, Shaykh Muhammad ibn Alawi al-Maliki al-, *Mafahim yajib an tusahhah*. Dubai: Hashr ibn Ahmad Dalmook, 4th ed. 1407/1986.
Hawwa, Said, *al-Sira bi lughati al-shir wa al-hubb*.
Haytami, *al-Jawhar al-munazzam*.
Haytami, Ibn Hajar al-, *Fatawa hadithiyya* (Cairo: Halabi, 1390/1970).
Haytami, Ibn Hajar al-, *Kitab al-mawlid al-sharif al-muazzam*.
Haytami, Ibn Hajar al-, *Mawlid al-Nabi* (Damascus, 1900).
Haythami, Ibn Hajar al-, *al-Jawhar al-munazzam*.
Haythami, Ibn Hajar al-, *Majma al-zawaid*.
Hibban, Ibn, *Sahih*.
Hisham, Ibn, *Sira* (Beirut, dar al-wifaq ed.).

Hisham, Ibn, *Sirat Rasul Allah*. trans. A. Guillaume. 9th printing (Karachi: Oxford U. Press, 1990).

Humayri, Shaykh Issa ibn Abd Allah ibn Mani al-, *Al-ilam bi istihbab shadd al-rihal li ziyarati qabr Khayr al-anam alayhi al-salat was-salam.*

Iyad, Qadi, *al-Shifa fi marifat huquq al-mustafa*, ed. al-Bajawi.

Iyad, Qadi, *al-Shifa fi marifat huquq al-mustafa*. Trans. Aisha Bewley, Madinah Press.

Iyad, Qadi, *al-Shifa*.

Jamaa, Ibn, *Hidayat al-salik.*

Jawzi, Abu al-Faraj Ibn al-, *Mawlid al-Arus* (Cairo, 1850).

Jawzi, Ibn al-, *al-Wafa.*

Jawzi, Ibn al-, *Mawlid al-arus*. (Damascus: maktabat al-hadara, 1955).

Jawzi, Ibn al-, *Muthir al-azm al-sakin ila ashraf al-amakin.*

Jawzi, Ibn al-, *Muthir al-gharam al-sakin ila ashraf al-amakin* (Cairo: Dar al-hadith, 1415/1995).

Jawzi, Ibn al-, *Sifat al-safwa* (Beirut: Dar al-kutub al-ilmiyya, 1409/1989).

Jaziri, Abd al-Rahman al-, *al-Fiqh ala al-Madhahib al-arbaa.*

Jilani, *al-Ghunya*, ed. Farj Tawfiq al-Walid (Baghdad: *maktabat al-sharq al-jadida*, n.d.).

Jilani, Abd al-Qadir al-, *Futuh al-ghayb.*

Jubayr, Ibn, *Kitab al-rihal.*

Jubayr, Ibn, *Ribal.*

Jurjani, Al-Sharif al-, *Kitab al-tarifat.*

Kathir, Ibn, *al-Bidaya wa al-nihaya* (Beirut and Riyad: Maktabat al-maarif & Maktabat al-Nasr, 1966).

Kathir, Ibn, *Mawlid al-Nabi.*

Kathir, Ibn, *Mawlid Rasulillah sallallahu alayhi wa sallam*. Salah al-Din al-Munajjad (Beirut: Dar al-Kitab al-Jadid, 1961).

Kathir, Ibn, *Sirat al-Nabi.*

Kathir, Ibn, *Tafsir.*

Khatib, Abu al-Abbas Ahmad ibn al-, *Wasilat al-islam bi al-nabi alayhi al-salat wa al-salam*. (Beirut: Dar al-gharb al-islami, 1404/1984).

Khuzayma, Ibn, *Sahih.*

Lucknawi, Abu al-Hasanat al-, *Zafr al-amani sharh mukhtasar al-sayyid al-sharif al-Jurjani fi mustalah al-hadith* edited by Abd al-Fattah Abu Ghudda (Aleppo and Beirut: maktab al-matbuat al-islamiyya, 3rd ed. 1416).

Majah, Ibn, *Iqamat al-salat wa al-sunnat.*

Majah, Ibn, *Sunan.*

Malik, *Kitab al-ruh.*

Maliki, Al-hafiz al-Turtushi al-, *Kitab al-hawadith wa al-bida.*

Maliki, Ibn al-Hajj al-Abdari al-, *Madkhal al-shar al-sharif* (Cairo, 1336 H).

Maliki, Shaykh Muhammad ibn Alawi al-, *al-Bayan wa al-tarif fi dhikra al-mawlid al-sharif.*

Maliki, Shaykh Muhammad ibn Alawi al-, *Mafahim yajib an tusahhah.*

Maliki, Shaykh Muhammad ibn Alawi al-, *Shifa al-fuad bi ziyarati khayr al-ibad.*

Mindah, Ibn, *Marifat al-Sahaba.*

Misri, al-, *The Reliance of the Traveller*, trans. Noah Ha Mim Keller.

Mubarak, Ibn al-, *Kitab al-zuhd.*

Mundhiri, *al-Targhib wa al-tarhib.*

Mundhiri, *Talkhis al-habir.*

Muslim, *Sahih.*

Nabahani, *Jami karamat al-awliya.*

Nahrawali, al-, *al-Ilam bi-alam bayt Allah al-haram.*

Najjar, Ibn al-, *Akhbar al-Madina.*

Najjar, Ibn al-, *al-durra al-thamina fi akhbar al-madina.*

Naqqash, al-, *Shifa al-gharam.*

Nasafi, *Madarik al-tanzil.*

Nasai, *Amal al-yawm wa al-laylat.*

Nawawi, *Adhkar.* 1970 Riyadh edition.

Nawawi, *Adhkar.* 1988 Taif edition.

Nawawi, *Adhkar.* 1992 Mecca edition.

Nawawi, *al-Idah fi Manasik al-hajj* (Damascus: *dar ibn Khaldun*, n.d.)

Nawawi, al-Majmu.

Nawawi, *al-Rawda.*

Nawawi, *al-Taqrib wa al-taysir.*

Nawawi, *al-Tarkhis fi al-ikram bi al-qiyam li dhawi al-fadl wa al- maziyya min ahl al-islam ala jihat al-birr wa al-tawqir wa al-ihtiram la ala jihat al-riya wa al-izam.* ed. Kilani Muhammad Khalifa (Beirut: Dar al-Bashair al-islamiyya, 1409/1988).

Nawawi, *Idah fi Manasik al-hajj.*

Nawawi, *Kitab al-Adhkar* (Beirut: al-Thaqafiyya).

Nawawi, *Kitab al-Adhkar*, ed. Abd al-Qadir al-Arnaut. *Dar al-Huda, Riyadh*, 1409/1989.

Nawawi, *Sharh Sahih Muslim* (Khalil al-Mays ed., Beirut: Dar al-Qalam).

Nawawi, *Tahdhib al-asma wa al-lughat* (Cairo: Idarat al-Tibaah al-Muniriyah, 1927),

Nisaburi, Abu Sad al-, *Sharaf al-mustafa*

Nisai, *Sunan.*

Nuaym, Abu, *Akhbar Asbahan.*

Nuaym, Abu, *al-Targhib.*

Nuaym, Abu, *al-Tibb al-nabawi.*

Nuaym, Abu, *Hilyat al-awliya.*

Nuaym, Abu, *Marifat al-Sahaba.*

Qari, Ali al-, *al-Asrar al-marfua.*

Qari, Ali al-, *Jam al-wasail fi sharh al-shamail.*

Qari, Ali al-, *Sharh al-shifa* (Beirut: Dar al-kutub al-ilmiyya ed. 2:149).

Qastallani, al-, *al-Mawahib al-laduniyya bi al-minah al-muhammadiyya.*

Qayyim, Ibn al-, *Kitab al-ruh.*

Qayyim, Ibn, *Madarij al-salikin.*

Qudama, Ibn, *al-Riqqa.*

Qunfudh, Ibn, *Wasilat al-islam bi al-nabi alayhi al-salat wa al-salam* (Beirut: Dar al-gharb al-islami, 1404/1984).

Qushayri, al-, *al-Risala.* Translated by Rabia Harris. *Sufi Book of Spiritual Ascent* (Chicago: KAZI Publications, 1997).

Qushayri, *Risala* (Cairo, 1319 ed.).

Razi, Tammam al-, *al-Fawaid.*

Rifai, al-Sayyid Hashim al-, *Adilla Ahl al-sunna wa al-Jamaa.*

Sad, Ibn, *Tabaqat.*

Sakhawi, Shams al-Din al-, *al-Jawahir wa al-durar fi tarjamat shaykh al-islam Ibn Hajar.*

Sakhawi, Shams al-Din al-, *al-Qawl al-badi fi al-salat ala al-habib al-shafi* (Beirut 1987/1407).

Sakhawi, Shams al-Din al-, *Maqasid al-hasana.*

Sakhawi, *Tarjimat shaykh al-islam qutb al-awliya Abi Zakariyya al-Nawawi.*

Samhudi, *Khulasat al-wafa.*

Samhudi, *Saadat al-darayn.*

Samhudi, *Wafa al-wafa.*

Saqqaf, Shaykh Hassan ibn -Ali al-,*al-Ighatha bi adillat al-istighatha,* (Maktabat al-Imam Nawawi, Amman 1410/1990).

Shakir, Ahmad Muhammad, *Riyadh*. (1949 edition).

Shama, Al-hafiz Abu, *al-Baith ala inkar al-bida wa al-hawadith,* ed. Mashhur Hasan Salman (Riyadh: Dar al-Raya, 1990/1410). Cairo edition.

Sharani, *al-Tabaqat al-kubra* (1343/1925).

Sharawi, Imam Mutawalli, *Maidat al-fikr al-islamiyya.*

Shatibi, al-, *Kitab al-itisam* (Beirut ed.).

Shawkani, *al-Badr at-tali.*

Shawkani, *Nayl al-awtar,* Dar al-kutub al-ilmiyya.

Shawkani, *Tuhfat al-dhakirin.* 1970 Beirut: Dar al-kutub al-ilmiyya.

Shayba, Ibn Abi, *Musannaf.*

Shaykh, Abu al-, *Kitab al-Salat ala al-nabi.*

Siraj, al-, *al-Luma.*

Subki, *Shifa al-siqam.*

Suyuti, *al-Khabar al-dall ala wujud al-qutb wa al-awtad wa al-nujaba wa al-Abdal.*

Suyuti, *al-Khasais al-kubra.*

Suyuti, *al-Laali al-masnua.*

Suyuti, *Anba al-adhkiya bi hayat al-anbiya.*

Suyuti, *Hawi li al-fatawi.*

Suyuti, *Husn al-maqsid fi amal al-mawlid* in *al-Hawi li al-fatawi.*

Suyuti, *Jami al-saghir.*

Suyuti, *Manahil al-safa fi takhrij ahadith al-shifa* (Beirut 1988/1408).

Suyuti, *Tabyid al-sahifa.*

Suyuti, *Tadhkirat al-mawduat.*

Suyuti, *Tafsir al-Durr al-manthur*

Tabarani, *al-Awsat.*

Tabarani, *al-Mujam al-kabir.*

Tabari, Ibn Jarir al-, *Tafsir.*

Taftazani, al-, *Madkhal ila al-tasawwuf.*

Tahanawi, *Inja al-watan.*

Tahawi, *Mushkil al-athar.*

Taymiyya, Ibn, *al-Aqida al-wasitiyya* (Cairo: al-matbaa al-salafiyya, 1346).

Taymiyya, Ibn, *al-Furqan bayna awliya al-shaytan wa awliya al-rahman*, 2nd ed. (Beirut: al-maktab al-islami, 1390/1970).

Taymiyya, Ibn, *al-Ziyara.*

Taymiyya, Ibn, *Fatawa.*

Taymiyya, Ibn, *Iqtida al-sirat al-mustaqim.*

Taymiyya, Ibn, *Majma Fatawa Ibn Taymiyya.* King Khalid ibn Abd al-Aziz edition.

Taymiyya, Ibn, *Majmua al-fatawa al-kubra* (1398 ed.).

Taymiyya, Ibn, *Mukhtasar al-Fatawa al-Misriyya* (al-Madani Publishing House, 1400/1980).

Taymiyya, Ibn. *Dar taarud al-aql wa al-naql*, ed. Muhammad al-Sayyid Julaynid (Cairo: Muassasat al-ahram, 1409/1988).

Tirmidhi, Shaykh al-Hakim al-, *Adab al-muridin.*

Tirmidhi, Shaykh al-Hakim al-,*Aridat al-ahwadhi.*

Uwayda, Salah Muhammad ed., Nawawis *al-Taqrib wa al-taysir* (Beirut: dar al-kutub al-ilmiyya, 1407/1987).

Wahhab, Muhammad Ibn Abd al-, *al-Usul al-thalatha.*

Wahhab, Muhammad ibn Abd al-, *Three Principles of Oneness.*

Wansharisi, Al-, *al-Mustahsan min al-bida.*

Yala, Abu, *Musnad* (Dar al-Mamun ed. 1407/1987).

Zabidi, al-, *Ithaf al-sada al-muttaqin.*

Zahawi, Al-, *The Doctrine of Ahl al-sunna*, trans. Sh. Hisham Kabbani (Mountain View: ASFA, 1996).

INDEX TO QURANIC VERSES

Allah and His angels are praying on the Prophet, 2

Allah and His angels send blessings on the Prophet, 52

Allah has knowledge of the Hour, 108

Allah is enough for you against them, 119

And they say We will not put faith in thee till thou cause a spring to gush forth, 129

And We granted you knowledge of what you knew not, 108, 128

Be aware of Allah, and Allah Himself will teach you, 137

Destroying all things by commandment of its Lord, 22

He is not stingy of (his knowledge of) the Unseen, 115

He will find Allah forgiving, merciful, 145

His sight swerved not, nor swept astray, 115

If they had only, when they were unjust to themselves, 80, 85, 91

If they had only, when they were unjust to themselves, 80, 85, 91

If We had made him an angel, We would have made him a man, 130

Lo! Verily the friends of Allah are those on whom fear comes not, 132

Muhammad is only a Messenger, 130

No one in the heavens or earth knows the unseen except Allah, 147

Of the favor and mercy of Allah let them rejoice, 4

On that day tidings will be darkened for them, 110

On the day when it will (all) be heated in the Fire, 123

One of Our slaves, unto whom We had given mercy from Us, 134

Say to them If you love Allah, follow (and love and honor) me, 2

Say. . . Allah has already informed us of the true state of matters concerning you, 108

Therein lie portents for those who read the signs, 139

They prefer others above themselves though poverty become their lot, 40

They would have found Allah forgiving, merciful, 145

They [the devils] are prevented from hearing, 150

Those who remember Allah standing, and sitting, and on their sides, 31

Those who strive hard in Us, We shall most surely guide them in Our ways, 137

We did not send you except as a mercy to human beings, 4

We only sent Messengers before that ate food and walked in the markets, 130

Whoso obey Allah and the Messenger, 132

[[He is] the Knower of the Unseen, and discloses not His Unseen to anyone, 147, 149

HADITH INDEX

A city will be built between the Tigris and Dujayl and Qutrubull and al-Sara, 125

A group of my Community will remain constant to the truth, 118

A time is only followed by one worse than it, 121

A time will come when any of you will long to see me, 31

Adam and whoever is descended from him are under my flag on the day of Judgment, 3

Allah curses women who visit graves, 69

Allah has angels that roam the earth bringing me the greetings of my nation, 84

Allah has defended the earth from consuming the bodies of Prophets, 43

Allah has engraved truth on the tongue of Umar and his heart, 136

Allah has servants who know (the truth about people) through reading the signs, 139

Allah has taught modesty to His Prophet Muhammad, 130

Allah knows that my heart loves you / that in truth I love you, 47

And the Prophet of Allah is alive and provided for, 43

And, by Allah there is none among you except he has lusted for something, 125

Anyone who visits my grave, 69

As I was sitting by the grave of the prophet, 91

Ask his wife about him, I saw the angels washing him, 120

Be firm. On you is a Prophet , a true man, and a martyr, 125

Be quiet by Allah! If he does not have someone to inform him, 126

Between my grave and my pulpit lies a grove from the groves of Paradise , ,, 72

Beware the vision of the believer, for he sees with the light of Allah, 138

By Him in Whose hand my life is, I will proclaim my conversion loudly, 124

By Him in Whose Hand my life is, Paradise and Hell were displayed before me, 114

By the one in Whose hand is Abu al-Qasim's soul, 52

By this I shall know where the grave of my brother Uthman is, 65

Conquer what comes within your sight, 113

Decorate the Quran with your voices, 8

Did you see this, O Salman?, 112

Do not do as the Persians do with their great ones, 39

Do not get up in the manner of the foreigners who aggrandize each other, 39-40

Do not make (the visit to) my grave an anniversary festival, 67

Do not make my grave a place to gather as for visitation, 66

Do not make my grave an *id*, 66-67

Do not make your houses graves,

67

Do not praise me in the fashion that the Christians praised Jesus son of Mary, 35

Do not visit the graves of the disbelievers except weeping profusely, 66

Do you know where you prayed, 10

Do you love me?, 47

Every innovation is a misguidance, 21

Fulfill your oath, 9

Go and make ablution, 51

Go back to your people and inform them (about it) till you receive my order, 124

Has the man not known his dwelling place yet?, 124

He is of those who are spoken to, 148

He who performs pilgrimage then visits my grave after my death, 83

He who perseveres through the difficulties and hardships of Madina, 94

He who visits me in Madina counting on his visit to me, 83

He who visits my grave becomes eligible for my intercession, 83

He will be tested together with the Muslims although he is one of the people of the fire, 119

His grave is in it, 125

How are you this morning O Haritha?, 135

How will it be when you are driven from it?, 123

How will it be when you wear the trousers of Chosroes?, 125

I adjure you by Allah, Uthman, did you hear it?, 124

I am not made the same as you but my Lord gives me food and drink, 131

I am the master of the children of Adam, 3

I am the Prophet! This is no lie. I am the son of Abd al-Muttalib!, 7

I beg you, O Allah, to let me die on Monday, 10

I have forbidden you in the past to visit graves, 61

I have received the keys of the Unseen, 109

I have received the keys to everything (unseen) except the Five, 109

I have turned myself away from this world, 135

I saw Moses standing in prayer in his grave, 43

I say, and none can find fault with me but one lost to all sense, 8

I swear on Allah Almighty, neither your ruku is hidden from me nor your sajda, 127

I was digging in one corner of the trench, 112

I was ordered to a town which will eat up towns, 76

If I had taken a close friend from my Community, 131

If I had wanted to, I would have named them for you, 121

If one of you loses something or seeks help or a helper, 146

If the masjid of Quba was at the top of the skies, 64

If there were a prophet after me verily it would be Umar, 136

If this entire mountain of gold were mine to spend and it were accepted, 124

Iraq will be conquered and people will be attracted to it, 76

Is there any business between you and him?, 62

It blows for the death of a hypocrite, 121

It is the day on which Allah drowned Pharaoh and rescued Moses, 16

Jump to it, O sons of Arfada!, 46

Know that I am a Messenger from your Lord, 62

Leave him be, for perhaps there is good in it, 123

Let no man stand from his seat for another, 40

Let the camel choose, for she has her orders, 47

Let them sing because for every nation there is a holiday, and this is our holiday, 7

Madina is a great good for them, if they but knew, 72

Madina would have been better for them, had they but known, 76

May Allah bless you, 52, 70

May Allah curse the Jews and Christians who have taken the tombs of their Prophets for mosques, 58

May Allah fight the Jews and the Christians., 78

Mounts are not to be saddled except to go to three (mosques), 63, 105

My Community will be destroyed at the hands of young men from Quraysh, 121

My eyes sleep and my heart does not sleep, 131

My intercession is assured for all who visit me, 68

My life is a great good for you, 115

My Lord came to me in the best image, 110

My *minbar* overlooks my Pool, 92, 96

No man visits the grave of his brother and sits by him, 65

No one except she and I knew where it was, 122

No one greets me except Allah has returned my soul to me so that I can return his salam, 32, 44, 68

No one leaves Madina preferring to live elsewhere, but that Allah will give it better than him, 76

No one will be patient in hunger and hardship in it (Madina) except that I will be a witness or intercede for him on the Day of Rising, 75

None of you believes until he loves me more than he loves himself, 2

Nothing remains of prophecy except the glad tidings, 134

Nothing was darkened for your Prophet except five matters, 110

O Allah! Bless them in their measure, and bless them in their sa and mudd, 75

O Messenger of Allah, has the prayer been shortened?, 36

O Messenger of Allah, where else can I sleep?, 123

O people! I am your Imam, 127

O people! Listen to this, understand it, and know it -, 132

O Prophet, I love you more than myself, 2

O so-and-so son of so-and-so, 151

O you whose voice you have made me hear!, 146

On that day Monday I was born and on that day the first message was sent to me, 3

On which day did the Prophet die?, 10

One of his limbs will precede him to the garden, 125

One prayer in this mosque of mine is better than a thousand prayers in any other, 73

Pay visits to your dead and give them your salutations, 65

Perhaps you will survive until some people profit by you and others seek to harm you, 122

Praise be to Allah who stripped Chosroes of them and put them on Suraqa, 125

Put yourself at ease, for I am not a king, 38

Recite, 7-8, 60, 70, 85, 90-91, 123

Spread your covering sheet, 135

Stand up for your master, 33

Take care of what you say: what is the reality of your belief, 135

That is the day that I was born and that is the day I received the prophecy, 3

The actions of human beings are shown to me, 115

The actions of human beings are shown to me every Thursday, 115

The best of you are my generation, then those after them, 120

The earth was collected together for me so that I was shown its Easts and Wests, 113

The first time, Allah opened Yemen, 112

The flourishing of Jerusalem will prove the ruin of Yathrib, 127

The Haram of Madina is between Ayr and Thawr, 95

The Holy Prophet could see equally well during the darkness, 127

The Hour will not come until two parties fight each other with the same claim, 126

The last of you will die in a fire, 119

The messenger of Allah commanded me that I omit no honored tomb but to level it, 58

The Messenger of Allah gave us an address, 114, 116

The night I was enraptured, 43

The one of you sitting closest to me on the Day of Rising, 125

The one who breathes from the soil of Ahmad, 85

The people eventually were all dead except for me and one other man, 122

The Prophets are alive in their graves, praying to their Lord, 43

The time is near when there will be a lot of non-Arabs among you, 120

There are angels at the entries of Madina, and neither plague nor the Dajjal will enter it, 77

There is not anything that I have not seen before, 113

There is wisdom in poetry, 6

These people have submitted to your decision, 34

They are of the strangers from this and that place, 132

They are the fewest in number, but the greatest in rank before Allah, 133

This business began as prophethood and mercy, 120

This is a believer, Allah has illumined his heart, 135

This morning I am a real believer, 135

Those who were before you used to take tombs as mosques, 58

Today you are better than you will be on that day, 117

Treat people according to their station, 34

Two religions shall not co-exist in the Arabian Peninsula., 78

Two religions shall not co-exist in the land of the Arabs, 78

Uthman will be killed while reciting the Quran, 119

Visit the graves, 59, 61-62, 65-66, 81, 94

Visit the graves for they soften the heart, 65

Visit the graves, and you will be reminded of the afterlife, 65

We are the girls of the Sons of Najjar, 47

We found his head dripping with water, 120

We have more right to Moses than you, 4

What a fine innovation this is, 21

What is between her two tracts of black stones, 95

Whatever the majority of

Muslims see as right, then this is good to Allah, 11

When the Messenger of Allah left us, 114, 117

When the Time draws near, almost no vision or dream of the believer will be false, 134

When you were born, the earth was shining, 6

Who are these?, 13

Who does not sing the Quran is not from us, 8

Whoever comes to me as a visitor driven by no other need but my visit, 104

Whoever does not visit my grave has slighted me, 71

Whoever invokes blessings on me at my grave, I hear him, 31, 45, 52

Whoever is able to die in Madina let him die there, 72

Whoever likes for men to stand up for him let him take his place in the fire, 38

Whoever sees me in vision or dream sees me truly, 134

Whoever visits me after my death, it is as if he visited me in my life, 71

Whoever visits my grave after my death it is as if he visited me in my life, 71

Whoever visits my grave, my intercession becomes guaranteed for him, 45, 86

Whoso acts upon what he knows, Allah will make him inherit a knowledge, 137

Why should I not weep seeing you die in a desert land, 123

With us, O messenger of Allah!,

47

Woe to you! He is from Ghifar,
on the trade route to Damascus,
125

Yemen will be conquered and the
people will be attracted to it, 76

You are my freedman, 48

You are part of me and I am part
of you, 48

You have a good voice, 8

You have not satisfied me as to
what I wanted, 124

You resemble me in my creation
and my manners, 48

You will send him hunting for
wild cows, 126

Your Prophet has received everything except these Five, 109

GENERAL INDEX

12th of Rabi al-Awwal, 12
Abbas, 6, 11-12, 25, 33-34,
    41, 53, 93, 111, 119, 122,
    124-125, 127, 130, 134
Abd al-Fattah Abu
    Ghudda, 100
Abd al-Haqq, 28, 45, 57,
    65, 100, 128
Abd al-Haqq al-Ishbili, 57,
    65
Abd al-Haqq ibn al-
    Kharrat al-Ishbili, 45,
    100
Abd al-Haqq Muhaddith
    Dihlawi, 28, 128
Abd al-Hayy al-Amruni,
    15
Abd al-Hayy al-Lucknawi,
    28
Abd al-Karim, 15
Abd al-Karim Jawad, 15
Abd al-Karim Murad, 15
Abd al-Muttalib, 7, 19
Abd al-Rahman, 29, 33,
    57, 75, 104, 118-119, 124
Abd al-Rahman al-Jaziri,
    57
Abd al-Rahman ibn al-
    Qasim ibn Muhammad
    ibn Abu Bakr, 33
Abd al-Rahman ibn Awf,
    124
Abd al-Rahman ibn
    Mahdi, 118
Abd al-Razzaq, 65, 135
Abd Allah, 29, 33, 40-41,
    61, 66, 72-73, 75, 77, 84,
    112, 115, 118, 123, 125
Abd Allah ibn al-Zubayr,
    33, 72-73
Abd Allah ibn Masud, 84,
    123
Abd Allah ibn Umar, 66,
    75, 125
abdal, 132, 138, 152, 154
Abdullah, 7, 49, 76, 119,
    129

Abdullah ibn al-Zubayr,
    76
Abdullah ibn Rawaha, 7
Abdullah Muhammad
    Ghimari, 129
Abidin, 20, 102, 121
Abraham, 13, 49, 62, 73,
    77, 90
absolute obligation, 69
Abu Abd al-Rahman, 75
Abu Abd Allah, 29, 40-41,
    112
Abu Abd Allah Sayyidi
    Muhammad ibn Abbad
    al-Nafzi, 29
Abu al-Darda, 114, 125
Abu al-Darda, 114, 125
Abu al-Fath ibn Abi al-
    Fawaris, 142
Abu al-Hasan al-Ashari,
    103
Abu al-Hasan al-Shadhili,
    140
Abu al-Hasanat al-
    Lucknawi, 63, 100
Abu al-Hubab Said ibn
    Yasar, 76
Abu al-Khattab, 27
Abu al-Khattab ibn Dihya,
    27
Abu al-Khayr al-Aqta, 86
Abu al-Layth al-
    Samarqandi, 57
Abu al-Qasim Ibn Asakir,
    40
Abu Ali al-Fudayl ibn
    Iyad, 93
Abu Amama, 39
Abu Amr ibn Alwan, 139
Abu Ayyub, 47
Abu Bakr, 7, 10, 19, 25,
    33, 36-37, 39-41, 49-50,
    77, 80, 82, 86, 91, 96,
    113, 126, 131, 148, 155
Abu Bakr al-Khatib al-
    Baghdadi, 41
Abu Bakr al-Sawli, 41
Abu Bakr al-Siddiq, 10,
    33, 155
Abu Bakr ibn Abi Asim,
    39-40
Abu Bakr ibn al-Arabi, 50,

148
Abu Bakra, 40
Abu Bakrah, 57
Abu Darda, 117
Abu Dawud, 9, 32, 34, 38-
    40, 43-44, 46-47, 58, 65-
    66, 68, 84, 110, 117-118,
    125, 133, 136, 141, 152
Abu Dharr, 117
Abu Ghudda, 100
Abu Hanifa, 41, 57, 103,
    135, 141
Abu Hanifa al-Numan,
    103
Abu Hazim, 85
Abu Hurayra, 31-32, 44,
    52, 64, 66, 73, 76-77, 84,
    92, 94, 96, 112-113, 119,
    121-122, 127, 135, 141,
    149
Abu Imama, 51, 139
Abu Imran al-Fasi, 69
Abu Ishaq al-Shirazi, 63
Abu Jahl, 39
Abu Lahab, 5
Abu Mansur al-Maturidi,
    103
Abu Mijlaz, 38
Abu Muhammad, 39, 41,
    138
Abu Muhammad al-
    Akfani, 41
Abu Muhammad al-
    Jurayri, 138
Abu Musa, 8, 39-42, 82
Abu Musa al-Asbahani,
    39-42
Abu Musa al-Ashari, 8, 82
Abu Musa Muhammad
    ibn Umar al-Asbahani,
    39
Abu Musab, 141
Abu Nasir, 84
Abu Nasr Bishr ibn al-
    Harith al-Hafi al-Zahid,
    39
Abu Nasr ibn al-Harith,
    39
Abu Nuaym, 20, 32, 34,
    43-44, 48, 51, 84-85, 126,
    137, 139, 141-142
Abu Qatada, 2-3

Abu Qatada al-Ansari, 2
Abu Said, 34, 120, 139
Abu Said al-Khudri, 34, 139
Abu Shama, 13-15, 17, 20-21, 25, 29
Abu Sulayman Hamd ibn Muhammad ibn Sulayman al-Khattabi, 39
Abu Taher al-Khashawi, 41
Abu Umama, 118
Abu Yala, 10, 34, 43, 52, 64, 117-118, 146
Abu Zura al-Iraqi, 30
Abul Abbas, 11-12, 25
Abul Qasim al-Azafi, 11-12, 25
acts that are subject to more than one interpretation, 59
Ad, 12, 22
adab, 6, 34-35, 38-40, 46, 53, 57, 70, 137
Adab al-mufrad, 6, 53
adab of entering the Mosque of the Prophet, 70
Adam, 3, 9, 29, 137
adhan, 26, 30, 85
Adhkar, 20, 43, 45, 53, 56, 86, 97-98
*afdal al-ibada*t, 63
ahbar, 84
Ahl al-Bayt, 119
ahl al-gharb, 118
Ahl al-Sunna, 15, 51, 143
Ahmad, 5-6, 9, 11, 15-17, 25, 32-35, 38-39, 41, 43-45, 47-48, 50, 53, 57, 60-61, 63-66, 69, 71-73, 83-85, 92, 94, 101-103, 105, 109-110, 112, 114-115, 117-118, 121, 123-125, 132-133, 136, 141-142, 147, 151, 156
Ahmad al-Gangohi, 101, 105
Ahmad ibn al-Mughlis, 39
Ahmad ibn Hajar, 16
Ahmad ibn Hanbal, 15,

34, 41, 71-73, 118
Ahmad ibn Muhammad, 102
Ahmad ibn Zayni Dahlan, 17
Ahmad Zarruq, 25
Aisha, 7, 10, 34, 46, 59, 68, 77, 82, 113, 116, 119, 131, 149
Akhnai, 62
al-Abbas, 6, 33, 41, 93, 119, 122, 124-125
al-Ahbar, 84
al-Anam, 29, 61
al-aqida, 144
al-aqida al-wasitiyya, 144
al-Ashari, 8, 82, 103, 132
al-Aswad, 57
al-Awsat, 71, 83, 104
al-Azafi, 11-12, 25
al-Azraqi, 11, 24-25
al-Baghawi, 39, 118
*al-Baith ala inkar al-bida wa al-hawadit*h, 17, 20-21, 29
al-Baji, 70
al-Baladhuri, 57
al-Baqi, 53
al-Bara ibn Azib, 111
al-Barizi, 42
al-Barzanji, 48, 102
al-Baydawi, 109
al-Bayhaqi, 20, 43, 45, 83-84, 123, 126
al-Bazzar, 10, 19, 34, 43, 72, 86, 115, 135, 139
al-Bidaya, 3, 5, 27-29, 33, 47, 112
al-Bidaya wa al-nihaya, 27-28, 33, 47
al-Dajjal, 113
al-daraja al-rafia, 79
al-Daraqutni, 45, 83, 86, 142
Al-Darimi, 84
al-Dhahabi, 27, 29, 123
al-Dhuhli, 41
al-Durar al-kamina, 16
al-Durr al-manthur, 109, 137
al-Durr al-thamin, 28
al-fadila, 79

al-Faqih Abu al-Tayyib Muhammad ibn Ibrahim al-Sabti, 29
al-fasiq, 108
al-gharb, 33, 71, 118
al-ghawth, 147
al-ghayb, 107-110, 137, 147
al-Ghazali, 63, 150
al-Ghumari, 30
al-hadith, 34, 41, 45, 67, 83, 100
al-Hajjaj, 75, 119-120
al-Hajjaj ibn Yusuf, 75, 120
al-Hakim, 34, 41, 47, 50, 65-66, 84, 102, 117, 133, 137
al-Halimi, 92
al-Hanafi, 12-13, 21, 28, 74, 103
al-Harawi al-Ansari, 145
Al-Harawi Al-Ansari on the Levels of Kashf, 145
Al-Harith ibn Hisham, 126
al-Hasan, 22, 93, 101, 103, 118, 120, 122, 140
al-Hasan ibn Ali, 120
Al-Hasan ibn Habib, 22
al-Hasan ibn Muhammad al-Zafarani, 22
al-haththth, 67
al-hawadith wa al-bida, 20-21, 25, 28
al-Hawi, 17, 20, 29
al-Hawi li al-fatawi, 17, 20
Al-Haytami, 12-13, 18, 29, 42, 94, 96, 138, 147, 150
al-Haythami, 10, 43-44, 83, 110, 112, 135, 139
al-Husayn, 32, 39, 41, 125
Al-Husayn ibn Ali al-Jawhari, 41
al-Idah, 45, 56, 86
al-Idah fi Manasik al-Hajj, 56, 86
al-Ighatha bi adillat al-istighatha, 97
al-Ihtifal bi dhikra al-mawlid, 29

al-Ilam bi alam bayt
  Allah al-haram, 13
al-ilm, 142
al-Iman, 31-32, 44-45, 50,
  52-53, 83-84, 135
al-Iraqi, 29-30, 62-63, 65,
  104
al-Islam, 33, 42, 68, 71,
  86, 91, 100, 138, 147
al-Izz ibn Abd al-Salam,
  20
al-Jami al-latif, 13, 28
al-Jawahir wa al-durar,
  33-34, 42
Al-Jazari, 29
al-jumhur, 99
al-Junayd, 139-140
al-Juwayni, 99-100
al-kafir, 108
al-kahf, 144
al-Kamil, 43, 45
al-Khasais al-kubra, 47,
  50, 84-85
al-Khatib, 33, 41, 126, 141
al-Khatib al-Baghdadi, 41,
  141
al-Khattabi, 39, 65, 96
al-Khazin, 130
al-Khidr, 134, 138
al-lafz al-raiq fi mawlid
  khayr al-khalaiq, 29
al-Layth al-Samarqandi,
  57
al-Luma, 21, 63, 138
al-Mabsut, 70
al-Madini, 41, 118
al-Madkhal, 3, 20
al-mahall al-ala, 133
al-Majmu, 56, 78
al-Mamun, 52, 102
al-Mankhul, 63
al-maqam al-mahmud, 79
al-Maturidi, 103
al-Mawahib al-laduniyya,
  29, 50, 115
al-Mawrid al-rawi, 28
al-Mawrid al-sadi fi
  mawlid al-hadi, 29
al-Mawrid ar-Rawi fi al-
  Mawlid al-Nabawi, 17
al-mikhlat, 108
al-Mughni, 45, 104

al-Mujam al-kabir, 147
al-Mukhtar ibn Ubayd,
  120
al-Mulla, 104
Al-Mundhiri, 32, 44, 83-
  84, 115
al-muslim al-sadiq al-
  salih, 108
al-mutafarrisin, 139
al-mutawassimin, 139
al-Muttalib, 7, 19, 58, 76
Al-Muwatta, 75
al-Nahrawali, 12-13
al-Nakhi, 98
al-Naqqash, 11, 24-25
al-Nasai, 61, 118
al-Nawawi, 20, 68, 86, 98,
  138
al-Nisaburi, 47
Al-Nuri, 138
Al-Qadi Iyad, 68
al-Qadi Iyad al-Maliki, 68
al-Qarawiyyin, 15
Al-Qari, 13, 28, 74-75, 78,
  98, 100, 110-111, 116,
  124, 126, 137
al-qasas, 110
al-Qasim, 29, 33, 40, 52,
  70
al-Qastallani, 115
al-Qurtubi, 42, 108
al-Qushayri, 86, 141
al-Razi, 43, 45
al-ridda, 120
al-ruya al-saliha, 134
al-Safa, 115
al-Sakhawi, 29, 42, 67,
  138-139
al-Salafiyya, 144
Al-Salamu alayka, 88, 91
Al-Samarqandi, 57
al-Sara, 125
Al-Sayyid Hashim al-
  Rifai, 15
al-Shadhakuni, 41
al-Shafii, 20, 22, 72, 86,
  97, 102, 104
al-Sharid ibn Suwayd al-
  Thaqafi, 7
al-Sharif al-Jurjani, 100,
  132
al-Shatibi, 20, 25

al-Shatti, 103
Al-Shaykh Abd Al-Qadir
  Al-Jilani Al-Hasani Al-
  Hanbali on, 79
al-Shaykh Abu
  Muhammad, 41
al-Shifa, 45, 50, 53, 68,
  71, 74-75, 78, 98, 115-
  116, 130-131
al-Shifa fi marifat huquq
  al-mustafa, 115
al-Shubi, 98
al-Siddiq, 10, 33, 100, 155
al-Siraj al-Tusi, 138
al-Subki, 42, 45, 68, 71,
  100
al-Sunan al-kubra, 71
al-Suyuti, 16, 20, 25, 30
al-Tabarani, 125, 151
al-Tabari, 12, 133, 139
al-Tahanawi al-Hanafi, 21
al-Tahawi, 61
al-Taj al-Subki, 42
al-Tali al-said, 29
al-Tamim, 23
al-Tanwir fi mawlid al-
  bashir al-nadhir, 28
al-Tarkhis fi al-ikram bi
  al-qiyam, 33, 42
al-Thawri, 124
al-Turkumani al-Hanafi,
  21
al-Turtushi, 20, 25-26, 28
al-ulama, 141
al-Utbi, 82, 91, 98
al-Walid, 25, 55, 81, 125-
  126, 155
al-Waqidi, 6
al-wasila, 79
al-Yafii, 42
Al-Zafarani, 22
al-Zahawi, 143
al-Zarqani, 30
al-Zubayr, 33, 38, 72-73,
  75-76, 119, 125
al-Zuhri, 78
ala al-dawam, 32, 44
Albani, 1, 19, 43, 45, 53,
  55
Alexandria, 25
Ali, 17, 28, 32, 34, 38, 41,
  47, 58, 71, 74, 78-79, 84,

86, 89, 93, 95, 97-98,
100-103, 110-111, 116-
120, 124-126, 133, 142
Ali al-Qari, 28, 74, 78, 98,
100, 110-111, 116, 126
Ali al-Qari al-Hanafi, 74
Ali ibn Abi Talib, 32, 58,
95, 119, 133
Ali ibn al-Madini, 41, 118
Ali ibn Umar al-
Daraqutni, 142
alim, 29
Alive, 32, 43-44, 92, 119,
157
All-Knower, 149
All-Powerful, 42
All-Saying, 47
Allah, 1-5, 7-11, 13-19, 23,
27-36, 38-41, 43-53, 56-
62, 66, 68-70, 72-73, 75-
99, 102-105, 107-120,
122-157
Allah said: Invoke bless-
ings on the Prophet, 4
Allah said: Rejoice in the
Prophet, 4
Allah's Apostle, 113, 135
Allah's friends, 132-133,
138
Allah's Messenger, 34-35,
80, 83-87, 91-96, 112,
114, 117-118, 123
Allah's will, 81, 143
Allahu akbar, 112
ambiguous, 5
Amin, 81
amir, 13, 33, 38, 110
Amir ibn Abd Allah ibn al-
Zubayr ibn al-Awamm
al-Asadi, 33
amirs, 120
Amman, 97, 115, 129
Amr, 33-34, 41, 57, 76,
126, 139-140
Amr ibn al-Abbas al-
Khazzaz, 41
Amr ibn Ali, 41
Amr ibn Maymun, 57
analogy, 14, 143
Anas, 7, 19, 35, 43, 46-47,
75-76, 83, 92, 115, 127,
137, 139, 141, 154

Anas ibn Malik, 43, 75-76,
92, 115
angel, 52, 62, 70, 83, 130,
134, 146-147
angelic attributes, 131
angelic nature of
prophets, 130
angels, 2, 5, 52, 70, 77, 82,
84, 110, 120, 129-131,
136, 138, 141, 149-150
anniversary, 17, 66-67
anniversary festival, 66-
67
anomalous, 20
Ansar, 34, 47, 121
anthropomorphic, 129
Antichrist, 120, 139
apostasy, 120
apostate, 122
aqida, 144
aqiqa, 19
aql, 20
Arabic, 22, 51, 62
*arbab al-hal wa al-
maqam*, 110
Arch-helper, 146
arfa al-taaat, 63
Aridat al-ahwadhi, 50,
148
arraf, 150
*as-salamu alayka ayyuha
al-nabi wa rahmatullah
wa*, 49
As-salamu alayka Ya
rasul Allah, 1, 49
*as-salatu khayrun min al-
nawm*, 26
asbab an-nuzul, 129
Ashari, 8, 82, 103, 132
Asharis, 145
Ashhab, 74
Ashraf, 71, 83, 101
Ashura, 4, 16, 18-19
Asif ibn Barkhya, 134
Asma bint Abu Bakr, 113
aspiration, 145
Asqalani, 13, 16, 20-21,
29, 34, 36, 42, 44, 52,
107, 109, 139
Assault on All
Innovations, 14
astrologers, 150

Aswad, 57
Ata, 154
aunt of Allah's Messenger,
93
awe, 41, 46, 88
awliya, 20, 42, 81, 107,
133, 136-138, 140, 143-
146, 148-149
ayat, 6
ayyada, 66
Ayyub, 47, 152
ayyuha al-nabi, 49
Badai al-fawaid, 78
Badr, 17, 122
Baghawi, 39, 67, 110, 118,
133
Baghdad, 81, 125, 140-141
Bakr, 7, 10, 19, 25, 33, 36-
37, 39-41, 49-50, 77, 80,
82, 86, 91, 96, 113, 115,
126, 131, 148, 155
balaghani, 46
Balqis, 133
banging the drum, 48
Banu Amir, 110
Banu Hashim, 127
Banu Najjar, 47
Banu Shayba, 12
Baqi, 53, 93
baraka, 10, 61, 81-82, 93
barr, 57, 62, 65, 154
barzakh, 46
Basra, 119, 121
battle, 7, 27, 111, 122,
126, 154-155
Battle of Ahzab, 111
Battle of Hunayn, 7
Battle of the Trench, 7
Battle of Yamama, 122
baya, 7
Bayazid al-Bistami, 137,
140
Bayhaqi, 9, 19-20, 22, 31-
32, 34, 43-45, 47, 50-53,
71-73, 83-84, 123, 126,
135, 141-142
Bayt Lahm, 10
Bazzar, 10, 19, 34, 43, 65,
72, 86, 115, 135, 139
Beauty, 81, 127, 155
Bedouin Arabs, 132
Beginning of Creation,

115

belief, 24, 107, 130, 135, 142, 144

believer, 2, 95, 113, 134-135, 138, 147-148

beloved, 3, 37, 49, 72, 89, 128

best acts of worship, 63

bestowed, 17, 46, 90, 108, 128, 157

Bestowed Knowledge, 128

Bethlehem, 10

bi al-tajalli al-suwari, 110

bi haqqihi, 80

bida, 14-15, 17, 19-21, 23, 25-26, 28-30

bida hasana, 19

bida mustahsana, 20-21, 26

bida mustaqbaha, 21

Bilal, 77

Bilqis, 23

Bin Baz, 1, 19, 99

birthplace of prophets, 10

Bismillah, 103, 112

bismillah al-rahman al-rahim, 103

blameworthy innovation, 20

blessed, 11, 15-16, 31, 55, 60, 72, 87, 104-105, 128

blessing, 10-11, 17, 25, 61, 68-69, 80, 82

boast, 109, 128, 130

Book, 2-3, 5-6, 8, 10-11, 15-17, 25, 27, 30-31, 33-34, 40-41, 45-47, 57-58, 65, 68, 71, 75, 79-80, 85, 87, 94, 97, 101, 111, 113-116, 124, 129, 133-135, 138-141

Book of *Mawlid*, 27

Book of Pilgrimage, 97

bounty, 85, 87, 92, 95, 108, 128

Bringer of glad tidings, 28

budala, 142

build the grave up slightly into a convex mound, 58

Bukhari, 2-6, 10, 16, 21, 30-31, 33-36, 42, 47, 53, 72, 82, 95, 107, 110, 113-

115, 117-118, 124, 127-128, 131, 134-136, 139, 141, 146, 149

Bukhari and Muslim, 2-3, 16, 72, 95, 114, 131, 134, 146

Burayda, 47, 61

Burayda ibn al-Hasib, 61

burial ground, 86

Byzantium, 118

Caesar, 117-118

Cairo, 20-21, 29, 42, 83, 111, 141, 144

Caliph, 13, 118, 123

caliphate, 119-120, 123, 126

calling his gracious form and qualities to mind, 48

cause, 39, 64, 81, 129

celebrate, 4, 13-14, 17-18, 24, 27, 53, 67

Certainty, 113, 150

certitude, 149

chain of transmission, 19, 84, 133, 147

chamber, 81-82

charity, 17-18, 27

Chosen One, 8

Chosroes, 117-118, 122, 125

Christians, 14, 35, 58, 67, 78

church, 59

church in Ethiopia, 59

City of the Prophet, 56, 118

coincidence, 150

collection-box, 26

coming to Your House, 81

command, 5, 79, 118, 155-156

commemorate, 17-18

commemoration, 1-2, 11, 13-16, 18-19, 21, 25, 30, 32, 53

common people, 93, 96

Community, 2, 13, 19, 24, 32, 55-56, 59, 68, 84, 89-91, 113, 117-118, 120-121, 126, 131, 136-137, 140-142, 144, 147, 149-150

Companions, 4, 6-7, 24, 30, 32-33, 35-36, 41, 43-44, 47, 70, 72, 74, 80-81, 90, 92-93, 95, 101, 104, 114, 116-117, 119, 121, 124, 126, 138, 144-145, 153-156

Companions to the Successors, 138

companionship, 37

Concerning the claim of the contemporary , 19

condemn, 13, 40, 48

condemnation, 38, 60, 152

Congregation, 32, 96

connection, 4-5, 138

consensus, 20, 23, 56, 68, 78, 99, 101, 103, 143

consensus of the scholars, 20, 143

Constantinople, 127

contentious, 108

context for revelation, 129

corruption, 97-98, 120

creation, 9, 46, 48, 59, 61, 87, 90, 101, 108, 115, 130-131

Creator, 42, 128

creed, 144

cup, 80

custom, 23, 37, 151

daif, 53

dajjal, 77, 113, 120, 139, 147

Dalail al-nubuwwa, 9, 43, 47

Damascus, 8, 18, 29, 86, 125, 150

dancing, 46, 48

Dar al-Huda, 97-98

Darimi, 43, 45, 84, 141

darkness, 127, 138

David, 157

dawn prayer, 94

Dawud, 8-9, 32, 34, 38-40, 43-44, 46-47, 58, 65-66, 68, 84, 110, 117-118, 125, 133, 136, 141, 152

Day of Judgment, 3, 83, 94, 96, 123, 132

Day of Resurrection, 59, 104, 113, 133, 144, 148

Day of Rising, 75, 125
Daylami, 83
Death, 10, 23, 33, 41, 51, 64-65, 71, 77, 79, 83, 87, 115, 121-124, 126, 131, 150, 152-155
death of the heart, 150
decoration of the Quran, 15
definitive knowledge, 43
deity, 90, 116, 147
derivation, 143
descendants of the Prophet, 12
desirable, 11, 25, 33-34, 40, 42, 68-69, 71, 79-80, 93-97
desolate, 133
destroyer, 120
deviation, 14, 62-63, 80
devoted, 68, 127, 133
Dhahabi, 8, 27, 29, 43, 45, 50, 64, 71, 83-84, 92, 123
Dharwan, 127
dhikr, 12, 15, 29, 44, 49
dhikr With the Name
Dhu al-Yadayn, 36
dignity, 32, 129
Dihya al-Kalbi, 28
disapproved, 21, 96
disbelief, 99, 129-130
disbeliever, 99, 108, 139
disclosure, 138, 145
disliked, 20, 35, 37, 39-40, 68-69, 129
disobedience, 63, 99
disordered, 39
display, 33, 42, 46
distinction, 33, 42
divine favors, 148
divine inspiration, 149-150
Divine Presence, 111, 145
Diyarbakri, 13
Doctrine, 51, 129, 143
Doctrine of Ahl al-Sunna wa al-Jamaa versus the , 62
doing-without, 24
doorkeepers of the Kabah, 12
doubt, 5, 9, 18, 35, 40, 48,

50, 74, 80, 98, 128, 149, 157
dream, 5, 86, 134-135, 138, 142, 154-155, 157
dreams, 108, 134, 142
drum, 9, 46-48
drum-playing, 9
dua, 11, 13, 25-26, 39, 44, 51, 59-60, 75, 81-82
Dubai, 60-61
Dujayl, 125
dunya, 65, 84, 115, 133, 142
dying on Monday, 3, 10
dynasty, 119
earth was rolled up, 118
eclipse, 113
efficient intermediary, 81
eight Paradises, 108
elite, 132
encouragement, 45, 67-69
endowed, 57, 105, 139
endowed with understanding, 57, 105
Enter, O Aba Amr, 140
Entering Madina the Illuminated, 79
Epidemic, 77
Epidemic of Madina, 77
Ethiopia, 59
Eve, 151
events of the Rising, 127
evil, 114, 118, 131
evil ones, 118
Exalted, 41, 46, 72, 79, 90-91, 110-111, 113, 137-139, 149
exalted station, 79, 90
exceeded proper bounds, 99-100
excellence, 33, 42, 68, 70-71, 74
excellent, 18-19, 23-24, 48, 54, 60, 68, 71, 90, 97-98, 111, 115
excellent innovation, 19
exemplar, 6
Explanation of Gilans Dua
Exposure of Deviation for the Healing of the Sick, 63
expression, 129, 152

Expulsion of the Jews from Madina, 77
extinction, 3, 111
fadila, 69, 79
fadl, 42, 105, 122
fair, 34-35, 38-39, 45, 65, 72-73, 99-100, 112, 139
Fajr, 147
false deity, 116, 147
familiarity, 17, 116, 145
family, 5, 31-32, 58, 77, 79, 89-90, 101, 117, 120, 133
faqih, 29, 42, 69, 102
farahan, 46
fard, 69
farrata, 99
Farthest Mosque, 64
Fasi, 69
fasiq, 108
fast, 3-4, 16, 66, 95, 155
fasting, 3-4, 16-18, 24
Fatawa, 14-16, 28-29, 42, 57, 138, 141, 145, 148-150
Fatawa Abd al-Hayy, 28
Fatawa hadithiyya, 29, 42, 138, 150
Fatawa mazhari, 28
Fath al-bari, 7, 10, 20-21, 31, 33, 42, 45, 52, 56, 64-65, 99, 108-109, 115, 123, 136
Fatima, 84, 120
Fatimi regime in Egypt, 25
fatwa, 9, 15, 20, 101, 103, 132, 138, 147
favor, 3-6, 18, 128, 132, 138, 143, 156-157
Fawaid, 43, 78, 137
Fayruz, 122
Fayruzabadi, 119
fear, 23, 37-38, 76, 132-133, 137, 154
festival, 66-67
figurative interpretation, 111
figurative interpretation, 111
fikr, 109
Final Hour, 150

fiqh, 24, 41, 56-57, 78, 135, 139, 141
firasa, 138-139, 145
firasa sadiqa, 145
fire, 3, 38, 73, 119-121, 123, 127, 135, 152
fitna, 114, 117, 147
Five, 20-21, 42, 86, 101, 109-110
five things, 109
flute, 8
followers, 1, 16, 103, 144-145
foot, 13, 87, 123
for his sake, 62, 80
forbidden, 8-9, 13, 20, 34, 53, 59-61, 63, 95, 101
foremost, 4, 19, 133
forgive, 14, 80
Forgiving, 145
form, 3, 48, 57, 67, 93, 110-111, 130-132, 134, 142
formal manifestation, 111
fortune-tellers, 150
fragrant herbs, 77
free of any possibility of alteration or evil, 131
Friday, 9, 12, 26, 32, 93, 115, 148
Friend of the Merciful, 96, 131
friends, 37, 81, 111, 119, 132-133, 138, 141, 146, 148-149
friends of Allah, 81, 132, 146, 148-149
frown, 48
fudala, 12
fulfilled, 59, 90, 134
fundamentalists, 129
funeral prayer, 125
funerals, 10
fuqaha, 12, 105
Futuh, 137, 140
Fuyud al-haramayn, 28
Gabriel, 10, 70, 125, 134
Gangohi, 101, 105
Garden, 119, 125, 127, 129, 135, 154-155
Garden of Paradise, 135
gathering, 5, 18, 22, 66-

67, 123, 127
gatherings, 49
generosity, 130
ghawth, 146-147
ghayr mashru, 99
Ghazali, 42, 60-61, 63, 65, 150
Ghumari, 30
ghusl, 87, 120
gifted, 22, 107, 126
giving, 3, 17-18, 37, 40, 125, 146-148
glad tidings, 28, 82, 86, 89, 92, 134, 138
Glorified, 79, 113, 129
Glorious, 28, 110, 149-150
goal, 90, 101, 111
God, 124-125, 129, 151-152
Godwariness, 41
good, 3, 6, 8-9, 11, 14-15, 18-22, 25-27, 31, 45-46, 52-53, 64-65, 71-72, 80-82, 92-93, 109, 114-115, 118, 123, 125, 127-128, 134, 142, 146, 150, 152
good innovation, 21
good vision or dream, 134
grace, 103, 128
grave, 5, 27, 31, 43-45, 50-52, 55-72, 74-75, 78-88, 91-93, 95-97, 99-100, 104-105, 115, 120, 125, 151-152
grave, 5, 27, 31, 43-45, 50-52, 55-72, 74-75, 78-88, 91-93, 95-97, 99-100, 104-105, 115, 120, 125, 151-152
graves as directions for their prayers, 59
graves for mosques, 59
Great Apostasy, 120
great benefit, 69
greatest imam, 103
Greatness, 9, 56, 87
Greetings to you, 71, 91
guards, 149
Habib Allah, 28, 49, 88
hadith, 2-5, 9-10, 13, 16, 18-19, 21, 24, 27, 31-42, 44-45, 50-52, 55, 59-68,

71-74, 83-84, 86, 94-96, 100, 104-105, 109-111, 113-118, 120, 123-125, 127-128, 132, 135-139, 141-142, 145-146, 148, 150
hadith hasan, 45, 71, 86
hadith master, 16
hadith masters, 13, 50, 118
hafiz, 5-6, 10, 18, 20-21, 27-30, 39-42, 50, 62-63, 67-68, 83, 86, 107, 118, 123, 137, 145
hafiztu, 135
Hajar, 5, 7, 10, 12-13, 16, 18-21, 29, 31, 33-34, 42, 44-45, 50, 52, 56, 63-65, 67, 94, 96, 99, 107-109, 123, 125, 135-137, 139, 146-147
hajj, 3, 21, 25, 35-38, 56, 69, 71, 83, 86, 96, 100, 102
Hakim, 34, 41, 43, 47, 50, 65-66, 78, 84, 102, 117, 133, 137
Halabi, 21, 42, 150
Hamza, 94
Hanafis, 27-28, 57, 63, 78, 99
Hanbalis, 30, 57, 63, 78, 99-100
hand, 21, 30, 51-52, 58, 72, 86-87, 92, 97, 110, 113-114, 124-125, 132, 142-143, 156
Hanzala al-Ghasil, 120
haqiqi, 111
Haqq, 28, 45, 57, 65, 79, 100, 128, 152
Haqqi, 42, 91
haram, 8-9, 13, 20, 53, 64, 76-77, 95, 102, 123
hardship, 68, 75
Harmala ibn Yahya, 20
Harun ar-Rashid, 11
hasan, 20, 22, 34-35, 38-39, 45, 47, 64-65, 71-73, 86, 93, 99-103, 110, 112, 118, 120, 122, 136, 139-140

Hasan, 20, 22, 34-35, 38-39, 45, 47, 64-65, 71-73, 86, 93, 99-103, 110, 112, 118, 120, 122, 136, 139-140

Hasan ibn Ali, 120

hasan sahih, 34-35, 47, 72, 110

hasan sahih gharib, 47, 72

hasana, 19-21, 45, 71

Hashim, 15, 127

Hassan, 7-8, 97, 129, 142

Hassan ibn Thabit, 7-8

Hassan Saqqaf, 129

Hatib, 122

hatred, 98

hayatihi, 110

Haytami, 12-13, 18, 29, 42, 44, 94, 96, 104, 138, 147, 150

Haythami, 10, 19, 32, 43-44, 51-52, 65, 83-84, 109-110, 112, 114-115, 117, 133, 135, 139, 147

Hayy, 15, 28

He of the Long Hands, 36

head judge, 12

heart, 4-5, 42, 47, 49, 65, 87-88, 94, 104, 128, 131, 135-136, 140, 150, 157

hearts, 17, 48, 60, 72, 80, 111, 133, 138, 149

heaven, 110, 124, 129-130

heedlessness, 93

hell, 6, 113-115

help, 97, 123, 146, 156-157

Help with the Proof-Texts of Seeking Help, 97

helper, 146-147

hereafter, 13, 61, 66, 95

heresy, 143

high rank, 41, 79, 104

highest acts of obedience, 63

Highest Assembly, 131

highest authenticity, 61

highest regard, 133

highly desirable, 69, 71

hijab al-sura, 111

Hijaz, 126

himma, 145

Hira, 117, 125

His attributes, 38

his body is in the earth tender and humid, 44

His commands and prohibitions, 131

His creation, 130-131

His Elect, 90, 107

His knowledge, 108, 115, 157

His presence, 18, 35, 87, 92

His qualities, 110

His vision, 110, 128, 155

Hisham ibn Urwa, 76-77

Holy Mosque, 55, 64, 72-74

holy place, 82

honor, 2-3, 6, 9, 11, 14, 19, 30, 34-37, 87, 104

honored tomb, 58

honorific difference, 50

honoring persons of merit, 34

horn, 8, 153-154

Hour, 108-110, 114, 116, 118, 120, 126-127, 150

Hour, 108-110, 114, 116, 118, 120, 126-127, 150

Hudhayfa, 114, 116-117, 119

huffaz, 13

hujja, 22

Humankind, 132-133

humble, 128

humbleness, 32, 38, 130

Hunayn, 7

hunting, 95, 126

hurmat, 33

Husayn, 32, 39, 41, 102, 125

Husn al-maqsid, 7, 18, 20, 29-30

Husn al-Maqsid fi amal al-Mawlid, 18, 20, 30

hypocrites, 119, 126

ibadat, 63

Ibn Abbas, 34, 53, 111, 124, 127, 130, 134

ibn Abd al-Aziz, 15, 56, 70, 74, 76, 78, 84

Ibn Abd al-Barr, 57, 62, 65

Ibn Abd al-Salam, 20-21

Ibn Abd al-Wahhab, 116, 147

Ibn Abd al-Wahhab, 116, 147

Ibn Abi al-Dunya, 65, 84, 133, 142

Ibn Abi Asim, 39-40

Ibn Abi Baltaa, 122

Ibn Abi Fudayk, 52, 70, 83

Ibn Abi Hatim, 133, 139

Ibn Abi Lahab, 122

Ibn Abi Mulayka, 83

Ibn Abi Shayba, 43, 65, 135

ibn Abi Talib, 32, 47, 58, 95, 119, 133

Ibn Abi Waqqas, 122

Ibn Abidin, 20, 102, 121

Ibn Ahmad, 60, 102-103, 121

Ibn al-Athir, 118, 126

Ibn al-Hajj, 3, 21, 25, 35-38

Ibn al-Hajj al-Abdari, 21

Ibn al-Humam, 68, 111

Ibn al-Kharrat al-Ishbili, 45, 100

Ibn al-Madini, 41, 118

Ibn al-Mubarak, 135

Ibn al-Najjar al-Hanbali, 63

Ibn al-Qasim, 29, 33, 70

Ibn al-Qayyim, 8, 44, 46

Ibn al-Salah, 34

Ibn al-Sani, 146

Ibn al-Zubayr, 33, 38, 72-73, 76

Ibn Alawi al-Maliki, 15, 47, 60, 101

Ibn Amir, 38

Ibn Aqil, 78

Ibn Arabi, 29, 140-141

Ibn Asakir, 32, 40, 43-44, 71, 83-85, 133, 142

Ibn Badran, 63

Ibn Battal, 64-65

Ibn Battuta, 12

Ibn Dihya, 27-28

Ibn Dihya al-Kalbi, 28

Ibn Hajar, 5, 7, 10, 12-13,

16, 18-21, 29, 31, 33-34, 42, 44-45, 50, 52, 56, 63-65, 67, 94, 96, 99, 107-109, 123, 125, 135-137, 139, 147
Ibn Hajar al-Haytami, 12-13, 18, 29, 42, 94, 96, 147
Ibn Hajar al-Haythami, 44
Ibn Hajar Asqalani, 16
ibn Haritha, 47
Ibn Hawshab, 64, 123
Ibn Hibban, 43, 69, 71-72, 83-85, 112, 117, 141
Ibn Hisham, 6, 8, 22-23, 112-113, 126
Ibn Ishaq, 23, 112, 123
Ibn Jarir, 133, 139
Ibn Jarir al-Tabari, 133, 139
Ibn Jubayr, 11, 25
Ibn Kathir, 3, 5, 7, 13, 16, 27-29, 32-33, 44, 47, 84, 109-110, 112
Ibn Kathir praises the night of Mawlid, 16
Ibn Main, 41, 45
Ibn Majah, 38-39, 43, 47, 50, 65-66, 72, 141
Ibn Majah, 38-39, 43, 47, 50, 65-66, 72, 141
ibn Malik, 43, 75-76, 92, 115, 125, 135
Ibn Mardawayh, 110, 133, 139
Ibn Masud, 11, 38-39, 84, 109, 115, 123, 125
Ibn Nafi, 74
Ibn Nasir al-Din al-Dimashqi, 5-6, 29
Ibn Qayyim, 7-8, 78
Ibn Qudama, 64-65, 85
Ibn Qunfudh al-Qusantini al-Maliki, 32-33, 71
Ibn Rahawayh, 34, 123
Ibn Rajab, 20, 62
Ibn Rajab al-Hanbali, 20, 62
Ibn Rawaha, 7
Ibn Rushd, 25
Ibn Sadaqa, 111

Ibn Shihab, 78, 154
Ibn Shihab al-Zuhri, 78
Ibn Taymiyya, 13-16, 19-20, 25, 30, 50, 53, 62-63, 78, 99-100, 141, 144-145
ibn Thabit, 7-8
Ibn Umar, 29-30, 39, 45, 49, 53, 66, 68, 71, 75, 83, 86, 94-95, 102, 104, 109-110, 125, 142
Ibn Uyayna, 118, 136
Ibn Wahb, 71-72, 75, 122, 136
Ibn Zahira, 12-13, 28
Ibn Zara, 111
ibn Zuhayr, 7
Ibrahim, 13, 29, 41, 49, 69, 79, 85, 90, 93, 96, 102
Ibrahim ibn Shayban, 85
Ibraz al-ghayy fi shifa al-ayy, 63
id al-adha, 66
id al-fitr, 46, 66
idhkhir, 77
idolatry, 58, 60
idols, 8, 59
ignorant, 23, 35, 133
Ihya, 61, 65
ijma, 56, 63, 78, 99, 143
ijtihad, 143
ikram, 33, 42
Ikrima, 39
Ikrima ibn Abu Jahl, 39
ilham, 137, 150
illumination, 28, 138
Illumination Concerning the Birthday of the Bringer of, 28
ilm al-ghayb, 107
ilman qatiyyan, 43
Ilqima, 57
Imam, 10-13, 15-20, 22, 27-29, 32-33, 36, 40-41, 45-46, 48, 53, 56-57, 60-61, 63, 67, 69, 71-75, 86, 92-93, 97-98, 100, 102-104, 109, 118, 127, 132, 138-139, 141-142, 144, 151
Imam Ahmad, 11, 15, 41, 45, 48, 53, 57, 63, 92,

132, 142, 151
Imam Bayhaqi, 22
Imam Ghazali, 60-61
Imam Malik, 33, 46, 56, 69, 71-73, 75, 100, 141
Imam Nawawi, 17, 33, 36, 72-73, 86, 93, 97-98, 138
imam of
Imam Suyuti, 18-19, 32
imams of the madhhab, 104
imams of theology, 104
iman, 2, 31-32, 44-45, 50, 52-53, 83-84, 135
Imdad Allah Muhajir Makki, 28
immense mercy, 46
impermissible, 24, 92
Inayat Allah Kakurawi, 28
incompatible narrations, 39
incumbent, 4, 96-98, 104, 141
inheritance from the Prophet, 142
inner detachment, 111
innovation, 1, 14-17, 19-22, 24, 26, 30, 49, 53, 55-56, 146
innovation (*bida*), 15, 19-20
innovations in religion under the Fatimis, 25
innovators, 144
inspiration, 108, 137, 145, 149-150
inspired, 136-137, 148-149
Intellect, 39, 128
intent, 26, 40, 67, 133
intention, 9, 15, 18, 62, 69-70, 87, 93-94, 101, 104, 157
interceding on our behalf, 43
intercession, 43, 45, 58, 68, 71, 80, 82-83, 85-86, 91
intermediaries, 130
intermediary, 45, 81
interpretation, 58-59, 69, 111, 134

interpreting in the worst sense, 59
intimacy, 36-37, 133
intimate friend, 49, 91
intuition, 150
intuitive knowledge, 132
invent, 23
invocation, 50-51
Invocations of blessings on the Prophet, 28
inward parts, 131
inward thoughts, 126
iqama, 85
Iqtida, 14, 30
Iqtida al-sirat al-mustaqim, 14, 30
Iraq, 13, 27, 76, 117, 123, 126, 142
Iraqi, 29-30, 62-63, 65, 104
Isa, 49, 52, 61
Ishaq, 23, 34, 41, 63, 69, 75, 112, 123
Ishaq al-Shahidi, 41
Ishaq ibn Abd Allah ibn Abi Talha al-Ansari, 75
Ishaq ibn Ibrahim, 41, 69
Ishaq ibn Ibrahim al-Qazzaz, 41
Islam, 3, 8, 16-17, 33, 42, 45, 56-59, 68, 71, 80, 86, 91, 94, 100, 115, 118, 124, 126-127, 129, 131, 138, 142-143, 145, 147, 150-151, 157
Islamic Beliefs and Doctrine According to Ahl al-Sunna:, 51
Islamic countries, 13
Islamic sciences, 23
Ismail, 77, 102, 154
isnad, 39, 152
Isra, 10
istighatha, 97
istihbab, 61, 68
istinbat, 143
Itab ibn Usayd, 126
itikaf, 93
ittila, 108, 116
ittisal, 138
Jabir, 48, 154
Jafar, 29, 32, 47-48, 93

Jafar ibn Muhammad ibn Ali ibn al-Husayn ibn Ali ibn Abi, 32
Jahiliyya, 7
Jahmiyya, 145
jaiz, 69
Jalal al-Din al-Kattani, 29
Jalal al-Din al-Suyuti, 16
jalil, 77
jamaa, 15, 53, 56, 84
Jami al-athar fi mawlid al-nabi al-mukhtar, 29
janaba, 120
Janaiz, 10, 58, 66
Jawziyya, 151
Jazak Allahu ya, 88
Jerusalem, 64, 96-97, 117-118, 121, 127
Jesus, 10, 14, 35, 50, 52, 147
Jesus son of Mary, 35, 52, 147
Jesus son of Mary will descend, 147
jihad, 7, 34, 120, 125
jinn, 133, 147
jiran, 95
Joseph, 156-157
joy, 4, 46-48
Julays, 142
Juma, 9, 26, 32
jumhur, 99, 134
jump, 46
Junayd, 139-140
jurisprudence, 27, 41, 56-57, 139, 156
jurist, 25, 42
jurists, 24
justice, 156
Juwayni, 99-100
Kab, 7, 84, 124
Kab al-Ahbar, 84
Kab ibn Zuhayr, 7
Kabah, 12, 25, 60, 75, 105, 117, 124-125
kafir, 6, 99, 108
Kamal al-Din al-Adfawi, 29
kamil, 43, 45
karama, 137, 144, 150
karamat, 13, 42, 136, 140, 148

karamat al-awliya, 42, 136, 140
Karbala, 125
karim, 15
kashf, 65, 131, 134-135, 138, 140-143, 145, 149
Kashf al-astar, 65
Khalaf, 56, 122
Khalaf, 56, 122
Khalid, 15, 126, 154-155
Khalil, 49, 73, 96, 101-102
Khandaq, 7
Kharijis, 119, 121
Khattabi, 39, 65, 96
Khawarij, 119, 121
khawass, 132
Khaybar, 78, 117
Khazars, 118
Khidr, 134, 138, 148
Khubayb, 23
Khubayb ibn Adi, 23
Khuzayma, 34, 43, 45, 117
killer, 119
killing, 119, 122, 125
Kitab al-adhkar, 20, 97-98
Kitab al-hawadith wa al-bida, 20, 25, 28
Kitab al-mawlid, 13, 29
Kitab al-zuhd, 135, 142
Kitab Mawlid an-Nabi, 29
Knowers, 40, 140-141
knowing, 57, 148
knowledge, 6, 24, 34-35, 37-38, 40-44, 48, 53, 64, 75, 99, 107-111, 113-119, 121, 123, 125-129, 131-135, 137, 139, 141-150, 157
Knowledge of the Unseen, 107, 113-117, 119, 121, 123, 125, 127-129, 131, 133, 135, 137, 139, 141, 143, 145, 147, 149
known, 6, 8, 21, 29, 31, 33, 36-37, 43, 50, 66, 71, 76, 93-94, 99, 103-105, 110, 113-114, 116-117, 121, 124, 128, 138, 143, 145-146, 148
Koran, 148-149
Kufa, 72
kufr, 60

kull, 22
kullu, 21-23
kursi, 105
la asl, 128
la ilaha illallah, 12
la yajuz, 92
Labid ibn al-Asim, 126
lamp, 83
large candles, 12
Last Hour, 109, 114, 116, 120
Law, 12, 15, 21, 24, 48, 56, 62, 100, 103, 107, 140, 156-157
lawful forms of merriment, 48
legal desirability, 68
legal rulings, 150
legally speaking, 23
Letters, 9, 70, 139
liar, 71, 120, 157
Life, 3, 6, 14, 16, 23, 26, 28, 30-31, 33, 43-44, 49, 52, 71, 85, 95, 104, 114-115, 123-124, 143
light, 5-7, 17-18, 46, 55, 64, 104, 107, 115, 124, 133, 138, 145
light of unveiling, 145
light-giving daybreak, 18
lights, 16, 31, 138
limbs, 125
limits, 95, 155
linguistically speaking, 23
Lisan al-arab, 119
literal, 66, 111
literal manifestation, 111
literal meaning of *id* is , 66-67
literally, 12, 67, 132, 135
Lord, 22, 43, 50, 58, 62, 80-82, 85, 89, 91, 108, 110-111, 129, 131, 135, 139, 151
love, 2, 7, 14, 17, 24, 30, 35, 37, 39, 46-49, 62, 77, 92, 104, 133, 155
Love for the Prophet, 14, 17, 92
love of and obedience to the Prophet, 24
lover, 27, 37, 49

Ma thabata min al-sunna, 28
Maalim al-Sunan, 65
madhhab, 104
Madina, 4-5, 18, 31-32, 44, 46-47, 49, 52, 55-57, 59, 61, 63-65, 67, 69-77, 79, 81, 83-87, 89, 91, 93-95, 97-99, 101-103, 105, 109, 111, 117, 121, 123-126, 142
madrasa, 27
Mafahim yajib an tusah-hah, 15, 60
Maghrib, 12, 112, 118
magistrates, 12
Magnificent, 2, 16, 57, 149
Mahdi, 118-119
Mahmud Said, 22
mainstream, 14, 30, 59, 115, 144
mainstream Islam, 59, 115
mainstream Islamic, 14
mainstream Muslims, 30
Majesty, 38, 131
Majma al-zawaid, 10, 19, 32, 43-44, 52, 65, 83-84, 104, 109-110, 114-115, 117, 133, 135, 139, 147
Majmu sharh al-muhad-hdhab, 78
major ablution, 120
Major schools, 28, 44, 53, 55, 57, 59, 107
majority, 11, 13, 19, 22-23, 28, 34, 54, 56-57, 72-74, 99, 119, 125, 134, 136, 154
Makhruh, 20
makruh, 21, 92
makruha, 20-21
Malik, 33, 43, 46, 56, 69-78, 92, 99-100, 115, 117, 125-126, 132, 135, 141-142, 154, 156-157
Malik ibn Anas, 141
Maliki, 15, 20-21, 25-26, 32-33, 47, 60, 68, 71-72, 74, 101-102, 131, 139
Maliki al-Hasani, 60
Malikis, 28, 42, 57, 63, 78,

99
Manasik, 32, 44, 49, 56, 83-84, 86, 105
Mandub, 18, 20
manduba, 57
manifestation, 110-111
mankind, 4, 72, 103, 130
mantle, 126
manumission, 5
maqam, 13, 79, 87, 110-111
Maqam Ibrahim, 13
mark, 37, 83, 92-93, 121
martyr, 125, 154-155
martyrs of Uhud, 94
Marwa, 146
Mary, 35, 52, 81-82, 130, 147
Masabih, 67
Masabih al-Sunna, 67
masajid, 63-64
Mashhur Salman, 1, 14, 19
masjid, 15, 64-65, 67, 71, 85, 87, 93, 97, 102, 123
Masjid al-haram, 102, 123
Master, 3, 16, 33, 60, 79, 86, 89-90, 93, 104, 122, 137, 144
Mawlana, 105
Mawlid, 1, 3, 5-7, 9, 11-21, 23-33, 35, 37, 39, 41, 43, 45, 47-49, 51, 53, 84
Mawlid al-arus, 18, 29
Mawlid rasul Allah, 16
Mawsuat al-ijma fi al-fiqh al-islami, 56, 78
May Allah bless you, O Muhammad, 52
Maymun ibn Abi Shabib, 34
Meadow, 69
means, 32-33, 44-45, 50, 63, 69, 71, 73, 79, 82, 90-91, 121, 136, 148-149, 154, 157
Medina, 16, 148
meeting the Prophet in dreams, 142
melodious voice, 8
memorization, 142
Merciful, 80-81, 85, 91, 96,

131, 145
merits, 21, 54, 75
Messenger, 1, 8, 17, 23, 34-36, 47-49, 57-58, 60, 62, 69, 72, 75-78, 80, 83-87, 89-96, 107, 112, 114, 116-118, 120, 122-125, 128-130, 132, 134, 143, 149-151, 153-155
midafternoon prayer, 41
Mighty, 91, 154
migration, 5, 123
minaret, 41
minbar, 69, 71, 79, 81, 86-87, 92, 96, 142
miracle, 145
miracles, 6, 13, 42, 116, 129, 136, 140, 143-144, 148
miracles of saints, 42, 136, 143-144
miracles will not cease to take place, 144
Miraj, 10
misguidance, 19-21, 60, 93
mizmar, 8
modality, 44
Monday, 2-3, 5-6, 10-11, 19, 25
morals, 24
Moses, 4, 16-17, 43, 50, 134
mosque in Quba, 64
mosques, 26, 58-59, 61-65, 69, 74, 81, 105
Mother of Cities, 11
Mount Hira, 125
Muadh, 33-35, 110
Muadh ibn Jabal, 110
Muawiya, 38, 118-119
Mubah, 20-21
mubaha yuthab alayha, 21
mubashshira, 138
mubashshirat, 134
mudd, 75, 77
mudtarib, 40
mufahhamun, 136
mufassir, 25
Mufti, 17, 28, 102
muhaddath, 136
muhaddathun, 136

Muhaddith, 9, 16, 28, 101-102, 128
Muhammad, 5-7, 12, 14-15, 20, 22-23, 25, 28-30, 32-33, 39, 41-42, 46-48, 50-53, 60, 70, 79-80, 83, 85, 90-91, 93, 101-103, 113, 116, 124-125, 129-130, 138, 142, 147, 149-151, 154
Muhammad Hamid, 14, 149
Muhammad Hamid al-Fiqqi, 14
Muhammad ibn Abd al-Wahhab, 116, 147
Muhammad ibn Alawi al-Maliki, 15, 47, 60, 101
Muhammad ibn Alawi al-Maliki al-Hasani, 60
Muhammad ibn Harb al-Hilali, 85
Muhammad ibn Hibban, 85
Muhammad ibn Jar Allah ibn Zahira, 28
Muhammad ibn Siddiq al-Ghumari, 30
Muhammad ibn Yusuf al-Salihi al-Shami, 29
Muhammad Mazhar Allah Dihlawi, 28
muharrama, 20-21
muhibb, 139
Muhibb al-Din al-Wahidi al-Maliki, 139
muhtasiban, 83
Muhyi Al-Din Al-Nawawi, 86
Muhyiddin, 12
Mujam, 92, 135, 147, 151
mujawara, 95
mujiza, 137, 141, 149
mujizat, 148
mujma alayha, 68
mukashafat, 138, 144-145
mukhataba, 138
mukhatabat, 144-145
mulhamun, 136
Mulla Ali al-Qari, 28, 98, 100
Mullah Ali Qari, 17

multiple paths of transmission, 116
munharif, 97
Munkar, 151
muntasibun, 103
muqallidun, 103
murad, 15, 67
murghabun fiha, 69
Musa, 8, 11, 39-42, 45, 49, 82, 102
Musa al-Hadi, 11
Musannaf, 43, 65, 135
Musaylima, 120
mushahada, 138
Mushkil al-athar, 33, 65
Muslim, 2-3, 5-7, 10-11, 13, 16, 18, 30, 33-34, 36, 42-44, 46, 53, 55, 61-62, 64-66, 69, 72-73, 78, 94-95, 103, 108, 113-114, 117, 122, 126-128, 131, 134, 136, 139, 144, 146, 148-149
Muslims, 4, 6, 11, 16-17, 24, 30, 44, 49-51, 53, 56, 59-60, 68, 70, 78, 92-93, 98, 100, 119, 123, 126, 129, 136-137, 141, 144, 147-148, 155-156
Musnad, 9, 11, 32, 34, 43-44, 48, 52, 64, 72-74, 84, 115, 132, 147
Musnad al-Humaydi, 74
Mustadrak, 43, 84, 133, 137
mustahabb, 11, 15, 25
mustajab, 59
Muta, 122
mutaammamin, 12
mutabarrikin bihi, 11
mutamaslif, 97
Mutazili, 111, 143
Mutazili leanings, 143
Muthir Al-Gharam Al-Sakin Ila Ashraf, 83
muttabiun, 103
mutual vision, 138
Muzaffar the King of Irbil, 27
Muzahim, 76
My Face, 140
Nabahani, 140

nadhr, 65
Nafi, 40, 45, 74
nafs, 24
Najmuddin Muhammad
   Ibn al-Imam Muhyiddin
   al-Tabari, 12
Nakir, 151
naql, 20
narration, 5, 34, 52, 61,
   64, 71, 92, 94, 104, 107,
   109-112, 132, 136
NasaI, 5, 43, 50, 61, 66,
   118
Nasir al-Din Albani, 55
Nasir al-Din ibn al-
   Tabbakh, 29
national holiday, 13
nations, 18, 118, 136, 149
Nawawi, 17, 20, 29, 33-38,
   40-45, 53, 56-57, 64-65,
   68, 72-73, 78, 83, 86, 93-
   94, 96-98, 136, 138, 142,
   148
*Nayl al-awta*r, 45, 56-57,
   74, 78, 99
nearly all, 22
nearness, 18, 41, 45, 137
nearness to Allah, 18, 45,
   137
necessary, 36-37, 39, 52,
   60, 69-70, 99-100, 143,
   145
necessity, 36-37, 44, 69
Negus, 122
new practice, 23
next world, 44, 65, 146
Night Journey, 10, 127
nikah, 5, 47
Nisaburi, 47
Nisai, 43, 65, 72, 84
noble, 12, 16, 27, 45, 50,
   60, 63, 68, 82, 90, 104-
   105
Noble Grave, 45, 50, 60,
   63, 68
not been established, 151
notables, 12
Nuaym ibn Abd Allah al-
   Mujmir, 77
Nuh, 17, 129
Nuh Keller, 129
number, 23, 30-31, 68, 75-

78, 84, 113-115, 118, 124,
   133, 135, 137, 144, 154
nur *al-kashf*, 145
obedience, 24, 31, 63
obligations, 140
obligatory, 20, 44, 56-57,
   62, 71, 97, 99, 148
Oneness, 116, 147
oneness, 116, 147
pagans, 124
pale, 33, 98
paradise, 8, 72, 92, 96,
   113-115, 135
parts, 117, 131, 151
passive receptivity, 135
patient, 75
pedestals of light, 133
people of Badr, 122
People of his house, 119
People of knowledge, 48,
   99
people of the Fire, 119,
   135
people of the Garden of
   Paradise, 135
perceptions, 149
perfect, 35, 48, 90, 151
perfected individuals, 132
perfection, 2, 135, 137
perfection of *ilham*, 137
permanently, 32, 44
permissibility of Mawlid,
   19
permitted, 15, 20-21, 61,
   69
permitted indifferently, 21
permitted innovation
   which merits reward, 21
Persia, 3, 112, 118, 121,
   148
Persian, 122
person, 4, 26, 34-35, 37-
   38, 41, 46, 52, 58, 61, 82,
   93, 108, 113, 124, 129,
   140, 143, 147-148
piercing sight, 128, 138,
   145
pilgrimage, 26, 44, 49, 56-
   57, 61, 71, 81, 83, 85-86,
   92, 96-97, 104
pious, 8, 11, 16, 32, 42, 59-
   60, 105, 132, 139, 143

pious believers, 42
pious early generations,
   60
Pious Predecessors, 32, 60
place, 9, 11, 13-15, 25, 30,
   38, 40-41, 51, 62, 64, 66-
   67, 70-73, 75-76, 80-82,
   87, 94, 96, 113, 119, 124,
   126-127, 132-133, 141,
   144, 148, 153, 155
place of prostration, 67
plague, 77, 121
play, 9, 46
poetry in praise, 28
poets, 6, 27
Pond, 80
pool, 92, 96
Power, 23, 128, 131, 137-
   138
powers, 133, 140, 144, 157
powers and influences,
   144
praiseworthy, 13, 15-16,
   20, 37, 43, 48, 53, 57, 90
praiseworthy innovation,
   15-16, 20
prayer, 11-13, 23, 26, 32,
   36, 40-41, 43, 49, 63-64,
   67, 71-74, 82, 85, 87, 92,
   94, 96, 113, 120, 125,
   132, 141-142, 147, 157
Predecessors, 32, 60
presence, 18, 32-33, 35,
   38, 72, 87-88, 92, 108,
   111, 134, 145
primacy, 56
principles, 103-104, 116,
   144, 147
Priority, 71, 79
prohibition, 34, 38-39, 49,
   55, 58-59, 61, 63-65, 67-
   68, 105
proof, 22, 32, 34-35, 38-40,
   44-45, 49, 58-59, 74, 97,
   103, 105, 156
proof-texts, 45, 97
proofs, 2, 38, 44, 46, 133
Prophet, 1-105, 107-152,
   154, 156-157
Prophet Abraham, 62
Prophet emphasized the
   birthplace of prophets,

10

Prophet hears and sees us, 43

Prophet is alive, 32, 43-44

Prophet is alive and tender, 44

Prophet is alive permanently, 32, 44

Prophet marked one grave with a rock, 58

Prophet Muhammad, 46, 50, 130

prophets, 9-10, 43-44, 49-50, 58-60, 62, 67, 69, 71, 78, 81, 85, 89-90, 107-108, 111, 123, 129-130, 132-133, 136-137, 141, 147, 149-150

Prophets and Messengers are intermediaries, 130

Prophets title

prostration, 17-18, 67, 78

protected, 56, 93

protectors, 149

psychic, 150

pulpit, 30, 69, 72, 80, 87, 142, 148

punctuating the Quran, 26

punished, 119

pure Arabic, 22

pure intent, 133

Pure Religion, 57

purity, 33, 35, 81-82, 85, 89, 92

purpose of *mawlid*, 24

qabr, 56, 61, 97

Qadariyya, 121

Qadi Iyad, 34, 45, 50, 53, 68, 70, 72, 74, 78, 99-100, 115-116, 126, 130-131

Qadi Iyad al-Maliki, 68, 74, 131

*qadi*s, 12

Qahtan, 120

qalbi, 47

qarn, 55

qasd, 101

Qastallani, 10, 29, 50, 115

Qatada, 2-3

Qays ibn Sad ibn Ubada,

qibla, 71, 79, 83, 88, 92

qila innaha wajiba, 69

qiyas, 143

Quba, 64, 81, 94

Quds, 64

Quran, 1-2, 4-5, 8, 15, 17-18, 20, 22, 26, 49, 53, 103, 108, 119, 128, 133-134, 136, 139, 143-145, 150-151

Quranic verses, 150

Quraysh, 120-121, 127

Qurayza, 34

qurba, 18

Qurtubi, 42, 108, 137

qurubat, 97-98

Qushayri, 86, 141

Qutb al-Din al-Hanafi, 28

Qutrubull, 125

Quzman, 119

Rabi al-Awwal, 3, 11-12, 25, 27

radda, 32, 44

radiance of the bridegroom, 18

raf al-mashaqqa, 68

Rafidis, 119, 121

Raghaib, 26

rain, 110

Rajab, 20, 26, 62

rakat, 10, 36, 51, 80, 94-95

Rashid Ahmad, 101, 105

Rawda, 69, 80, 87, 92, 148

Rawdat al-Jannat fi Mawlid khatim al-risalat, 29

read the signs, 139

reading about his life, 30

reason, 10, 18-19, 33, 35-38, 46-47, 50, 56-57, 72, 82, 130, 139, 157

recitation, 7-8, 18, 30, 87

recitation of poetry in honor of the Prophet, 30

recitation of Quran, 18

reciting, 7-8, 17, 26, 30, 48, 60, 119, 142

reciting of poetry, 48

recommended, 15, 18-19, 28, 33, 42, 56-57, 81-82,

86-87, 94-95, 97-99

refutation, 36, 143

relatives, 5, 92

Reliance of the Traveller, 17, 129, 147

religion, 23, 25, 43, 57, 99, 103, 120-121, 140, 143, 145, 151

remembrance, 4, 15, 17, 40, 44, 65-66

Remembrance of Allah, 15, 44

reprehensible, 27, 92

Repudiation of , 14, 17, 19, 21, 23, 25-26, 51, 129

required, 49, 104

required act, 104

resource without equal, 22

Respect, 5, 31, 33, 36-37, 42-43, 46, 59, 107, 131, 143, 147

retreat, 93

return of his soul, 32

revelation, 70, 108, 129-131, 137, 145

reverence, 32-34, 36-37, 41-42, 88, 92, 94, 104

ridda, 120, 122

Rifai, 15, 129

righteous, 40, 82, 90, 108, 132, 146, 148

Righteous are the very purpose of all that exists, 146

Rightly-Guided Caliphs, 56

rightly-guided caliphs, 56

rigorously authenticated, 16, 50, 148

rigorously authenticated (*sahih*), 16

Rihal, 11, 25, 61, 63-64, 69, 105

Risala, 86, 89, 141

Rising, 36-37, 75, 125, 127, 149

rites of Pilgrimage, 49

Riyadh, 20, 48, 53, 97-98

ruasa, 12

rub the pulpit to take its blessing, 80

Ruhba, 139-140

ruku, 127
rule, 13, 25, 28, 63-64,
   118-119, 140, 155
ruling, 14, 23, 63-64, 104
rust of screens, 111
ruya, 134, 138
ruyatihi, 110
Sacred Law, 140
Sacred Mosque, 73-74
sacredness, 33
sacrifice for newborns, 19
sacrosanct, 76
Sad, 5, 33-35, 47-48, 75,
   102, 122, 125
Sad ibn Abi Waqqas, 122
Sad ibn Muadh, 33-35
Sad ibn Ubada, 47
Sada, 33, 111, 137
sadaqa, 27, 95, 111, 125
Safa, 115, 146
Safa and Marwa, 146
Safiyya, 91, 93
safwa, 86, 133, 140, 142,
   146
Safwan ibn Umayya, 122
sahaba, 4, 124-126
sahih, 3, 5, 16, 30-31, 33-
   35, 42-48, 50-52, 55, 62,
   64-65, 72-73, 78, 84, 94-
   96, 99-100, 104, 107,
   109-111, 114-115, 117,
   124, 127, 135-136, 141,
   146, 149
Sahih Muslim, 3, 33, 42,
   44, 55, 64, 72-73, 78, 94,
   136
Sahihs, 92, 94
Said, 2-10, 15-20, 22-23,
   25, 27, 29, 31-36, 38-42,
   44-48, 50-52, 56-60, 62-
   78, 80-86, 91-96, 98-104,
   108-115, 117-128, 130-
   136, 138-149, 151-155,
   157
Said Al-Khudri, 34, 139
Said Hawwa, 15
Said ibn al-Musayyib, 85
saint, 42, 108, 133, 137,
   141
saints, 40, 42, 58-59, 81,
   107, 113, 115, 117, 119,
   121, 123, 125, 127, 129,

131-133, 135-139, 141-
   147, 149
sajda, 127
Sakhawi, 13, 18, 29, 33-
   34, 42, 44-46, 56, 67, 71,
   138-139
salaf, 24, 56, 59-60
Salaf al-salih, 60
Salafi, 14, 19, 45, 51, 55,
   58, 97-99
Salafi Corruption of the
   Text of Nawawi's Adhkar,
   97
Salafi prohibition of travel
   for the purpose of visiting, 55
Salafis, 1, 13-14, 27, 55-
   56, 93, 107, 128-129,
   136, 142-147
salafiyya, 105, 144
salam, 1, 20-21, 31-33, 36,
   44, 58, 61, 68, 71, 84-86
Salama, 85
Salama ibn Dinar, 85
*salam*s, 91, 93
*salam*s to Abu Bakr, 91
Salat, 11-13, 21, 25, 31-33,
   45-46, 49-50, 52, 61, 63-
   64, 67, 71, 96, 99, 147
salat al-fajr, 147
salat al-Maghrib, 12
Salat al-Tarawih, 21
salawat, 1, 30, 32, 46
*sallallahu alayhi wa sal-
   lam*, 28
*sallallahu alayka ya
   Muhammad*, 52
Salman al-Farsi, 112
Samhudi, 45, 56-57, 84-86
Samura ibn Jundub, 119
Sana, 112
Sariya, 148
satan, 134
Saudi, 13, 97
Saudi Authority for
   Scholarly Research, 97
sayyid, 15, 20, 29, 43, 88,
   100, 102, 122
scholars, 1, 5, 10, 12-15,
   17, 19-20, 23, 25, 27-28,
   33-34, 40, 42, 44-45, 49-
   50, 52-53, 55, 57-59, 63-

64, 72-75, 78, 87, 93, 96,
   99, 101-105, 107, 115,
   129, 134, 136, 139, 141-
   144, 147
Scholars from al-Azhar,
   102
Scholars from India, 101
Scholars from Madina,
   102
Scholars from Syria, 102
scholars of hadith, 27
school, 15, 25, 72, 98, 156
schools, 1, 12, 24, 28, 44,
   53, 55, 57, 59, 78, 103,
   107
Science, 41, 118, 142
Scripture, 133-134
Seal of Prophets, 9, 50, 89
secret, 57, 122
secrets, 110, 126, 140-141,
   149
secrets of Allah Most
   High, 140-141
secrets of the hypocrites,
   126
seeing the Prophet, 42,
   138
seeking help, 97
self-adornment, 111
self-purification, 24
selling, 26
Servant, 6, 90, 125, 145
seven heavens, 108
Shaban, 26
shadd al-rihal, 61, 63, 69
Shaddad ibn Aws, 10
shadhdh, 20, 98
shafaa, 58
Shafii, 12-13, 20, 22, 52,
   72-73, 86, 97, 102, 104
Shafii *qadi*, 12-13
Shafii shaykhs, 52
Shafiis, 27, 29, 42, 57, 63,
   78
Shah Abd al-Rahim
   Dihlawi, 28
Shah Wali Allah Dihlawi,
   28
Shahr Ibn Hawshab, 64,
   123
Shahr ibn Hawshab, 64,
   123

Sham, 70, 76, 84-85, 112, 117, 125-126, 142
Shama, 13-15, 17, 20-21, 25, 29, 77
Shamail, 111
Shamaim imdadiyya, 28
Shams al-Din al-Jazari, 29
Shams al-Din ibn Nasir al-Din al-Dimashqi, 29
Shamsuddin Muhammad ibn Nasir al-Din al-Dimashqi, 6
Sharh al-Kawkab al-Munir, 63
Sharh al-mawahib, 30
Sharh al-shifa, 71, 75, 78
Sharh al-sunna, 110, 133
Sharh sahih Muslim, 33, 42, 44, 64, 72-73, 78, 136
Sharia, 8, 15, 17, 42, 53, 59, 83, 93, 143
sharif, 13, 21, 47, 100, 102, 131-132
shaved heads, 121
Shawkani, 13, 17, 45, 50, 53, 56-57, 74, 78, 99-100, 137
Shaykh Abd al-Haqq, 128
Shaykh Abd al-Qadir, 79, 81, 103, 137-138, 140, 146
shaykh al-islam, 42, 68, 86, 100, 138, 147
Shaytan, 144
Sheba, 133
Sheet, 135
Shia, 143-144
Shifa, 11, 24, 45, 50, 53, 63-64, 68, 71, 74-75, 78, 98, 101, 115-116, 130-131
Shifa al-siqam, 64, 68, 71
shirk, 53, 59-60, 146
Shuab al-iman, 31-32, 44-45, 50, 52-53, 83-84, 135
shurafa, 12
siddiq, 10, 30, 33, 100, 148, 155
siddiqin, 132
Sifat al-safwa, 86, 133, 140, 142, 146
Siffin, 119, 126

Sight of the Prophet, 127
sign, 43, 46, 113, 149
sign of gratitude, 46
Silah al-mumin, 67
similar to angelic attributes, 131
Sincerity, 82
sing, 7-8, 46
singing, 7-8, 30, 47-48
singing *qasida*s of praise, 30
sins, 80
Sira, 6, 9, 14-15, 17-18, 30, 112-113
siraj, 138
sirat, 5, 8, 14, 23, 30
Siyar alam al-nubala, 8, 27, 29, 84
Some Sayings That Were Retained From the Visitors to his, 84
sooth-saying, 150
soul, 23, 32, 44, 46, 52, 68, 84, 110, 113
souls, 46, 131
sound, 9-11, 19-20, 24, 31-32, 34-35, 42-45, 47-48, 50-52, 58, 65-66, 68, 72, 77, 84, 93, 96, 99-100, 104, 109, 111, 114-117, 132, 139, 146
sound chain, 11, 19-20, 32, 44, 48, 66, 68, 72, 84, 115
special blessing, 25
special clothes, 12
special sermon, 12
spiritual communications, 144
spiritual states, 110
spiritual unveilings, 144
standing for the sake of the Prophet, 42
standing place, 87
standing up, 33-36, 38, 42, 48
stars, 150
state of major ritual defilement, 120
Station of Divine Presence and Abiding, 111
Story, 17, 36, 82, 122, 125, 150, 154, 157

strangers, 70, 132
strict adherents, 103
strict followers, 103
strict imitators, 103
stylistic figure, 22
Subhan Allah, 113
Subki, 17, 42, 45, 64, 68, 71, 100
Substitute-saints, 138
Substitutes, 132, 142
Subul al-huda, 29
Successors, 35, 138, 144
Sufi, 103, 124, 143
Sufi-doctrine of
Sufis, 33, 138, 150
Sufyan, 41, 76, 124, 152, 154
Sufyan (al-Thawri), 124
Sufyan ibn Abi Zuhayr, 76
Suhayl ibn Amr, 126
Sulayman, 39, 71, 83
Sultan, 13, 140
Sultan of the Knowers of Allah, 140
sun, 38, 95, 105, 149
Sunan, 19, 34, 43, 46-47, 58, 65, 68, 71, 83-84, 100, 139, 152
sunna, 1-2, 15, 17-21, 24, 28, 30-31, 46, 51, 53, 57-58, 62, 67-69, 71, 81, 93, 95, 103, 110, 130, 133, 136, 140-141, 143
sunna manduba, 57
sunna wajiba, 57
*Sunna*s of Muslims, 68
Sunnis, 25, 28, 121
superstructure over the grave, 58
supplication, 11, 13, 44, 59-60, 75, 81-82, 92, 95
sura, 6, 111
Surah al-Naml, 22
Surah Luqman, 108-110
Suraqa, 125
Suyuti, 7, 13, 16-20, 25, 29-30, 32, 41, 43-44, 47, 50, 65, 83-85, 109, 115, 132, 135, 137-138
synecdoche, 22
Syria, 13, 101-102, 123-124, 126

Tabaqat, 5, 48, 137
Tabarani, 10, 19, 43, 45, 51, 65, 71-72, 83, 104, 109, 114, 117-118, 125, 133, 135, 139, 146-147, 151
Tabari, 12, 133, 139
tabarruk, 25
tabiin, 56-57
Taff, 125
Tafil, 77
tafsir, 32, 44, 84, 108-110, 134, 139
Tafsir Ibn Abbas, 134
taghut, 116, 147
Tahawi, 33, 61, 65
Tahiyya, 87
tahiyyat al-masjid, 71, 87
tahlil, 12-13
tahliq, 121
tahliyatihi, 111
tahmid, 13
tahrim, 64-65
Tahrir al-kalam fi al-qiyam inda dhikr mawlid sayyid, 29
tajalli, 110-111
tajalli haqiqi, 111
tajalli suwari, 111
takhliyatihi, 111
Talha, 75, 125
Tamhid, 65
Taqi al-Din, 45, 68
Taqi al-Din al-Subki, 45, 68
tarawih, 18, 21, 26
Tarh al-Tathrib, 63
Tarikh, 13, 28, 32, 43-44, 83-85, 139, 141
Tarikh Baghdad, 141
Tarikh Habib Allah, 28
Tariq, 79, 145
Tarkhis, 33, 42
tasawwuf, 24, 140
tashahhud, 49
Tashnif al-adhan, 30
tathwib, 26
tatrib, 26
tawaf, 69
tawassul, 50, 82
tawassum, 139
tawatur, 61, 116

tawil, 111
tazkiyat al-nafs, 24
tenth of Muharram, 16-17
Text of the *fatwa*, 103
Thabit, 7-8, 45, 92, 153-155, 157
Thabit al-Bunani, 92
Thanksgiving, 18
Thaqif, 120
theology, 104
they have the aspect of men as far as their bodies and, 131
those who curse the Companions and declare, 121
those who possess vision, 139
Three Holy Mosques, 81
three Mosques, 61-65, 105
Three Principles of Oneness, 116, 147
Throne, 75, 105, 133, 135
throne of Balqis, 133
Tigris, 125
time one observes with festive activities, 66
time that returns, 66
Tirmidhi, 9, 34-35, 38-39, 47, 50, 65-66, 69, 72, 94, 110-111, 136-137, 139, 141
to seek nearness to Allah, 18
tongue, 104, 136
Translating the Hadith
translation, 23, 44, 66, 68, 89, 116, 131, 141
transmitted texts, 44
travel for the purpose of visiting the Prophet, 55
travelling, 60-61, 77, 87, 99, 101, 104
Travels, 11
true dream, 134-135
trustworthiness, 98
trustworthy, 45, 64, 83, 110, 112, 121, 125, 133, 138
Truth, 42, 47, 82, 100, 118, 123-124, 128, 134, 136, 139-140, 149

truthful, 45, 68, 80, 85, 90, 108, 130, 132, 145, 156
truthful ones, 132
truthful piercing sight, 145
truthfulness, 156-157
Tuhfat al-akhyar fi mawlid al-mukhtar, 29
turba, 86
turban, 26, 111
Turkey, 13
Turks, 118
two Sacred Sanctuaries, 95
Ubayy ibn Khalaf, 122
Uhud, 77, 94-95, 122
Ukaydar, 126
ukrima, 108
ulama, 10, 17-18, 45, 50, 61, 141, 143
ulu al-albab, 57
ulum al-fiqh, 24
ulum al-tasawwuf, 24
Umar, 2, 21, 29-30, 36-37, 39, 45, 49, 53, 56, 64, 66, 68, 70-72, 74-76, 78, 80, 82-84, 86, 91, 94-96, 102, 104, 109-110, 113, 115, 119, 121, 125-126, 132, 136-137, 142, 148-150, 154-155
Umar ibn Abd al-Aziz, 56, 70, 76, 78, 84
Umar ibn al-Khattab, 2, 64, 74, 78, 136
Umayr ibn Wahb, 122
Umayya ibn Abi al-Salt, 7
Umayyads, 118
Umm al-Fadl, 122
umm al-muminin, 77
umma, 89, 103, 137, 142
umra, 86, 94
unbelief, 60, 148
unbeliever, 147-148
unbelievers, 5, 22, 127, 129
understanding, 24, 57, 105
unique sight, 128
United Arab Emirates, 61
units of measure used in

Madina, 77
uns, 17
Unseen, 107-110, 113-117, 119, 121, 123, 125, 127-129, 131-133, 135, 137, 139, 141, 143, 145, 147-150
unveilings, 144
urf, 29
Usayb ibn Hudhayr, 94
usul, 116
Utba ibn Abi Lahab, 122
Uthaymin, 1, 19
Uthman, 51, 58, 65, 93, 96, 113, 119, 123-125
Uthman ibn Affan, 51, 124
Uthman ibn Hunayf, 51
Uthman ibn Mazun, 58, 65
Uways al-Qarani, 120
vast majority, 22, 73, 99
veil of form, 111
Veils, 149
veils, 149
very purpose of existent beings, 146
Virgin Mary, 82
virtue, 82, 156
vision, 110, 127-128, 132, 134, 138-140, 145, 154-156
vision and true dream, 134
visit, 12, 27, 55-69, 71, 81, 83, 85-88, 94, 96-101, 104-105, 140
visiting graves, 58, 61, 65-66, 69, 98
Visiting the Grave of the Prophet, 68, 83
voluntary act of worship, 32
vow, 65
wafa, 50, 57, 84-86, 115
Wahb, 71-72, 75, 84, 122, 136, 142
Wahb ibn Munabbih, 84, 142
Wahhabi, 143
Wahhabi heresy, 143
Wahhabis, 50-51, 93, 121, 143

wahy, 137, 150
wajib, 20, 57, 62-63, 69, 99
Wajih al-Din Abd al-Rahman al-Zabidi al-Dayba, 29
wali, 28, 42, 107, 133, 150
wara, 41
Warner, 28, 89
Washed-by-the-angels, 120
wasila, 45, 79
waters of Majinna, 77
way, 8-9, 14, 18-19, 24, 27, 40, 48-49, 60, 62, 66-67, 73-74, 82, 95-98, 103-104, 115, 118, 123, 125-127, 129, 131, 138-140, 145, 150
weak, 37, 39-40, 71, 83, 99-100, 104, 112, 123, 151, 156
weak chain, 123
wedding celebrations, 7
well of Aris, 94
Why Bukhari emphasized dying on Monday, 10
Wise, 27, 52, 156
with a form, 110
witness, 75, 83, 90, 94, 124-125, 151, 156
wives, 89-90, 119, 124
Word, 22, 51, 62, 66, 69, 82, 103, 113, 134, 139, 145
work, 3, 17, 24, 26, 44, 138, 154
worship, 3, 6, 8, 17-18, 31-32, 48, 58-59, 63
wujubiyya, 69
Ya Allah, 51
Ya Habib Allah, 49, 88
Ya Khalil Allah, 49
Ya Muhammad, 50-53, 83
Ya Musa, 49
ya nabi, 49, 88
Ya Nabi Allah, 49, 88
Ya Naji Allah, 49
Ya Safi Allah, 49
Ya Yahya, 49
Yahya, 20, 41, 49, 75-78, 82, 102, 118, 154

Yahya al-Qattan, 41, 118
Yahya ibn Main, 41
Yahya ibn Sad, 75
Yahya ibn Said, 75
Yahya ibn Yahya, 75
Yamama, 122
yanbaghi, 64, 89, 97-98
Yathrib, 76, 127
Yazid ibn Abi Said al-Mahri, 70
Yemen, 13, 76, 112, 117
Yuhannas, 75
yukram, 107
yustahabb, 97-98
Yusuf, 29, 75, 120, 129
Yusuf, 29, 75, 120, 129
Yusuf al-Rifai, 129
Zahawi, 143
Zahir, 29
Zahir al-Din Jafar al-Misri, 29
Zahiris, 57, 99
Zakariyya, 81-82, 138
Zarqani, 30
zawiya, 12
Zayd, 47-48, 118, 125
Zayd ibn Haritha, 47
Zayd ibn Suhan, 125
Zayn al-Din al-Iraqi, 29
Zaynab, 125
Zaynab bint Jahsh, 125
Zaynab bint Jahsh, 125
Ziyad ibn Abih, 57
Zubayr, 33, 38, 72-73, 75-76, 119, 125
Zubayr ibn al-Awamm, 33, 75
Zuhayr, 7, 76
Zuhd, 24, 66, 135, 142, 145

ENCYCLOPEDIA OF ISLAMIC DOCTRINE SERIES

VOLUME 1:
ISLAMIC BELIEFS (*AQIDA*)

VOLUME 2:
REMEMBRANCE OF ALLAH AND PRAISING THE PROPHET
(*DHIKR ALLAH, MADIH, NAAT, QASIDAT AL-BURDA*)

VOLUME 3:
THE PROPHET: COMMEMORATIONS, VISITATION
AND HIS KNOWLEDGE OF THE UNSEEN (*MAWLID, ZIYARA, ILM AL-GHAYB*)

VOLUME 4:
INTERCESSION (*SHAFAA, TAWASSUL, ISTIGHATHA*)

VOLUME 5:
SELF-PURIFICATION: STATE OF EXCELLENCE (*TAZKIYAT AL-NAFS / TASAWWUF, IHSAN*)

VOLUME 6:
FORGOTTEN ASPECTS OF ISLAMIC WORSHIP: PART ONE

VOLUME 7:
FORGOTTEN ASPECTS OF ISLAMIC WORSHIP: PART TWO

VOLUME 8:
INDICES